BOCCONI
UNIVERSITY
PRESS

**Francesca Pecoraro · Alex Turrini · Mark Volpe**

# FUNDRAISING FOR THE ARTS

Foreword by **Andris Nelsons**

*Cover*: Cristina Bernasconi, Milan
*Typesetting*: Valentina Apolloni, Milan

*Cover photo*: Slabs from The Tomb of the Diver (© Parco Archeologico di Paestum e Velia / Ministero della Cultura)
*Cover photo credit*: Maria Cristina Richiardi



EGEA S.p.A.
Via Salasco, 5 - 20136 Milano
Tel. 02/5836.5751 – Fax 02/5836.5753
egea.edizioni@unibocconi.it – www.egeaeditore.it



First edition: May 2023

| | |
|---|---|
| ISBN Domestic Edition | 978-88-99902-94-0 |
| ISBN International Edition | 978-88-31322-63-8 |
| ISBN Digital Domestic Edition | 978-88-238-8637-7 |
| ISBN Digital International Edition | 978-88-31322-64-5 |

Print: Logo s.r.l., Borgoricco (PD)

*To Clement and Ephie: Thank you*

*To Giovanni and Renate: With gratitude*

*To Martino: A promise for the future*

# Table of Contents

# Foreword

by *Andris Nelsons*[*]

While my primary focus will always be on making music with some of the greatest musicians in the world, I am keenly aware that the arts are constantly in need of financial subsidy. Throughout history, geniuses such as Alvin Ailey, Ludwig van Beethoven, Leonardo da Vinci, Martha Graham, Wolfgang Amadeus Mozart and many others have created extraordinary works of art with the support of royalty, the church, government and, more recently, generous individuals, corporations and foundations. The arts, like education, medical research, social services and religion, are not sustainable in the market without underwriting. Yet virtually every society has concluded that the arts are essential as they define our humanity and enable self-expression and reflection. Therefore, I have tremendous appreciation for the benefactors and the fundraisers who make possible what we, as artists, do.

I have had the good fortune of conducting many of the leading orchestras in Europe and America and have a sense of the various approaches to funding culture. In Leipzig (the city of Bach and Mendelssohn), I serve as Gewandhauskapellmeister of one of the oldest orchestras in the world, which is greatly supported by the city of Leipzig. Elected officials serving in governance or ex-officio positions is not unusual in continental Europe where most of the cultural institutions receive substantial public sector support. In Boston, where I serve as Music Director of the Boston Symphony Orchestra (BSO) there is only incremental public sector sup-

* Music Director of the Boston Symphony Orchestra (BSO) and Gewandhauskapellmeister of the Gewandhausorchester Leipzig.

port, with the private sector providing roughly 50 per cent of the revenue needed for this great American cultural icon and the remaining 50 per cent coming from ticket sales and other earned income sources.

Of course, there are advantages and disadvantages of receiving public or private support, and this book written by an esteemed academic and two practitioners (one of them being my partner at the BSO for the first six years of my Boston tenure) outlines them. Beyond that, the book identifies the "actors" involved in funding the arts (individuals, corporations, foundations, government) as well as the process of fundraising, which involves the planning, measuring and communicating needed for annual fundraising as well as capital/endowment campaigns. Consequently, this book should serve as a template for those who want to ensure that the arts will continue to provide inspiration and spiritual nourishment and be accessible to all for generations to come.

# Authors' biographies

**Francesca Pecoraro** is a performing arts manager, with specific skills in Opera Management. Pecoraro defines herself as a passionate and eclectic professional, with a deep interest in the arts, nurtured at different levels. After completing her Bocconi MSc in Economics and Management for the Performing Arts (2008), Pecoraro worked in digital marketing and community management for the Marketing Department of Piccolo Teatro in Milan (after a period as a consultant) and also collaborated with several performing arts festivals, such as Benevento Città Spettacolo and the Festival Pergolesi Spontini. Since 2009, she has been working in the Marketing and Audience Development Department of Teatro di San Carlo in Naples (Italy), with specific responsibility for marketing and sales, business analytics and support for management control. She has been a visiting speaker at several performing arts management workshops and lectures, both in Italy (at Bocconi University in Milan, Università degli Studi di Napoli Federico II and Università degli Studi del Sannio) and abroad (among others, at the Hong Kong Arts Festival). Pecoraro worked in theatre education from 2017 to 2019, conducting workshops both for adults and for children, and she has also worked as an assistant director. In 2018, she was selected as a young ambassador for the very first World Opera Forum in Madrid, with a specific lecture focus on advocacy for the performing arts. *Fundraising for the Arts* is her first book.

**Alex Turrini, PhD** is Associate Professor in public and non-profit management and Director of the MSc in Arts and Cultural Management at Bocconi University, Milan. He has been Visiting Chair of the SMU Meadows Division of Arts Management and Arts Entrepreneurship as well as Visiting Professor in arts management and cultural policy at SMU Meadows and Cox School of Business (Dallas, TX). Previously, he was faculty director of the Government, Health and Not for Profit Division at SDA Bocconi School of Management, Milan. He has overseen several research, training and consulting projects with different national and international public sector organizations that are involved in the arts. His research activities center on two main areas: the first is cultural policies and arts management, with a particular focus on cultural philanthropy; the second is public sector leadership and change. Turrini is the author of numerous books and papers on these topics, the latter having been published in *International Journal of Arts Management*, *Journal of Arts Management, Law, and Society*, *International Journal of Cultural Policy*, *Public Administration Review* and *American Behavioral Scientist*, among others. He serves as reviewer of several national and international journals and is editor in chief for the *International Journal of Arts Management*. Turrini earned both his Laurea degree and his PhD in management from Bocconi University. Among other appointments, he has been visiting research associate at Goldman School of Public Policy, University of California, Berkeley; Richard Wagner School of Public Service, New York City; Research Centre for Social Innovation, Heidelberg University, Germany; and SKEMA Business School, Sophia Antipolis, France. In 2017, he received executive coaching certification from the Teachers College Columbia University Coaching Certification program.

**Mark Volpe** served as President and Chief Executive Officer of the Boston Symphony Orchestra (BSO) from September 1997 until June 2021. In this role, he was responsible for all activities of the BSO, Boston Pops and Tanglewood as well as the BSO's real estate holdings, the most extensive of any orchestra in the world. During his tenure, the BSO reaffirmed its status as one of the world's leading orchestras. As steward of the organization's finances, he oversaw an annual budget of $107 million, quadrupled its endowment (the largest of any orchestra in the world) to $540 million, raised more than $850 million in annual and capital funds, and secured $100 million from forty corporate sponsors. Other accomplishments during Volpe's tenure include the construction of Tanglewood's four-building Linde Center for Music and Learning (one of the buildings is named in his honor), the creation of the multidimensional Tanglewood Learning Institute, a significant touring program (fourteen international and forty domestic tours), the release of fifty recordings with six garnering Grammys, the development of the most visited web platform of any American orchestra, and twenty-three years of labor harmony. Prior to Boston, Volpe held leadership positions with the orchestras of Detroit, Minnesota and Baltimore. In Detroit, Volpe helped lead an initiative that resulted in the construction of the Fisher Music Center as well as the $100 million Detroit School for the Arts. The project helped inspire the resurgence of the Woodward Corridor, one of the central arteries in the city of Detroit. After his retirement from the BSO, Volpe has advised numerous orchestras and music festivals in the United States and Europe and lectured at Harvard University, Yale University, Massachusetts Institute of Technology, Boston University, the University of Rochester, Southern Methodist University and the University of Miami. During the autumn of 2022, Volpe taught at the Università di Bologna, the Università della Svizzera Italiana, the Università Ca' Foscari Venezia, Bocconi University and the University of Rome, as well as being a panelist at the Forum Impresa Cultura Italia in Rome. Volpe obtained his Juris Doctorate cum laude from the University of Minnesota Law School in 1983 and was awarded a bachelor's degree in music from the Eastman School of the University of Rochester in 1979. In 2017, Volpe was elected to the 237th class of the American Academy of Arts and Sciences, the first-ever chief executive of an orchestra to receive this honor. In 2020, he was awarded the Chevalier of the Order of Arts and Letters by France's Minister of Culture. Volpe holds honorary doctorates from Boston University, the University of Rochester, Northeastern University, the New England Conservatory of Music and Westfield State University. Volpe and his wife, Martha Volpe, have two daughters, Francesca and Madeline. He was raised in Minneapolis, Minnesota, where his father played trumpet in the Minnesota Orchestra for forty-three years.

# Contributors' biographies

*Fundraising for the Arts* was written after the Arts Philanthropy Talks Series, organized by SDA Bocconi, were held between February and July 2022. These talks involved various panels of arts management professionals who shared their experiences and knowledge about the topics discussed in each chapter. The biographies are presented in the order in which their contributions appear in this book. We warmly thank all of them for their involvement in this work. We would also like to thank Ludovica Anselmo for her support as research assistant to this project, as well as Maria Cristina Richiardi, her son and Museo Archeologico Nazionale di Paestum for the cover image.

*Francesca Pecoraro, Alex Turrini, Mark Volpe*

**Lanfranco Li Cauli (Teatro alla Scala)** was born in 1972. Since 2016 he has been the marketing and fundraising director of Teatro alla Scala, where he is responsible for around two-thirds of the theatre revenues, coming from both private contributions and ticket sales. From 2013 to 2015, he was the marketing and communication director at Piccolo Teatro di Milano – Teatro d'Europa, where in 1997 he started his career after a degree in Economics and Management at Bocconi University in Milan.

**James Ryan Jillson (Nasher Sculpture Center)** is an arts manager with a passion for helping cultural institutions take data-driven approaches to developing strategy, navigating change, building audiences and driving revenue. He currently serves as the director of development at the Nasher Sculpture Center, a non-profit modern and contemporary art museum in the Dallas Arts District. There, he leads a team in the planning, execution and evaluation of the museum's membership and annual giving programs, major gift efforts for exhibitions and special initiatives, and fundraising events. Previously, James worked with more than a half-dozen arts organizations and other non-profits – including The Arts Community Alliance, The Meadows Foundation, and the Undermain Theatre – in various capacities related to fundraising, marketing, planning, research and operations. James teaches arts management and arts entrepreneurship as an adjunct faculty member at Southern Methodist University's Meadows School of the Arts. He has led workshops and presented research on fundraising and marketing in the arts at industry conferences nationally and internationally. Additionally, he regularly volunteers as a grants panelist for the City of Dallas Office of Arts and Culture. James has earned an MBA, an MA in Arts Management and a BA in Music from SMU.

**Alessandro Borchini (Piccolo Teatro di Milano)** graduated with a degree in Violin Performance from the Istituto Superiore di Studi Musicali of Reggio Emilia and Castelnovo ne' Monti in 1998. After working for several years as a professional violinist in various orchestras and chamber music groups, he decided to pursue a managerial career in arts and culture in 2005. The same year, he received a Master's degree (with honors) in Music Enterprise Organization and Management from the University of Parma. Throughout his career, Borchini has held roles of increasing responsibility in important organizations such as Reggio Parma Festival, Solares Fondazione delle Arti, Filarmonica del Teatro Comunale di Bologna, Teatro Regio di Parma and Teatro Eliseo in Rome. He holds the role of marketing and communication director of the Piccolo Teatro di Milano – Teatro d'Europa since 2016. Borchini's work has always been oriented towards the research and development of new business models and management practices, as well as the delineation of marketing, communication and fundraising strategies. In addition to his role at the Piccolo, he carries out consultancy and training activities for arts and cultural organizations. He also hosts courses and lectures in universities and training institutions, including the Università Cattolica del Sacro Cuore di Milano, Università di Verona, Università Bocconi and SDA Bocconi School of Management, Università IULM, Accademia della Scala, POLIMI Graduate School of Management, RCS Academy and Sole24Ore

Business School. Borchini is a member of the Faculty Advisory Committee within the Psychology department of Università Cattolica del Sacro Cuore di Milano, and of their Master's program in Modern Philology; he also sits on the advisory committee for the Bachelor's and Master's Degree Courses in Foreign Languages and Literatures at Università di Milano. Borchini holds an Executive MBA (cum laude) from the Milan POLIMI Graduate School of Business.

**Piergiacomo Mion Dalle Carbonare (SDA Bocconi)** is SDA Junior Lecturer of the Government, Health and Non-Profit Division and Coordinator of the Master in Arts Management and Administration (MAMA) at SDA Bocconi School of Management. He is deputy director of the Master of Science in Economics and Management for Arts, Culture, Media and Entertainment (ACME) at Bocconi University; he also teaches courses related to Cultural Policies, Public Management and Territorial Marketing at Bocconi University and SDA Bocconi School of Management. He holds a PhD in Marketing from the University of Valencia.

**Marek Prokůpek (KEDGE)** is Assistant Professor in Arts Management at KEDGE Arts School, KEDGE Business School. He is also a member of the Creative Industries & Culture Research Center at KEDGE. His research interests lie primarily in the areas of museum fundraising and philanthropy and its ethical dilemmas, the art market and innovative business models of arts and cultural organizations.

**Kim Noltemy (Dallas Symphony Orchestra)** has served as President and Chief Executive Officer of the Dallas Symphony Orchestra (DSO) since 2018. During her tenure, the DSO took over management of the Meyerson Symphony Center, appointed Fabio Luisi as music director (through 2029) and launched an expansive new educational initiative for students of color. The DSO performed live throughout the COVID-19 pandemic period, utilizing strict health and safety protocols for the orchestra and audience. In addition, Noltemy added media infrastructure to the concert hall, resulting in forty concerts being distributed digitally each season, plus seven programs distributed on television by Bloomberg Media and PBS. Noltemy was previously the Chief Operating and Communications Officer of the Boston Symphony Orchestra where she oversaw digital media, earned revenue, events, marketing, public relations, education and special projects. She was executive producer of the award-winning Boston Pops July 4th television programs and produced the PBS and online series New Tanglewood Tales.

**Agustí Filomeno (Cultural Department, Catalan Regional government)** is a performing arts manager, a growth-oriented professional with extensive experience of organizational understanding in defining strategies for transformation, positioning, revenue growth, resource optimization and improvement of brand value. He is highly skilled in problem-solving and efficient decision-making through the analysis and synthesis of complex economic, social and environmental data. With a sound history of success in management, especially in the areas of marketing, commercial operations and communication, his consumer orientation stands out. Filomeno has been the marketing and sales director of the Liceu Opera House in Barcelona, a €45m budget theatre, where he has reorganized the whole department and executed a major change in brand image and positioning of the institution. Managed audience development has increased business, and he has also devised and executed new pricing strategies to ensure achievement of full business potential. As a result, income from ticket sales and subscriptions has increased by up to 43.5 per cent and the total public opera attendance has increased by up to 23 per cent. In addition, he has encouraged tourism development for growth and boosted economic activities, capturing 30 per cent of total ticket customers and ensuring young audience development resulting in a youth share of 21 per cent of total ticket customers. In parallel, he has overseen the development of business intelligence, which has improved operational efficiency and increased competitive advantages. Filomeno has strengthened the business brand with a new image and advertising approach to theatre campaigns, even achieving recognition as winner of the Cannes Lion for an advertising campaign for the year 2018–2019. A member of the European steering committee of marketing and communication for European opera theatres, he was appointed as fundraising and marketing director of the Teatro Regio di Torino, the opera house of Turin (Italy), with a budget of €80m. As part of his responsibilities, he defined and implemented the marketing strategy and the operational marketing plan, while developing and strengthening the theatre's brand equity. He developed a strategic and commercial plan that recruited and monitored sponsoring companies and patrons, increasing sponsor revenue by more than 14 per cent, and he also reviewed the hospitality policy and benefits for sponsors. As part of his responsibilities, he also relaunched the institution's merchandising activities as well as devising new business development opportunities to increase the theatre's revenue. Since 2018, he has also been Marketing and Communications Professor for Culture and Performing Arts at Barcelona University. As of 2021, he has been the marketing and audience development advisor to the cultural department of the Catalan regional government.

**Janet Clarkson Davis (Clarkson Davis Consulting).** Thirty years in the non-profit sector have informed Clarkson Davis's beliefs that creativity is a basic human need, and that authentic gratitude is the heartbeat of successful fundraising efforts. As a founding principal of the consulting firm Clarkson Davis, she provided guidance on annual and capital fundraising, strategic planning, and governance to arts and cultural clients including the North Carolina Stage Company, Kitchen Dog Theater, Second Thought Theatre, Dallas Film Society, Big Thought, Lone Star Circus Arts and Encore Park. Janet has held in-house positions leading the fundraising teams at the Dallas Theater Center, Dallas Symphony Association, the Nasher Sculpture Center and the Ogunquit Playhouse. She has served as adjunct professor for the Master of International Arts Management program at Southern Methodist University, as a faculty member for the Certified Fund Raising Executive organization and the Association of Fundraising Professionals, and as a lecturer for non-profit industry organization conferences including Theatre Communications Group, the Center for Nonprofit Management, NH Center for Nonprofits and United Way of America. She holds a BFA in Musical Theater from University of Michigan and is an alumna of Philips Academy Andover. Parents of three grown children, she and her husband Wyatt live with their two Labrador retrievers in Rye, New Hampshire, USA.

**Pilar Cárdenas (Advisory Board for the Arts)** is senior director at Advisory Board for the Arts and is based in Madrid. She joined the Advisory Board for the Arts (ABA) in the summer of 2019 immediately after the inception of the company. Besides being responsible for several ABA European members, she is also in charge of developing ABA's presence in Europe. Previously, she worked at the Albeniz Foundation – Reina Sofía School of Music in Madrid. She completed her Master's in Arts Management and Administration from SDA Bocconi School of Management in Milan, Italy. Following this, she worked at Postclassical Ensemble, an orchestra in Washington DC. Cárdenas is a graduate in law from the University of Navarre in Spain, where she worked for several years developing an arts and culture extracurricular program for university students.

**Dan Wakin (Metropolitan Opera)** is the senior director of communications at the Metropolitan Opera, overseeing the media operations of the company and liaising with the marketing and editorial teams. Before starting at the Met in the spring of 2022, he had been a journalist at the *New York Times* for twenty-two years, including eight years as the classical music and dance reporter. He was also a deputy editor of the culture desk, overseeing the daily report and international coverage. In addition, he covered religion; was deputy editorial director of NYT Global, a strategic team focused on building international audience; and an editor on the obituary news desk, where he led the project "Those We've Lost," a chronicle of the victims of the COVID-19 pandemic. As a reporter, he covered stories in two dozen countries in Asia, the Middle East, Europe and Latin America, including the New York Philharmonic's visit to North Korea, the death of Pope John Paul II and the conclaves that elected Benedict XVI and Francis. He also wrote a series of stories on the rise of classical music in China and on the West Bank. He helped lead the team that produced the Emmy-nominated multimedia project "Inside the Quartet." Earlier in his career, Dan worked for the Associated Press, serving as a correspondent in bureaus in Newark, New Jersey, and Rome and as news editor for southern Africa, based in Johannesburg. A graduate of Harvard University with a degree in the classics, he is an avid amateur clarinetist and co-founder of the chamber music collective Hellgate Harmonie. Dan is the author of *The Man With the Sawed-Off Leg and Other Tales of a New York City Block* (Arcade, 2018). He lives in Manhattan.

**Edilia Gänz (FEDORA Circle)** is the director of FEDORA – The European Circle of Philanthropists of Opera and Ballet. A graduate of the University of Mannheim and ESCP Business School, she helped launch the non-profit in 2013 and has been responsible for its growth and management ever since. In 2019, she was named by ***Forbes*** magazine as one of Europe's most promising cultural managers, and was listed among the

"Forbes 30 under 30 Europe in Arts & Culture." In 2020, she was selected by Mariya Gabriel, European Commissioner for Innovation, Research, Culture, Education and Youth, as one of the #EUwomen4future representatives leading innovation in these areas. As part of this, Gänz was invited to participate in a panel discussion on International Women's Day at the European Parliament in Strasbourg, co-hosted by its President, Roberta Metsola, and Mariya Gabriel.

**Stefano Prestini (Bocconi University)** is lecturer at the Marketing Department at Bocconi University. He holds his PhD in Management and Innovation at Catholic University of the Sacred Heart, Italy. He coordinates the specialized Master's in Marketing and Communication at Bocconi University. His current research interests are in consumer behavior (CCT perspective), luxury shopping experience, arts marketing, LGBTQ+ studies, advertising and digital marketing. His papers have been published in *Industrial Marketing Management*, *Journal of Consumer Behavior* and *Italian Journal of Marketing*. He teaches marketing, digital and social media marketing, strategic marketing and planning in undergraduate, graduate and executive courses.

**Michele Mario Stanta (Jakala)** graduated with a Master of Science in Art, Culture, Media & Entertainment at Bocconi University. He is now a partner and digital and media director at Jakala, a leading European martech company. He is in charge of digital strategy implementation for recognized brands, institutions and non-profit organizations. Before joining Jakala, he was country manager at 77Agency, a key Italian digital agency. During over twelve years in digital marketing, he has built digital acquisition and fundraising strategies for many projects and institutions – with a particular passion for hedonic and arts organization. He currently teaches digital and social media marketing in the specialized Master's in Marketing and Communication (MiMeC) at Bocconi University.

# Part I
# Context

# 1 Why This Book About Fundraising for the Arts

## 1.1 Arts organizations, civil economy and fundraising for the arts

Arts organizations operate in an increasingly complex and multifaceted environment. This complexity is the result of internal and external pressures that deeply influence the way in which cultural institutions carry out their activities and pursue their mission. Some of these tensions have always been faced by arts managers: the constant necessity of developing creative strategies for attracting new audiences and for meeting community needs; the increasing number of competitors operating in other not-for-profit fields and able to attract funds from public agencies and private donors; the concentration of wealth in the hands of a few rich individuals or corporations, which makes the competition for funds even more fierce; the decrease in public funding; and the challenge of supporting artists' creativity and innovation while pleasing audiences' (mostly) conservative tastes.

The COVID-19 pandemic and its severe consequences have dramatically exacerbated these challenges. Even if in the first year of the pandemic – both in Europe and the United States – governments, donors and the community stepped forward to grant arts institutions resources to survive, these organizations are now experiencing massive economic setbacks, with dramatic effects both on their earned revenues and contributed income (Guibert and Hyde, 2021). Furthermore, many not-for-profit organizations had to cope with the changing financial behaviors of donors and consumers, who began to use data to better ground their strategic intentions while focusing on measuring and communicating their impact on the community (Van Steenburg et al., 2022).

Post-COVID-19-pandemic social distress (together with geopolitical turbulence, climate change threats and a burst of new "culture-wars" – escalated by the social justice movement) has also prompted cultural institutions to rethink their true reason for existence. Are arts institutions in the business of providing "experiences" and "entertaining" their loyal audiences and tourists, or is their legitimization rooted in their capacity to capture and activate social and cultural change in their local communities? Are arts institutions there as "dispatchers" of their artistic productions (being supported by public or private funding to cover the high fixed costs of production), or is their role (and justification for public or private support) to proactively serve the community and support younger generations of artists? And to what extent are arts executives committed to and aware of their civic role? All these questions and dilemmas have emerged from the turbulent times many arts organizations are experiencing.

One of the possible answers that we propose in this book is directly linked to the debate about how and why the arts might contribute to the redesign of welfare systems in developed and underdeveloped countries and how they might support the economic and social development of communities. In these regards, Zamagni (2018), among others, claims that we are experiencing a shift from a traditional "political economy" paradigm to a "civil economy" paradigm (Bruni and Zamagni, 2016; Bechetti and Cermelli, 2018). He explains the dualism by tracing it back to two fundamental texts in the history of economic thought: Adam Smith's *An Inquiry into the Nature and Causes of the Wealth of Nations* (1776) and one of his slightly earlier texts, *The Theory of Moral Sentiments* (1759). In *The Wealth of Nations*, Smith introduces the idea that the pursuit of personal interests by individuals can produce a substantial increase in the wealth of a country. Motivated by their self-interest and by the possibility of achieving their own "private" gains, each person carries out a greater and greater number of economic exchanges, creating an even greater amount of wealth for the community in which they live. An example Smith gives is very famous, and may be summarized as: "it is not from the goodness of the brewer that we obtain one or more beers, but from his own interest in providing them to us" (Turrini, 1999). From this simple principle we can derive all the assumptions of modern economic theory (and a good part of the neo-liberal rhetoric), which portrays a "*homo oeconomicus*," incurably individualistic and busy pursuing his own interests. From here it also follows that the State, and only the State, intervenes when wealth is not equally redistributed (a function that competitive markets do not effectively address) or when market mechanisms fail (especially in the provision of public goods such as the arts).

Mainstream economists' focus on the role of markets and the State represents an erroneous simplification of Smith's thought (Bruni and Zamagni, 2016; Turrini, 1999). In his writings prior to *The Wealth of Nations* (in which the theoretical assumptions that led to the elaboration of the 1776 masterpiece can be traced), Smith reiterates that the fundamental condition for an efficient market system is the existence of a civic framework and a system of relationships that are based on "moral sentiments" that indissolubly bind a group, a community, a territory, a nation. Smith identifies these moral feelings in the traits of sympathy and benevolence – that is, in the ability to put oneself in the other's shoes and to make oneself responsible for the fate of others. The market and even the State, according to what Putnam et al. (1992) have more recently evidenced, are therefore more efficient and effective if immersed in a fabric of social relations that integrates the economic actors and citizens who operate within it. The market is a positive-sum game if it is part of a civil society (where sympathy and benevolence are practised) and not in the so-called forest (where the Hobbesian *homo homini lupus* rule holds): "Moral Spirits" versus "Animal Spirits" as John Maynard Keynes, another famous English economist, would say (Turrini, 1999).

At the heart of the civil economy approach, defined for the very first time in 1753 in Naples by another enlightened economist, Antonio Genovesi,[1] one can find a focus on the importance of nurturing trust, reciprocal relationships and gift exchanges (Polanyi ([1944], 2001), Mauss, ([1925] 1950)) to strengthen the social and human capital necessary for local development (Bruni and Zamagni, 2016; Sugden, 2021). However,

---

[1] In his lectures as chair of the first Faculty of Economics in Europe at the University of Naples (1755), Antonio Genovesi, a contemporary of Adam Smith, questioned the reasons for the economic decline of Naples and the south of Italy – an incomprehensible decline given the presence of a port that was beneficial to trade, a good climate that favored agriculture and a young population ready to work. Among other reasons, Genovesi found the roots of the crisis in the cultural backwardness that was imposed by the Bourbon monarchy. This backwardness (manifesting itself in a complete lack of trust and civic virtues in the cities) hampered the social and economic development of society as a whole (Genovesi, 1769).

there is a difference between development and growth (Zamagni, 2018). Development includes three key dimensions, which relate to growth, society and spirituality. Growth is the hard and materialistic aspect of development, related to the achievement of positive economic results. The social and spiritual dimensions cover intangible aspects of development, related to the "*civitas*" and to the connection between citizens participating in civic life. Growth alone might be granted by markets or through the redistributive function of the State. The other two dimensions of development magnify the effects of mere growth, strengthening connections among people and nurturing their personal feelings and well-being (and happiness) in the community to which they belong.

In the theoretical perspective that we have briefly outlined here, arts, heritage and cultural organizations might find answers to the questions and dilemmas about their mission, as they re-emerge in the post-COVID-19 pandemic epoch. More than protecting the arts or heritage, these institutions are pivotal in creating bonds of trust, nurturing social capital, facilitating social development, serving younger generations and granting cultural access to all citizens. Cultural institutions are urged, more than ever, to express and demonstrate how they can help to "produce" citizenship. They are pushed to articulate why they should be supported, enriching the traditional art for art's sake argument (Turrini and Voss, 2020). As "commons," they are the repository of shared values within their communities and, in the face of a fractured civil society, they have to consistently reinforce their civic value through the clear implementation of their mission and activities. They are engaged in the development of a territory, not just its growth.

Cultural philanthropy, conceived as any act of altruism that sustains the arts and culture, is inevitably linked with and essential to the civil economy approach. As we see in Chapter 2, a cultural philanthropy approach is different from mere fundraising, which is focused on techniques for securing gifts that are intended to provide for the financial sustainability of arts organizations. Consistent with what we have described so far, cultural philanthropy might be traced back to the epoch when cities and civic life re-emerged as a social and political phenomenon in Europe (see Box 1.1).

**Box 1.1 The historical roots of cultural philanthropy**

In order to profile different models of cultural philanthropism, we might go back to the 13th and 14th centuries in Italy – an epoch that experienced the resumption of cultural life and the flourishing of a new model of social order that was centered on a community of "free" men, the city, which emerged as a reaction to feudalism. In those times, in central-northern Italy, there were already ninety-six cities with more than 5,000 inhabitants – fifty-three of them with more than 10,000 inhabitants – and 21.4 per cent of the total of the population resident there, compared with Europe as a whole, which saw an average of 9.5 per cent of the population in cities. Only the Netherlands reached quite the same level of "citizenship," while in 1500 England still had just 4.6 per cent of its population living in urban areas (Bruni and Zamagni, 2016). It was in these centuries that humanism – and then the Renaissance – blossomed in Italy: religious and secular patronage of the arts and forms of civic philanthropy became common practice, their different forms representing the social and economic turmoil of the epoch.

The first kind of cultural philanthropy can be well illustrated by the story of a businessman named Oliviero Forzetta, who lived in Treviso, near Venice, between 1300 and 1373 (Gaffuri, 1997). Son of a notary, Niccolò, who had accumulated a considerable amount of money through usury loans, Oliviero was given the title of notary when he was twenty, but, following his father's example, preferred the profession of moneylender. Forzetta was a man "without letters," but he had an intense passion for codices, books and antiquities: he was able to form a library and an archaeological collection that compared with a later Renaissance collection. His attention fell, among other antiquities, on two important marble high-reliefs, which came from the throne of Saturn of the Ravenna Basilica of St Vitale and dated back to the first centuries after Christ; they are now preserved in Venice's Archaeological Museum (see Fig. 1.1). These *putti* were later the source of inspiration for artists such as Mantegna, Lombardo, Sansovino. On 16 July 1368, still in good health, Forzetta dictated his will. Having no children, despite having had five wives, he left his estate to the Confraternity of Santa Maria dei Battuti of which he was a brother, noting that after his death all his art should be sold and the revenue from the sale given to poor girls. In this way, his collection was rapidly dispersed. Even though Forzetta wanted his codices secured to benches by chains, at the Confraternity's Oratory, they were also soon lost. The Forzetta collection is famous because he listed all the purchases he made in Venice, thus leaving us the oldest known evidence of an art and archaeology collection. The document notes various sculptures, paintings and drawings by different artists, and we can conclude that this collection helped culture to blossom in Venice.

*Figure 1.1* Relief on Saturn throne with angels (*c.* 50 ad)

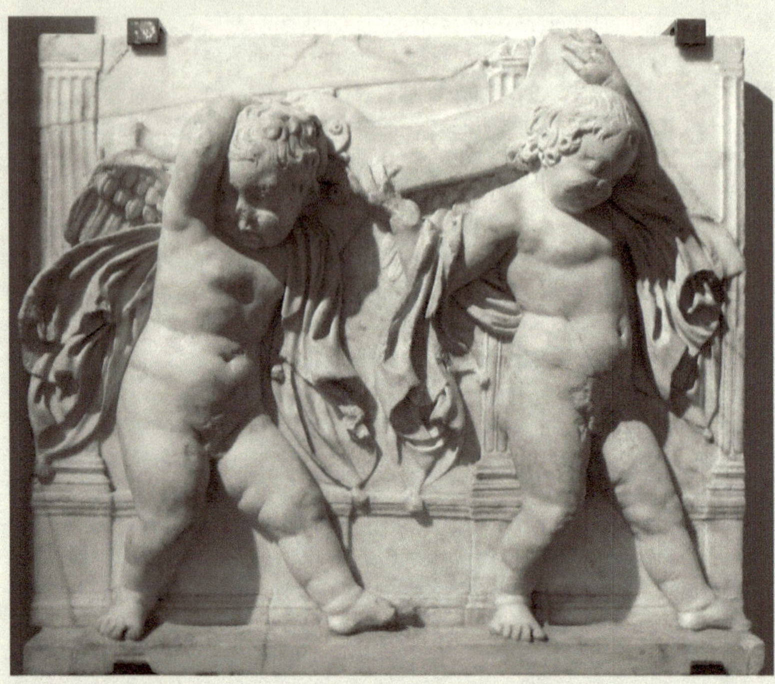

*Credit*: Sailko, CC BY-SA 4.0, via Wikimedia Commons

Oliviero Forzetta represents the first type of cultural philanthropist, namely a private art collector. One might argue that the act of collecting cannot be envisioned as a form of giving, and cultural economists would include collecting as a paradigmatic form of household consumption: the open-endedness of a collection resonates with the continuous search for novelty in contemporary consumer behavior. Far from being donors, collectors are also fiercely competing in art markets to own the best pieces on the market (Bianchi 1997).

However, portraying arts collectors (and cultural philanthropists) as fully rational and self-interested economic agents is not useful. It would not explain Forzetta's will or some results from a study about Texas art collectors by one of this book's authors (Turrini, 2020). When arts markets are geographically limited, people know each other and disintermediation is not fully developed; in addition, art collectors' network dynamics today resemble those we might have found in Florence or Venice in the 14th century. Art market exchanges are embedded in social networks that "punish" speculative behavior and rely upon trust and friendship. Texas art collectors competitively bid in auctions to purchase the best pieces of Texan art, but at the same time they are members of art associations (such as the Texas Arts Collectors Organization). Within these associations, they organize seminars, exchange information and news about Texas arts, meet monthly at different collectors' homes to see new purchases – and also to have a beer together. Their collections seldom begin purposefully (sometimes it is fascination about a single item or the need to furnish a new home), and artworks are gathered together for a range of purposes: aesthetic pleasure (which is emotional), economic investment (which is rational), exhibitionism and social advancement (which is political), education and refinement (which is intellectual) or to broaden their social life instead of "bowling alone," as Robert Putnam put it. For collectors, social relationships and trust count: when a Texas art piece is sold at an auction, the collectors' network begins to fight any bidder from outside Texas who wants to "steal" the work of art. They care that this piece of heritage remains in Texas – think of Forzetta and his chained books – and they support and organize self-funded travelling exhibitions of Texan art both to increase its value (and that of the paintings they own), but also to reinforce Texan cultural identity. Above all, an explicit philanthropic aim emerges when collectors think about the future of their collections – but we need more studies and research to understand and explore when, how and why arts collectors become philanthropists. Regarding them as more than economic speculative agents, we would align collecting and collectors with Walter Benjamin's ([1935] 2008) portrait of collectors as those individuals who through their purchases save art from commodification that markets trigger.

Returning to the 14th century in northern Italy, we can detect two other types of cultural philanthropism: patronage of the arts and capitalist philanthropy. To do so, we can briefly refer to two other patrons of the arts at that time who were in some way linked: Cangrande I della Scala from Verona and Enrico Scrovegni from Padua. Della Scala lived in Verona between 1291 and 1329, at a time when Verona – thanks to the Scaligeri family – had become a city of great political importance. With Cangrande, it also became a cultural center, anticipating the splendor of Renaissance patronage that developed shortly thereafter in Florence with Cosimo de' Medici. It is interesting to focus on the patronage relationship that Cangrande built with Dante Alighieri, Italy's most famous poet, one of the founding fathers of Italian literature. Being exiled from Florence and in need of a patron from 1312 to 1318, Dante was hosted by Cangrande della Scala, who appears in the seventeenth canto of *The Divine Comedy*, Dante's masterpiece:

> So recognised shall his magnificence
> Become hereafter, that his enemies

Will not have power to keep mute tongues about it.[2]
("Paradiso," canto XVII, verses 85–87).

The Dante–della Scala relationship is a good example of patronage in which reciprocity matters. A famous and widely debated epistle that Dante wrote to Cangrande in which the poet dedicates the entirety of "Paradiso" to his patron is an enactment of the oath of friendship, a return on a promise and a gesture of sincere gratitude for an invaluable gift. In this sense, as Paul McLean (2005, 640) recently wrote, "Patronage did not simply signify the top-down distribution of material rewards, nor [...] a lavish support of philosophy and the arts. It was a pervasive, bottom-up, political cultural phenomenon – an *institution* in the sociological sense of a set of relatively routine or 'standardized activity sequences' or 'organized, established procedure[s]' that support and reproduce a set of shared expectations about the world and how it operates."

The life of Enrico Scrovegni, the founder of Cappella Scrovegni in Padua, was also influenced by Dante. Enrico Scrovegni was from a family of moneylenders, and Dante put Scrovegni senior in a special place in hell (the Inferno) reserved just for him so he could repent for his sins as a moneylender and as an exploiter of the less fortunate. Either to give back what his father had taken away or as a strategic move to launch his political career in Padua – as Chiara Frugoni (2008) recently indicated – Enrico Scrovegni decided to devote part of his accumulated wealth to the construction of a chapel, now known as Cappella Scrovegni. He hired Giotto, the most celebrated fresco painter of the day, to decorate the inside of the chapel with scenes from the life of Christ. In the frescoes, Scrovegni is depicted as kneeling in an act of devotion, presenting a model of the chapel. He is not only depicted in Paradise, but also appears the same size as the other saints, in order to portray himself as one of the just, as a figure who could play a role in the city's future fortunes (see Fig. 1.2).

Enrico Scrovegni represents a different type of giving, triggered by different motivations. He could even be considered a precursor of welfare capitalism or capitalist philanthropy, a 14th-century Carnegie, Rockefeller or Gates. Scrovegni wanted to give back something that his family had taken from the community (in a primitive example of the restitution principle), just as American welfare capitalism is based on the agreement under which companies have the task of considering the fate and well-being of their employees and their employees' families. According to the restitution principle, a capitalist returns part of his or

---

[2] This is the English translation of these lines:
*Le sue magnificenze conosciute*
*saranno ancora, sì che 'suoi nemici*
*non ne potran tener le lingue mute.*

*Figure 1.2* Enrico Scrovegni in the Cappella Scrovegni fresco by Giotto (1303–1305)

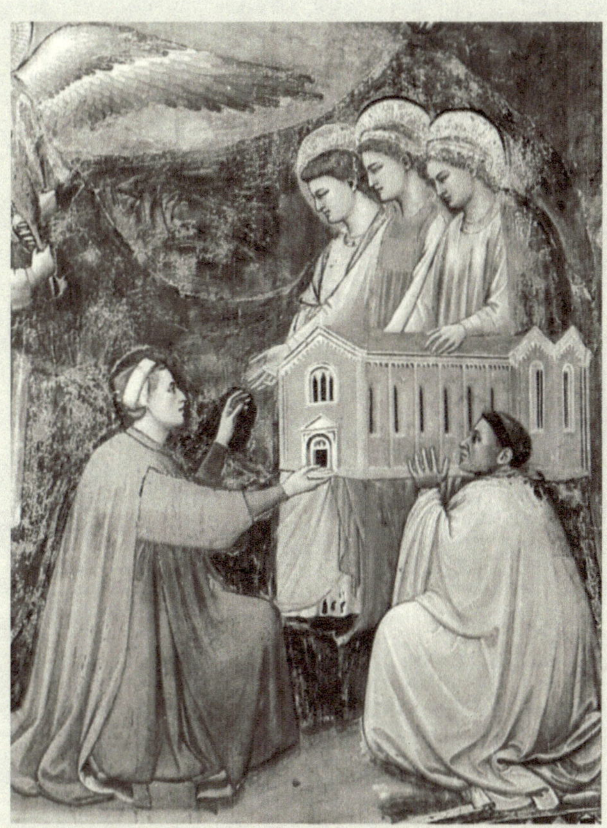

*Credit*: Wikimedia Commons

her profits to those who have contributed to them. For Scrovegni, this type of giving resulted in the building of a chapel; in modern times, the result of a gift of this nature is often the constitution of a foundation. What is remarkable here is the different kinds of motivation that ground cultural philanthropy: For Scrovegni, it was an obligation to give back or an attempt to increase his reputation in the community. For della Scala, a patron and a cultural entrepreneur who had a direct relationship with an artist, it was establishing long-term collaborative and reciprocal relationships. However, we might attribute both of these motivations to cultural philanthropists who placed resources and entrepreneurial know-how at the service of a cause of collective interest.

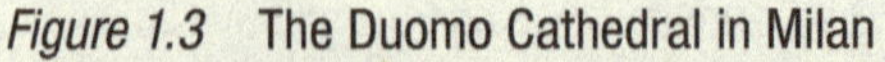

*Figure 1.3* The Duomo Cathedral in Milan

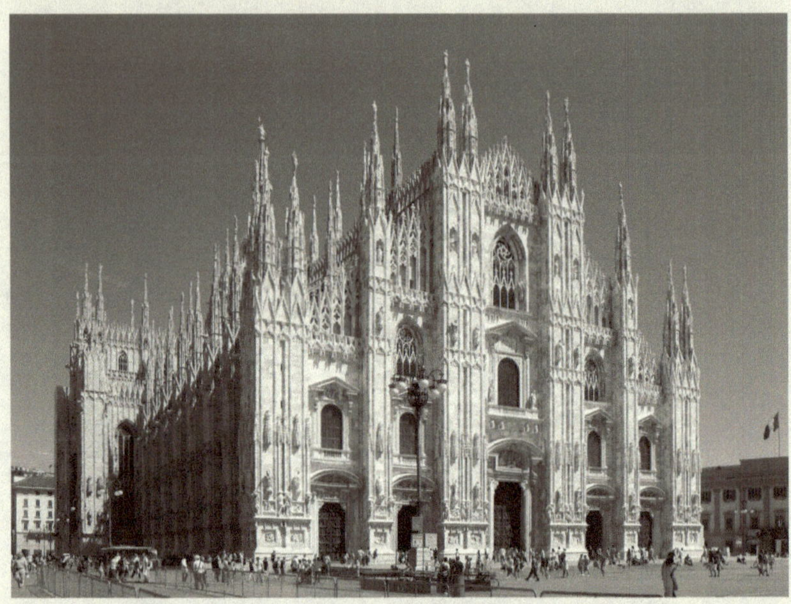

*Credit*: Jiuguang Wang, CC BY-SA 3.0, Wikimedia Commons

The final form of cultural philanthropy that we can trace back into the past, one that is currently becoming more popular, is what we might label as crowdfunding. Rather than speaking about a digital crowdfunding platform such as Kickstarter, we can go back to the 14th century, even if we move a little bit westward in Italy – from Venice to Milan. As recent studies by Martina Saltamacchia have shown, the Duomo Cathedral in Milan (see Fig. 1.3), like many other cathedrals in Europe, was not only built thanks to the munificence of a prince or a duke (in this case the Visconti family), but also because of the contributions made by Milan's "crowd" – the city's Christian community.

The organization in charge of the building of the cathedral was the *Fabbrica*, which drew together the philanthropic efforts of all Milan's citizens. As Saltamacchia (2011: 171) describes:

> Especially in the first decades, when much effort was needed for the excavation of the foundations, the chronicles of the *Fabbrica* often noted "labor pro nihilo," work for nothing, literally. Citizens of any craft – tailors, millers, butchers, carpenters, fishermen, goldsmiths, jurists, doctors, pharmacists, bakers and procurators

– went to the cathedral on their day off to offer their hands generously and with no monetary remuneration.

Alongside this form of volunteering, donations from the crowds were constantly solicited. Saltamacchia continues (180):

> The *Fabbrica* had also implemented an effective network of fundraising, employing an organized system of multiple instruments. [...] The main place for the collection of donations was the altar in the church of Santa Maria Maggiore [...] Four deputies from the *Fabbrica* welcomed donors at the altar, received offerings and recorded them in their registers. [...] Not everyone had time to bring their donation to the altar. So, in order to reach all the people, boxes were located at major crossroads of the city and the countryside, as well as in places where people might gather: churches and chapels to be sure, but also at the gates of the city, in front of the room used by the archbishop's vicar for audiences, and even at the quarries outside Milan. [...] Teams formed by two priests, two lay officials of the *Fabbrica* and two boni homines of Milan would go to countryside villages around the city to celebrate the morning mass, announcing on that occasion the news of the cathedral's construction. At the conclusion of the mass, after a sermon focused on the virtue of charity and the rewards that awaited generous donors in heaven, the group of six people passed door to door throughout the village, requesting donations. Also the *puellae cantagolae*, the girls with the singing throats, helped the *Fabbrica* in its devout fundraising. These young ladies, dressed in white, paraded through the streets of the city and the villages nearby singing and dancing in the squares and at the crossroads to encourage popular donations. The *Fabbrica*'s firm commitment and sense of mission, the large number of dedicated mendicant friars and volunteers, along with the capacity to organize them efficiently, had the result of making men and women in the city and the countryside aware of the construction work, and gave each member of the diocese the possibility of partaking in the effort with his or her donation entrusted to the collectors.

The collective giving effort was mirrored by the *Fabbrica*'s democratic governance structure: all the donations were recorded, with the destination of each gift being specified, and all major decisions were collectively taken through its elected council, which met weekly to deliberate on all matters regarding the construction, management and administration of the cathedral. The three main stakeholders – the prince, the Church and the people – were all represented on the council. The citizens, for example, were represented by fifty residents per district, who convened weekly not to address emergencies but to monitor a long-term project. This flat governance structure was quite common at the time. Similar organizations could be found in other Italian cities, together with corporate guilds (which were engaged in cultural philanthropism as well as supporting their members) and confraternities (Tepstra, 1999).

*Source*: Author's adaptation from Turrini (2021)

In our post-COVID-19 pandemic present, arts institutions are therefore being pushed to elicit contributions from donors in other ways, without appearing to be selling or begging. The fundraising model described in this book is based on several assumptions. It is grounded in the idea that at the heart of philanthropic processes there is the building of a stable relationship between cultural institutions and their constituents as well as the entire community. In other words, if fundraising for the arts is focused on transactional exchanges (i.e., money in return of specific individual benefits), it will fail. Cultural philanthropy, however, is another way in which relational goods can be produced[3] (Nussbaum, 1986; Gui, 1987; Bechetti et al., 2008; Bruni and Stanca, 2009), building ties and increasing awareness around the arts and heritage as "commons," the meaning of which has to be agreed together – and this requires donations in order to be realized.

This approach also responds to the practical needs and challenges that arts organizations face, as will become clear in the following section. A philanthropic culture is key to achieving financial sustainability and to further protect these organizations from the possible crises that are inevitable in an ever more complex environment.

## 1.2 The relevance of fundraising for arts organizations

In contrast to for-profit entities, the development (or acquisition) of resources in the not-for-profit world is often detached from service delivery. These organizations frequently provide their services with a low (or no) charge for the final recipients, and sometimes their "customers" are members of the community at large (e.g., in the case of advocacy organizations). This implies that organizations have to raise funds from other sources to be able to cover their costs. In contrast, clients of for-profit companies are always expected to pay a price for the services or products they purchase, in order to cover the company's production costs with any surplus to be defined as profit. For these businesses, there is only one system (service production and source of income), as the purchasers are those who pay to cover costs at a minimum. In the not-for-profit space,

---

[3] Relational goods are "non-material goods, which are not services that are consumed individually, but are tied to interpersonal relations" (Gui, 1987: 37).

income from the purchase of services only covers a portion of the costs, and therefore another source of revenue (resource development, i.e., fundraising) is required. Mason (1984) labelled this characteristic a "dual internal system" for voluntary enterprises.

As Mason (1984) highlights, the presence of this duality in not-for-profit organizations has some important consequences for their leaders. These organizations do not enjoy the built-in self-regulation mechanisms that other businesses have. Donors are not necessarily the not-for-profit service users. Consequently, those who pay cannot directly control or express satisfaction about the service encounter (Normann, 1986). Adding to the complexity, the two systems might not be well aligned: an increase in the financial needs of the service production system might come at a time of government cuts or when there is a shortage of private contributions; there might be conflicting views expressed when marketing to two different publics; there might be a different balance in skills and competencies of professionals who are working in the two systems – just to name a few. These concerns hold for arts organizations, which can affect the consistency of their actions, especially in respect to their fundraising choices.

However, some clarifications should be made. Museums and theatres cannot cover the full costs of their operations with earned income, but part of their revenue still comes from commercial activities (ticket sales, venue rental, merchandising, sponsorship, etc.). This situation might bring about opportunities to mitigate the dual system trap, but at the same time it poses some threats.

The opportunities derive from a functional overlap between what we may call the resource development system and the service production system. A large overlap might be decreased if, for example, there is the possibility of transforming ticket holders into arts organization members or cultural philanthropists who support the organization. The threats are linked to the possibility that the appetite (and need) for more commercial revenue weakens the mission-driven nature of an arts organization.

Taking this perspective into account, fundraising is therefore vital for arts institutions if they want to keep a focus on their social and cultural mission: fundraisers are the key-people who can help secure the funds need to implement mission and fulfil community cultural needs (Van Steenburg et al., 2022). If this holds true for the United States, a healthy fundraising culture in arts organizations is even more important in Europe, where government cuts are forcing such organizations to cultivate and solicit gifts from private donors.

Today, strengthening development departments in arts organizations is taking place in parallel with a greater awareness about the public nature of arts institutions: they exist not only to market their services and sell tickets, but also to serve the community at large. Still, internal negotiations often take place when fundraisers try to emphasize the relevance of their work for the organization's survival (Herrero and Kraegen, 2020), and it is only during the past several decades that arts institutions have acknowledged that there is an increasing demand for specialized and skilled professionals (Suarez, 2010; Kuenzi and Stewart, 2017). Recruiting the right people to cover positions in their fundraising departments is becoming an increasing challenge. What are the key skills needed for effective fundraising and what are the trends in the market for development professionals? In the following paragraph, we will briefly respond to these concerns.

## 1.3 Arts fundraisers' expertise and career trajectories

It is only fairly recently that scholars have begun to examine various profiles for fundraising professionals and to study the reasons for and ramifications of their frequent career switching and erratic career trajectories (Norris-Tirrell et al., 2018). This is surprising, because such information would help arts institutions to identify candidates possessing the most appropriate characteristics, skills and professional knowledge better and more easily. In the following paragraphs, we note the expertise that previous studies have evidenced as being important for fundraising careers, as well as the career paths that fundraising professionals are currently experiencing.

### 1.3.1 *Arts fundraisers' expertise*

Even if the majority of case histories show that personal skills are the most important attribute for skilled fundraisers, Norris-Tirrell et al. (2018) indicate that higher education is still very important in the career trajectories of not-for-profit executive leaders. Furthermore, Nathan and Tempel (2017) demonstrate in various studies that fundraisers with high levels of formal education and professionalization have distinct advantages during their careers.

The increasing availability of business education has allowed fundraisers to acquire managerial skills, including financial management, technical abilities, proficiency in program analysis and a global perspective on change (Haggerty, 2015). Mor Barak et al. (2001) also reveal the existence of a negative relationship between education and turnover intentions among service organization workers. In their recent study, Turrini et al. (2022) clearly show that arts fundraisers with a business education background have a longer tenure and a lower likelihood of career switching than those with a non-business education background.

All this provides useful insights that should inform human resources (HR) selection processes within arts and culture organizations. Indeed, despite cultural institutions lacking a business-like orientation (Kolb, 2013), arts organizations should care about the different skills and competencies of their fundraising professionals. In his research, for instance, Breeze (2017: 57) lists the following traits and skills as the most common among fundraisers:

- they have formative experiences involving helping behaviors;
- they can rely on high levels of generalized trust;
- they have a greater predilection for gift-giving to loved ones and donating blood to strangers;
- they have a willingness to facilitate social situations;
- they have a preference for community-oriented and intellectual hobbies;
- they present positive personality traits and higher levels of emotional intelligence.

Broadly speaking, fundraisers are motivated by what has been labelled a public service motivation (PSM), which is generally defined as a calling to serve a specific mission (Perry and Wise, 1990) or a higher purpose. PSM can be rational, such as an interest in public policy; normative, such as a desire to achieve social justice; or affective, such as a compassionate attitude (Norris-Tirrell et al., 2018). Empirical studies have shown how PSM has changed over time: younger generations are often motivated to pursue not-for-profit careers by a willingness to address a certain issue or to impact a specific community based on their personal experiences;

while older leaders have been motivated by a general desire to "change the world" (Kunreuther, 2006: 3). All these reflections bring us back to the previously mentioned paradigm of the civil economy.

One of the most powerful levers in the accrual of skills and competencies is the on-the-job training that fundraisers experience over time. In most of the studies about careers in fundraising, deeper acquaintance with the third sector is linked to a longer tenure in fundraising positions. In their pivotal study about fundraising jobs, for example, Tempel and Duronio (1997) found that fundraisers with ten or more years' experience stayed in their jobs two years longer than less experienced fundraisers. More recently, Nathan and Tempel (2017) have found that, on average, individuals who have ten or more years of experience in fundraising and earn the highest levels of compensation tend to keep working in fundraising for long periods of time. Similarly, Shaker et al. (2022) have found that older and more experienced fundraisers had longer job tenures. In addition, more experience in the field (i.e., working in a single sector for a long time) was found to be negatively correlated with turnover intentions (Mor Barak et al., 2001).

Turrini et al. (2022) confirm this picture for the arts field: individuals working in a single sector for a long time are more likely to have longer tenures and less likely to switch careers than those who have been in the sector for a shorter time. These results imply that the most committed employees are those who show a high rate of sector experience and indicate a commitment to one sector.

### 1.3.2 *Arts fundraisers' career trajectories*

Careers in fundraising either start accidentally or because practitioners are motivated by the personal desire to serve a higher purpose. Many fundraising professionals enter the not-for-profit sector from the business sector (Schlosser et al., 2017). This trend is particularly evident in the United States (Suarez, 2010), where fundraising is recognized more widely as an independent managerial function than it is in Europe. Moreover, Bozeman and Ponomariov (2008) found that professionals in technical jobs are more likely to switch careers than those employed in managerial positions.

Scholars have noted various motivational factors that lead professionals to begin a career in fundraising:

1. *Falling into a career.* In this group, fundraisers do not plan to start their career in not-for-profits. Their entry into the profession is accidental, stemming from an organization- or mission-based interest rather than a job-based one (Farwell et al., 2020). Farwell et al. (2020) also state that individuals who fall into the profession do not necessarily have specific skills that are relevant to the fundraising position.
2. *Life changes, personal relations and interests.* In this group, individuals begin their collaboration with a not-for-profit institution because of unexpected changes in their lives such as redundancy, a firm's shutdown or a workforce shrinking in their original field. Some professionals in this category are driven towards a career in fundraising thanks to professional or personal contacts (Nelson, 2017). Occasionally, volunteers who have encountered the interesting work and compelling mission of a not-for-profit organization apply for a staff position (Krumboltz, 2009).
3. *Looking for a higher purpose.* Some professionals may decide to enter the not-for-profit sector to pursue a meaningful and gratifying job that supports charitable activities (Levy, 2004). Scholars highlight how fundraisers in this cohort have often worked previously in "people-oriented" fields such as education, advertising and promotion, and also in general business (Dale, 2017). These individuals are more likely to be "attuned to the societal value" and "the common good" than to the "dollar value" and "the company good" (Marion, 1997: 72).
4. *Interest in the sector and investing in a specific education.* Even if there has been little research into education and career experiences as drivers towards the highest-paying jobs in not-for-profit organizations, the number of individuals entering the sector after obtaining fundraising-specific degrees at higher education institutions is clearly growing (Norris-Tirrell et al., 2018). Another relevant feature is that trained not-for-profit executives with fundraising-oriented careers display loyalty to their organization and its purpose (Kuenzi and Stewart, 2017). Individuals with specific education in fundraising also have a short tenure in their first position and experience rapid quick career growth thereafter because of their potential (Kuenzi and Stewart, 2017). Many arts practitioners consciously choose to forego careers in the for-profit sector, and such

> individuals are often reluctant to intermingle arts and culture with anything that could be considered commercial or profit oriented. The logic behind this attitude seems to be a conception of art as superior to any purely commercial activity and therefore a commitment to not-for-profit orientation.

Looking at career trajectories, previous studies have indicated that a strong commitment towards an arts organization and its mission – inspired by values and a specific vision of the world – rather than towards personal achievements is a common trend among high tenure or non-switching fundraisers (Tempel and Duronio, 1997).

Some individuals tend to hold parallel titles in their organizations, which may indicate that they are less focused on fundraising. Therefore, one specific function (fundraising as opposed to, for example, marketing) should be prioritized to avoid dispersion and loss of focus, thus encouraging role specialization. Data demonstrate that individuals with parallel titles in the same organization (i.e., marketing and development director) are likely to have a shorter tenure in their current job (Turrini et al., 2022)

As we discuss in more detail throughout this book, fundraising relies on personal, trust-based relationships more than on transactional exchanges between the arts organization and its donors. Building long-lasting relationships requires time and effort, especially in the case of substantial gifts; otherwise, donors may be confused and see their contribution not as added value for the organization but as a mere commercial exchange. Consequently, changes and turnover in development staff can have an impact on the level of donations. Losing momentum in development can translate immediately into losing money and opportunities. That being said, since fundraisers develop skills and build relationships with donors over long periods, arts organizations should prefer to invest in long tenures for their development team. Luckily, Schneider (2009) states that career switching in fundraising is problematic because of several key reasons. First, fundraisers are recognized as part of the organization and as one of its "assets," and they serve as points of reference for the organization's internal groupings. Consequently, switching careers within the organization may be easier than switching from one organization to another. Secondly, the fundraising function is often shared with the board, the chief executive officer (CEO) or the board chair: the opportunity to make a career within an organization might lower turnover especially when internal advancement is supported by senior leaders. Consequently, the opportunity for advancement within the organization is recommended to those cultural institutions that want to attract and retain talented and experienced fundraising professionals.

## 1.4 Concluding thoughts: the rationale behind *Fundraising for the Arts*

The work of fundraising has been transformed into a sophisticated and competitive profession, attracting talented and dedicated leaders who wish to use their skills to contribute to a secure financial future for their organizations. The arts and cultural field has not been an exception, as cultural institutions in the United States and Europe are becoming more and more reliant on contributed income because ticket sales and public sector funding are flat at best.

As the competition for contributed income increases, individuals with specific fundraising education and experience become ever more attractive to cultural institutions that are hiring development staff. Furthermore, scholars and practitioners are continuing to refine and clarify the role of development professionals within the arts sector as arts institutions embrace the notion of a culture of philanthropy.

This book aims to be a reference point for upper-level undergraduate students, graduate students and junior practitioners in the arts management field. It provides core insights about and inspiration for careers in fundraising for the arts and high-quality content (including on advanced topics such as the organizational dynamics of creating a culture of philanthropy, EDI (equity, diversity and inclusion) in fundraising, the use of digital and social media platforms, board involvement, performance management and accountability) that will appeal to novice or experienced practitioners.

The book supports learning, lecturing and understanding by providing examples and mini-cases in each chapter. Each chapter ends with a list of keywords for arts fundraisers and suggested questions for meetings and discussion relating to the topic that has been covered.

We begin our discussion by providing a definition of the culture of philanthropy and its implications for arts institutions. The subsequent chapters are organized in two parts: Actors (Chapters 3–6) and Processes

(Chapters 7–10). The first part focuses on fundraising actors, analyzing the role played by small and large individual donors, corporations, public agencies and private grant-makers. In respect to processes, we discuss planning in fundraising, capital campaigns and the necessity of evaluating and communicating the impacts of fundraising for the arts. The book ends with an overview on the implications of digital fundraising in the arts sector.

*Fundraising for the Arts* includes contributions from American and European practitioners, which are intended to offer varying perspectives on the trends, opportunities and challenges faced by cultural institutions on two continents.

Let us start our journey!

## Keywords for arts fundraisers

Civil economy, post-COVID-19 pandemic social distress, trust, reciprocity, commons, cultural philanthropy, art collector, patronage of the arts, capitalist philanthropy, give back, crowdfunding, relational goods, dual internal system, fundraising careers, public service motivation (PSM), third sector, fundraising careers, turnover, career trajectories

## Suggested questions for meetings and discussions

- What duality between income and fundraising systems exists in arts organizations? Do you see any difference between European and American arts organizations in respect to this?
- What can help arts organizations to enhance the alignment of their fundraising actions with their income system?
- How can arts organizations play an active civic role in their community?
- What are the main challenges that arts organizations face when recruiting arts fundraisers?
- What are the key-skills of an effective arts fundraiser?

## References

Becchetti, L. and Cermelli, M. (2018). "Civil economy: Definition and strategies for sustainable well-living," *International Review of Economics*, 65: 329–357.

Becchetti, L., Pelloni, A. and Rossetti, F. (2008). "Relational goods, sociability, and happiness", *Kyklos*, 61 (3): 343–363.

Benjamin, W. ([1935] 2008). *The work of art in the age of its technological reproducibility*. Cambridge, MA: Harvard University Press.

Bianchi, M. (1997). "Collecting as a paradigm of consumption," *Journal of Cultural Economics*, 21: 275–289.

Bozeman, B. and Ponomariov, B. (2009). "Sector switching from a business to a government job: Fast-track career or fast track to nowhere?" *Public Administration Review*, 69 (1): 77–91.

Breeze, B. (2017). *The new fundraisers: Who organises charitable giving in contemporary society?* Bristol: Policy Press.

Bruni, L. and Zamagni, S. (2016). *Civil economy another idea of the market.* New York: Agenda Publishing, Columbia University Press.

Bruni, L. and Stanca, L. (2008). "Watching alone: Relational goods, television and happiness," *Journal of Economic Behavior & Organization*. 65 (3–4): 506–528.

Dale, E. J. (2017). "Fundraising as women's work? Examining the profession with a gender lens," *International Journal of Nonprofit and Voluntary Sector Marketing*, 22 (4): e1605.

Farwell, M. M., Gaughan, M. and Handy, F. (2020). "How did we get here? The career paths of higher education fundraisers," *Nonprofit Management and Leadership*, 30 (3): 487–507.

Frugoni, C. (2008). *L'affare migliore di Enrico. Giotto e la cappella Scrovegni.* Turin: Einaudi.

Genovesi, A. (1769). *Lezione di commercio o sia d'economia civile.* Venice: A spese Remondini.

Gui, B. (1987) "Eléments pour une définition d'économie communautaire," *Notes et documents*, 19–20: 32–42.

Guibert, G. and Hyde, I. (2021). *Analysis: COVID-19's Impacts on Arts and Culture.* Available at https://www.arts.gov/sites/default/files/COVID-Outlook-Week-of1.4.2021-revised.pdf (accessed 26 May 2021).

Haggerty, A. L. (2015). *Turnover intentions of nonprofit fundraising professionals: The roles of perceived fit, exchange relationships, and job satisfaction* (unpublished PhD thesis). Richmond: Virginia Commonwealth University.

Herrero, M. and Kraemer, S. (2020). "Fundraising as organizational knowing in practice: Evidence from the arts and higher education in the UK," *International Journal of Nonprofit and Voluntary Sector Marketing*, 25 (4): e1673.

Kolb, B. M. (2013). *Marketing for cultural organizations: New strategies for attracting audiences*. London: Routledge.

Krumboltz, J. D. (2009). "The happenstance learning theory," *Journal of Career Assessment*, 17: 135–154.

Kuenzi, K. and Stewart, A. J. (2017). "An exploratory study of the nonprofit executive factor: Linking nonprofit financial performance and executive careers," *The Journal of Nonprofit Education and Leadership*, 7 (4): 306–324.

Kunreuther, F. (2006). *Up next: Generation change and the leadership of nonprofit organizations*. Baltimore, MD: The Annie E. Casey Foundation.

Levy, J. D. (2004). "The growth of fundraising: framing the impact of research and literature on education and training," *New Directions for Philanthropic Fundraising*, 43: 21–30.

Marion, B. H. (1997). "The education of fundraisers," *New Directions for Philanthropic Fundraising*, 15: 69–81.

Mason, D. E. (1984). "Dual internal systems," in Mason, D. E., *Voluntary Nonprofit Enterprise Management: Nonprofit Management and Finance*. Boston, MA: Springer.

Mauss, M. ([1925] 1950). *Essai sur le don*. Paris: PUF.

McLean, P. (2005). "Patronage, citizenship, and the stalled emergence of the modern State in Renaissance Florence," *Comparative Studies in Society and History*, 47 (3): 638–664.

Mor Barak, M. E., Nissly, J. A. and Levin, A. (2001). "Antecedents to retention and turnover among child welfare, social work, and other human service employees: What can we learn from past research? A review and metanalysis," *Social Service Review*, 75 (4): 625–661.

Nathan, S. K. and Tempel, E. R. (2017). *Fundraisers in the 21st Century*, Academic Studies Collection, IUPUI Lilly Family School of Philanthropy, Indianapolis (US).

Nelson, E. (2017). "The accidental nonprofiteer: Chance events and the selection of a nonprofit career," *The Journal of Nonprofit Education and Leadership*, 7 (4), 287–305.

Norman, R. (1986). *Service management: Strategy and leadership in service businesses*. London: John Wiley and Sons

Norris-Tirrell, D., Rinella, J. and Pham, X. (2018). "Examining the career trajectories of nonprofit executive leaders," *Nonprofit and Voluntary Sector Quarterly*, 47 (1): 146–164.

Nussbaum, M. (1986). *The Fragility of Goodness: Luck and Ethics in Greek Tragedy and Philosophy*, Part 2, 2nd ed. Cambridge: Cambridge University Press.

Perry, J. L. and Wise, L. R. (1990). "The motivational bases of public service," *Public Administration Review* 50 (3), 367–373.

Polanyi, K. ([1944] 2001). *The great transformation: The political and economic origins of our time*. Boston: Beacon Press.

Putnam, R. D., Leonardi, R. and Nanetti., R. Y. (1992) *Making democracy work: Civic traditions in modern Italy*. Princeton, NJ: Princeton University Press.

Putnam, R. D., *Bowling alone: The collapse and revival of American community* (New York: Simon & Schuster, 2000).

Saltamacchia, M. (2011). "The Prince and the prostitute: Competing sovereignties in Fourteenth-Century Milan," in: Sturges, R. (ed.), *Law and sovereignty in the Middle Ages and Renaissance*, 173–191. Turnhout: Brepols.

Schlosser, F., McPhee, D. M. and Forsyth, J. (2017). "Chance events and executive career rebranding: Implications for career coaches and nonprofit HRM," *Human Resource Management*, 56 (4), 571–591.

Schneider, J. A. (2009). "Organizational social capital and nonprofits," *Nonprofit and Voluntary Sector Quarterly*, 38 (4): 643–662.

Shaker, G. G., Rooney, P. M., Nathan, S. K., Bergdoll, J. J. and Tempel, E. R. (2022). "Turnover intention and job tenure of US fundraisers," *Journal of Philanthropy and Marketing*, 27 (4), e1742.

Suarez, D. F. (2010). "Street credentials and management backgrounds: Careers of nonprofit executives in an evolving sector," *Nonprofit and Voluntary Sector Quarterly*, 39 (4), 696–716.

Sugden, R. (2021). "The correspondence of sentiments. An explanation of the pleasure of social interaction" in: Bruni, L. and Pier, P. (eds), *Economics and Happiness: Framing of analysis*, 91–115. Oxford: Oxford University Press.

Tempel, E. R. and Duronio, M. A. (1997). "The demographics and experience of fundraisers," *New Directions for Philanthropic Fundraising*, 15: 49–68.

Terpstra, N. (ed.) (1999). *The politics of ritual kinship: Confraternities and social order in early modern Italy*. Cambridge, Cambridge University Press.

Turrini, A., Massi, M., Mion, P. G. and Prokupek, M. (2022). *Exploring fundraising executives' careers in the arts and culture: The role of tenure and career switching*, Working paper series, SDA Bocconi Arts Knowledge Center.

Turrini, A. (1999). *Appunti del Corso di Storia del Pensiero Economico* (PhD thesis). Milan: Bocconi University.

Turrini, A. (2020). *Texas arts collectors as cultural philanthropists*, Working paper, SMU-Meadows School for the Arts, Dallas Texas.

Turrini, A. (2021). "Io ho quello che ho donato." *Exploring the institutionalization of cultural philanthropy*, "Collecting as Giving" Public Lecture Series, Heidelberg University, Heidelberg.

Turrini, A. and Voss, Z. (2020). "Strategic fundraising in the arts" in Addis, M. and Rurale, A. (eds), *Managing the cultural business: Avoiding mistakes, finding success*, 180–198. London: Routledge.

Van Steenburg, E., Anaza, N. A., Ashhar, A., Barrios, A., Deutsch, A. R., Gardner, M. P. and Taylor, K. A. (2022). "The new world of philanthropy: How changing financial behavior, public policies, and COVID-19 affect nonprofit fundraising and marketing," *Journal of Consumer Affairs*, 56 (3): 1079–1105.

Zamagni, S. (2018). "Beni comuni territoriali e economia civile," *Scienze del territorio*, 6: 50–59.

# 2 Introducing a Culture of Philanthropy in Arts Organizations

with *Lanfranco Li Cauli*

## 2.1 Culture of philanthropy: concepts and definitions

Traditionally, individuals within an arts organization had very distinct roles. The second oboist played the second oboe parts. The actor playing Hamlet just played Hamlet. The curator for Ancient Egyptian, Nubian and Near Eastern Art only focused on art from those regions. And the development director solely raised money. While this approach worked in the past, the digital revolution, the proliferation of not-for-profits arts institutions competing for funds and the evolving sensibilities of younger generations have led to rethinking about who is responsible for fundraising. As Cynthia Gibson noted in her article "Beyond Fundraising," when considering who was responsible for fundraising in arts organizations, it might have seemed weird for a development director to state that fundraising was "everyone's job." Similarly, a request by fundraisers to be involved in key organizational planning meetings, including those focused on artistic and mission topics, would not have been welcomed (Gibson, 2016: 4). In other words, development professionals were just expected to raise money and not to be involved in decision-making regarding the core activities of the arts institution.

Today, with the arrival of more enlightened thinking, the modern arts organization is best served if all employees and volunteers have "ownership" of fundraising success. Now, the second oboist may serve on an annual fund committee and occasionally might be asked to write thank-you notes to donors. The actor playing Hamlet might speak to a group of donors at a post-performance reception. The curator of Egyptian,

Nubian and Near Eastern Art might lead a group of donors on an excavation in Egypt. And the lead development officer should expect to be included in meetings in which strategic decisions are made. This is not to say that artists are being asked to replace the arts organization's development team or that the development director will be allowed to make programming decisions. Rather, such involvement has more to do with cultural attitudes and approaches than with functional responsibility and a team approach to management. In essence, everyone in the organization has "fundraising" as an element of their job description, whether directly or indirectly, as arts institutions realize that developing a culture of philanthropy is very important to achieve sustainability. Furthermore, this culture can unify the entire organization around a shared purpose (Gibson, 2016).

In order to understand how a shared culture of philanthropy has become a key factor for the success of an arts organization, we have to distinguish philanthropy from fundraising and fundraising from development. Fundraising is the technique, the plan, the programs and the tactics that are implemented to persuade individuals and organizations to make gifts to an arts or other type of not-for-profit institution. Typically, there is a reciprocal dimension to fundraising, as both the donor and the not-for-profit derive benefit from the transaction. Philanthropy is the cultural attitude that shapes and gives consistency to fundraising: its purpose is to build better and stable social infrastructure and relationships (Worth, 2016). Broadly speaking, philanthropy is an investment made by private entities (e.g., citizens, foundations, companies) to support the production of goods and services of public interest – such as the arts – to facilitate the improvement of communities. Representative examples of philanthropy in the arts might include gifts made to construct new arts venues, endow educational projects or fund new artistic productions. Philanthropy, as an attitude, is long-term oriented. Fundraising, as a technique, focuses on donor analysis, plans, programs and actions, and has a shorter-term orientation. Different arts organizations can rely on similar fundraising methods to implement their development strategies, but each has its own philanthropic attitude, as it is a further expression of its mission and general purpose. As we discuss in Chapter 1, philanthropy has to do with personal values, culture and vison of the world, and development officers should strive to scout and nurture philanthropic attitudes and interests among people – outside and inside the arts organization – in order to achieve their goals more effectively. Philanthropy is about people, not just money, as it leads to engagement and strong donor relationships. True philanthropy can turn the transactional approach, in other words asking for donations (that is, benefits in exchange for money), into the building of long-lasting relationships between the institution and its supporters around an arts organization's mission.

This wider perspective introduces the concept of development as it contrasts with that of fundraising. As Worth (2016) highlights, fundraising is often a collection of single actions and initiatives; while development is a continuous activity of relationship-building. Fundraising focuses on a particular target or set of goals, while development has a more holistic approach and is aligned with a long-term commitment to support the empowerment of an arts institution as a whole. A specific set of interpersonal skills is essential for successful fundraisers; development officers, instead, are focused on the mission of the arts institution, with a deeper understanding of the organization and its financial situation as well as a strong orientation towards the aim of building long-lasting relationships with donors. Their expertise and professional skill in soliciting gifts define fundraisers; being a strategist and (but not always necessarily) a skilled fundraiser is what characterizes a development officer. More than two thousand years ago, Aristotle stated: "To give away money is an easy matter and in any man's power. But to decide to whom to give it, and how much, and when, and for what purpose and how, is neither in every man's power nor an easy matter."[1]

To truly maximize their impact, arts organizations that aspire to build a strong culture of philanthropy should be more focused on the broader notion of development; this contrasts with fundraising, which is focused on securing gifts. Figure 2.1 provides an emotional visual example of the idea of culture of philanthropy that we discuss in this book.

---

[1] Quoted in Yoon (2014: 302).

*Figure 2.1* "Youth." Oil on Belgian linen by Hennie Niemann jnr, 2019

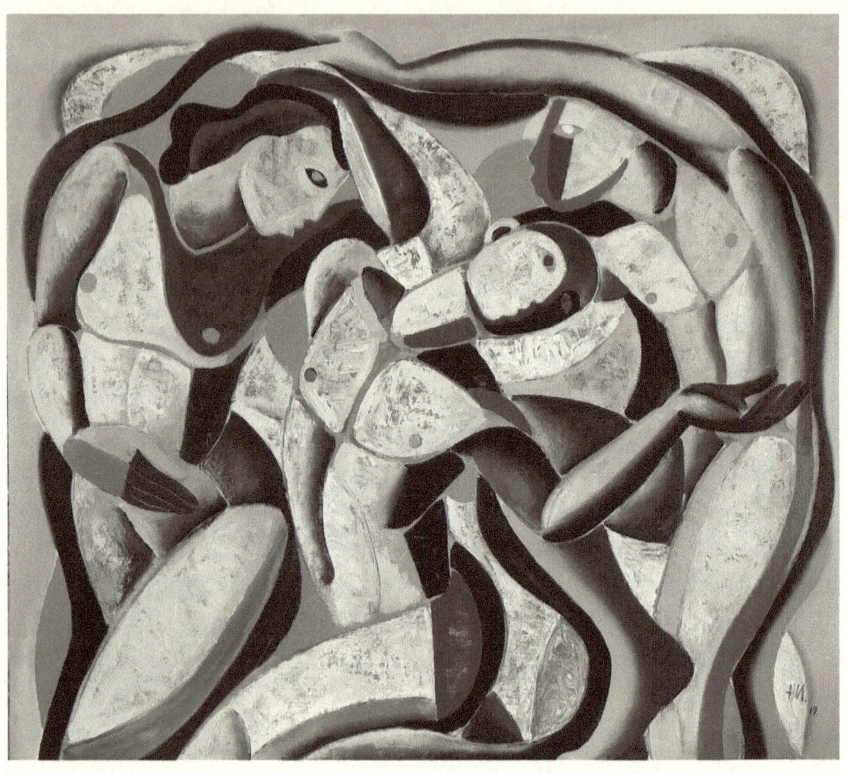

*Credit:* Hennie Niemann, CC BY-SA 4.0, via Wikimedia Commons

## 2.2 The importance of building a culture of philanthropy in arts organizations

A culture of philanthropy does not exist in a vacuum. Rather, it is a subset of the broader organizational culture of arts institutions. Furthermore, in the best cases, it helps foster staff, board and artist engagement with the organization's purpose or mission (Yoon, 2014; Gibson, 2016; Whitchurch and Comer, 2016; Zirkle, 2017).

While there are several ways of describing organizational culture, perhaps it can be best defined as the personality of an arts organization. This personality is the institution's tacit social order, mostly based on unwritten rules and relationships, and concerns the behavioral norms of people within an organization.[2] External factors (e.g., political, industry-related, societal, cultural, technological) can have a great influence on organizational culture, which can evolve as demands and opportunities emerge. For instance, in the United States and many other parts of the world, the social justice movement has altered the dynamics within arts organizations and is causing a cultural shift in many cultural institutions whose employees and audiences have been predominantly Caucasian or Asian. Furthermore, the digital revolution – which is undeniably systemic and hugely pervasive – has also sparked a change in their culture, especially in terms of ways to communicate.[3] Finally, the full and lasting impact of the COVID-19 pandemic on the arts sector is currently (2022) difficult to assess, but certainly has and will have ramifications for the organizational culture in arts institutions.

Organizational culture is therefore influenced by external changes even if the pace of change might be slow. Culture is less formalized and structured since it includes, as stated earlier, a set of behaviors, unwritten rules and social patterns. At the same time, it can be extremely important in driving motivation and focusing energy towards shared objectives.

So how does a culture of philanthropy fit into an organizational culture? As previously noted, a culture of philanthropy is based on the assumption that everyone in the organization should be aware that each member can do something to establish reciprocal relationships and effectively contribute to raising resources (Gibson, 2016). Consequently, in arts organizations where a culture of philanthropy is established, it is understood that development has a great value, aiding the realization of the institution's mission.

---

[2] Schein (2004: 17) summarizes the attributes of organizational culture as "a pattern of shared basic assumptions that the group learned as it solved its problems of external adaptation and internal integration and that has worked well enough to be considered valid and, therefore, to be taught to new members as the correct way to perceive, think, and feel in relation to those problems". Schein's definition is particularly interesting because it focuses on people's reactions and adaptations as their external environment evolves, as well as the internal dynamics of the organization. Furthermore, it embeds the possibility for people to "learn" the culture that will ultimately influence their approach to problem-solving. In managerial terms, organizational culture also impacts on various intangibles such as group dynamics and social balancing.

[3] See Section 2.3.

Understanding the importance of relationships with internal and external stakeholders of the arts organization is also key to fostering a culture of philanthropy. The organization perceives actual and potential donors as having something to give beyond money: by offering support, they are contributing to the common good (Payton and Moody, 2008). In other words, organizations that have embraced the notion of building a culture of philanthropy regard fundraising as a way in which new community relationships can be established and existing ones can be nurtured.[4]

It is easy to define the difference between a culture of philanthropy and a culture of fundraising. The former refers to the act of helping, giving and doing good, shared as a common attitude among all the members of the organization and with relationships as the main drivers. Money is just a means to give tangible support to a cause that the organization shares with its stakeholders through a high level of engagement. Conversely, a culture of fundraising focuses on the technical ability to raise money by using a more tactical and transactional approach. If there is a culture of fundraising, the entire institution assumes that fundraising is a function in the organizational structure and that the development department is tasked with the exclusive responsibility of soliciting contributions for the organization's various needs, with few connections being made with other departments. Consequently, shortfalls in fundraising are always the fault of the development department which can lead to staff burnout and turnover.

A culture of philanthropy, in contrast, involves everybody in the organization in the development process and shares fundraising accountability among the different levels of the functional hierarchy. Bell and Cornelius (2013: 22) comment on the vicious circle when blame is placed on poor fundraising performance, leading to short tenure and volatility in development director positions. They argue that building a culture of philanthropy can break this cycle, as capacity is built across the entire institution: everyone in all departments takes some responsibility for philanthropy, so the institution can succeed even during periods of development staff turnover. A cultural institution with a strong philanthropic culture can continue to perform well after the departure of a charismatic

---

[4] See also Chapter 1.

leader. Ultimately, this culture can outlast any leader and results in better results for fundraising activities. Moreover, a strong culture of philanthropy benefits organizational cohesion at all levels, strengthening trust, cooperation and engagement among internal groups and external stakeholders. It favors a greater alignment between the cultural institution's mission and its programs and goals, with a positive effect on revenue.

Given the challenges hastened by the COVID-19 pandemic, arts organizations that have not already done so should consider making a significant shift in how they think about and design their approach to raising funds. Establishing or reinforcing a culture of philanthropy and converting it into managerial practice are important steps towards organizational viability (see Box 2.1 for an example).

**Box 2.1 Culture of philanthropy at Teatro alla Scala in Milan**

Teatro alla Scala relies on private support for about one-third of its income. This support comes from both private donors and companies, who support the theatre through donations and sponsorship agreements. In order to secure these grants, the fundraising department works very carefully on the relationship with the organization's donors and sponsors. Teatro alla Scala creates different levels of engagement – according to contribution levels – with the aim of increasingly involving supporters in the life of the opera house. This approach has led to the creation of donor and sponsor categories, with different levels of involvement and participation. The common thread of these efforts is letting donors live a "unique experience." Everybody at La Scala is aware of this, starting with the front office staff and up to the executives. All play their role as "fundraisers," sharing the mission of La Scala in different contexts.

*Source*: Lanfranco Li Cauli personal communication

## 2.3 How to build a culture of philanthropy in arts organizations

The process of initiating and nurturing a culture of philanthropy in arts organizations is complex: it is incremental, gradual and requires time. It is a laborious process, but, if effectively implemented, a transition to such a culture can have a lasting impact on the institution. There are several elements to building a culture of philanthropy that should be noted (see Fig. 2.2).

*Figure 2.2* How to build a culture of philanthropy in arts organizations

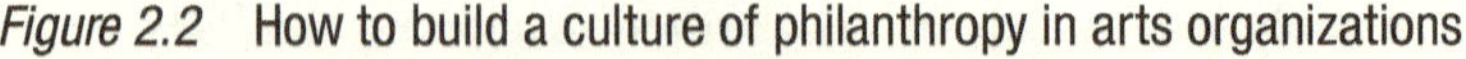

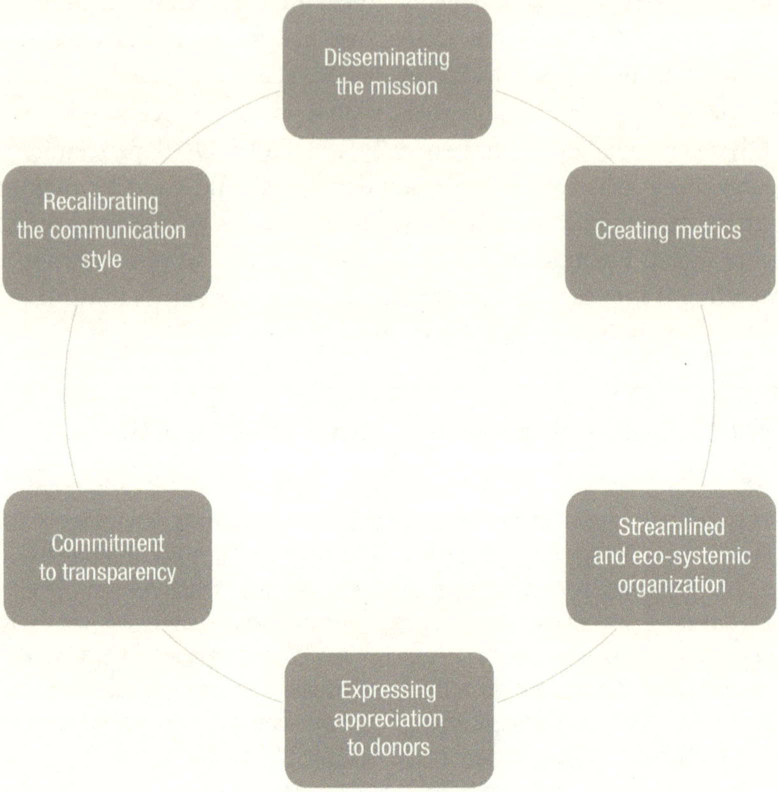

Effective communication/dissemination of an arts organization's mission is the first key element when building a culture of philanthropy. As previously mentioned, everyone in the organization must feel a responsibility to promote philanthropy and should be able to articulate, in their own words, a case for giving.[5] To do this effectively, all constituents should have a solid understanding of the organization's mission and activities. Typically, staff meetings should include a briefing on the institution's various activities and the need for philanthropic support, so that

[5] See the Essential Glossary for Arts Fundraisers, p. 297.

its mission can be realized. A discussion of mission should also be part of board members' agendas. When staff, artists and board members have a common understanding of the purpose of their organization, they can more effectively communicate to their respective networks, allowing the creation of connections and the building of relationships, something that will resonate with donors and others who are interested in supporting their particular organization. In sum, everyone can play a role in helping to acquire all the resources needed to do the organization's work: a clear and understandable mission statement can motivate all groups to participate, as they will have a coherent vision of what the arts organization can and will be if a culture of philanthropy is sustainably implemented. However, as Gibson (2016: 10) suggests, engaging donors as partners in the work does not mean that they are "driving the bus"; they are active players in the institution's life, rather than simple funders. With this in mind, Zirkle (2017) suggests that engagement with the organization's mission should start within it before extending to the external environment and donor base (the inside-out approach).

Creating metrics to evaluate process development and goal achievement is crucial in order to shift effectively and sustainably to a culture of philanthropy. When guided by a culture of philanthropy, arts organizations should broaden their definition of metrics, not only looking at traditional quantitative aspects, but also at other relevant features (e.g., donors' level of engagement and participation, grade of endorsement, quality perceived, communication) to evaluate success. For example, philanthropy reports should not only include metrics on numbers, size and source of gifts (e.g., individuals, foundations, corporations), but also the various ways in which donors are being engaged (including a listing of social appointments, concerts and events attended by donors) and other various "touch-points" that connect the institution and its supporters. The orientation towards development (and not just fundraising) is what helps managers to persuade every group within the arts organization that raising funds is a consistent and crucial way to feed organizational growth.

The shift from a culture of fundraising to a culture of philanthropy necessitates broader structural changes that make possible the alignment of fundraising with other activities (Whitchurch and Comer, 2016). This means the arts organization's structure has to be redesigned, moving from hierarchical structures that are characterized by rigid department boundaries to flatter, more streamlined and ecosystemic structures that facilitate collaboration, openness and horizontal decision-making. Organizations that understand the need for widespread awareness of the relevance of a philanthropic attitude tend to operate differently because they meld fundraising, communication, marketing and programs department functions into a collaborative whole. In these organizations, development and marketing departments are typically coordinated by a Chief Advancement Officer who is in charge of engagement with the stakeholders. The job description outlined in Box 2.2 emphasizes the requirements for such a professional at the Dallas Symphony.

**Box 2.2 The job description of a Chief Advanced Officer at Dallas Symphony (extract)**

**Summary:**

The Dallas Symphony seeks a seasoned Chief Advancement and Revenue Officer (CARO). This high-level executive position will be directly responsible for successfully leading and implementing an integrated revenue stream comprised of donations and earned revenue. Success will be achieved by leading the strategy of our development and marketing departments to build the organization's visibility, impact, and financial resources.

The Chief Advancement & Revenue Officer (CARO) brings strategic and analytic skills to the organization, and utilizes data and patron feedback to make decisions. The position will be responsible for the integration of the traditional marketing and development functions into a total patron relationship system that enhances the bond between patron and institution to maximize participation and total revenue.

This executive position is one of the key leaders in realizing the strategic objectives of the organization and creating a new, sustainable model among orchestras. He or she works cross-functionally with the senior management team and serves as an external ambassador for the organization. The position will lead a team of professionals responsible for fundraising, volunteer cultivation, corporate philanthropic support, marketing and social media functions for the organization. The Chief Advancement & Revenue Officer (CARO) is a member of the executive team and works together with the team to provide strategic leadership to the organization. The Chief Advancement & Revenue Officer will report to the CEO.

**Specific responsibilities:**

- Evaluate progress in achieving financial and moves management objectives:
- Identify and align on a set of key metrics to evaluate success.

- Monitor progress to goals and respond to feedback in order to improve results.
- Ensure key stakeholders are engaged and motivated to meet organizational targets.
- Develop and implement the overall strategic direction and supporting organizational structure for patron management in conjunction with the Vice President of Sales & Marketing:
- Develop overall structure for customer management across the patron life cycle and identify key touch point opportunities.
- Develop meaningful, customer-informed action plans with clear timelines and owners to move patrons to increasing levels of commitment to the organization.

*Revenue Generation*

- Lead the efforts to raise $8.5 million annually through corporate, individuals, foundations and/or auxiliary funding sources for the Annual Fund, with meaningful assistance from the CEO and Executive Board. Additional fundraising efforts include:
- Gala: $800,000.
- Corporate Event: $300,000.
- League & Auxiliaries $1M.
- Planned giving also falls under the purview of this position.
- Work closely with CEO on the capital campaign to raise $100 million dollars over the next five years with 1.2 million as a 2023 goal.
- Oversee earned revenues – Goal $11M in ticket sales with auxiliary revenue goals of 1.6M.
- Identify and implement new revenue streams, with a focus on increasing sustainable unrestricted, private revenue.
- Partner with CEO to deepen existing donor relationships and cultivate new supporters.
- Plan and evaluate marketing plans and fundraising plans for the organization's immediate and long-term future.

*Board and Senior Staff Leadership*

- Work closely with Executive Team and Development Board Committee on implementation of the Strategic Plan and the development/marketing strategy.
- Attend board meetings and board committee meetings (and oversee management of these meeting) and report on activities as needed, in coordination with the CEO.
- Work with the CEO to ensure board members are engaged and energized by their association with organization.

*Internal Management and Infrastructure*
- Effectively lead the Marketing and Development departments operations, budgets and income forecasts.
- Oversee the communications to ensure consistent messaging and branding throughout the organization in all materials and online.

**Qualifications:**
Bachelor's Degree with a minimum 10 years of executive level experience preferably in non-profit management coupled with past leadership experience representing the organization to external audiences. Demonstrated fundraising success from a variety of fundraising streams coupled with prior staff management and Board engagement experience. Exceptional communication and influencing skills; persuasive, credible and polished communicator both written and verbal. Creative, independent, strategic thinker with project and budget management skills are necessary to be successful. Experience in classical music beneficial.
Excellent computer skills, including Microsoft Office and database management, specifically Tessitura, a plus.

*Source*: https://www.dallassymphony.org

When constructing a culture of philanthropy, arts institutions must also reconsider and recalibrate their communications style, shifting from something that is simply functional or informative, to something more engaging and personal. Communications should make donors feel that they are part of the organization. In a world where, in spite (or because) of the digital revolution, more and more people feel isolated and disconnected, arts institutions can create a community and a sense of belonging through effective communication and engagement. This philosophy of communication is rooted in the co-creation of valuable experiences (common to people and the organization) and in strong community management activity. While this revamped messaging strategy should be employed in the traditional communication methods that relate to the current demographics of the arts audience, such institutions are remiss if this recalibration is not fully deployed in relation to its multiple social media platforms as well. Social media users might be younger on the whole, but they are also seeking connections and a sense of being part of something. In addition, digital communication is much more cost effective, and exponentially increases an arts organization's ability to connect and interact with an audience the size of which was unthinkable prior to the advent of such technology.[6]

Of course, expressing appreciation to donors and celebrating the impact they have are integral to fostering a culture of philanthropy. Expressions of gratitude can be as modest as a heartfelt letter or phone call or as massive in scale as a major event that celebrates those donors who contributed to a successful building campaign. While some donors prefer to remain anonymous, of course, many others want to feel appreciated and have others know of their generosity. Donor listings in programs and on an organization's website, named galleries in museums and performing arts venues, as well as donor celebration days are just a few of the ways in which arts institutions can thank their donors. Furthermore, sincere and authentic donor recognition frequently inspires others to give, and inherent in a culture of philanthropy is the notion that success breeds success. Clearly, the sensitivities and sensibilities of individual donors should be honored, so most celebrations should be tailored to those specific donors who are being acknowledged and be proportionate to the gift and the occasion. Just as in the case of family celebrations around birthdays and anniversaries, celebrations of philanthropy reinforce our collective humanity and bring together those individuals who support a cultural institution.

Finally, the cultivation of a culture of philanthropy includes a commitment to transparency. As they are engaged to share the arts organization's general purpose and their activities, donors should know how their contributions are used and what impact their donations have had. Philanthropists and donors want to change people's lives, and an arts organization needs to reassure them that their contribution is doing exactly that (Yoon, 2014: 301). This awareness and transparency should also characterize internal communication, increasing the engagement of "internal constituencies" in fundraising activities. Box 2.3 provides an example about the development of a culture of philanthropy at Boston Symphony Orchestra.

---

[6] See also Chapter 10, discussing digital fundraising.

**Box 2.3 Building a culture of philanthropy at the Boston Symphony Orchestra (BSO) (1997–2021)**

The BSO's culture of philanthropy has been an important component in the success of the orchestra, which has an annual income in excess of $100 million; this is equally divided between earned income (50 per cent) and support from contributions (25 per cent annual fund and 25 per cent draw from the BSO's $540 million endowment). Every internal group is engaged with fundraising: artistic leaders, paid staff, trustees and artistic staff. Objectives are discussed and reinforced in conversations with all groups. Philanthropic responsibility is sensed by everyone, including ushers and other front-line staff who all understand that they are the first, and sometimes only contact, with the patrons of the orchestra. In advancing this change in culture, the CEO made an analogy that compares attending a concert to eating at a restaurant.

He noted that a bad exchange with a waiter can ruin the evening for a patron even if the food is good. Such a patron would be very unlikely to return. Likewise, a bad experience with an usher or box office staff can lead to a loss of a donor/patron no matter how good the play, opera or concert is. Initially, there was some resistance as some musicians and staff felt that performing their jobs at a very high level should be enough. However, with the passing of time, every group came to understand that they had a role to play in furthering the BSO's philanthropic efforts and that part of their compensation depended on robust fundraising.

This change was evidenced when every musician of the BSO began annually contributing a minimum of $200 in 2005 to support a student fellowship at the BSO's summer academy at Tanglewood. The players' commitment then went beyond their personal giving to include service on an annual fund committee responsible for securing over $10 million in annual support for the orchestra. Musician participation on this committee inspired greater board involvement and commitment, further strengthening internal bonds., To further promote cohesion within staff, board, musicians and artistic leadership, social events were initiated to bring everyone together. Likewise, including everyone in celebratory events such as season openings, anniversaries of conductor tenure, the centennial of Symphony Hall, the seventy-fifth anniversary of Tanglewood Festival and the hundredth anniversary of Leonard Bernstein's birth, celebrated with the Bernstein family, was instrumental in embracing a culture of philanthropy.

*Source:* Mark Volpe personal communication

### 2.3.1 *The role of the board in building a culture for philanthropy in arts organizations*

As previously stated, successfully creating and fortifying a culture of philanthropy requires that all internal constituencies understand that they have a role to play in supporting the philanthropic efforts that sustain their arts institution. However, this will not happen unless executive and board leadership provides the necessary inspiration and guidance.

As fiduciaries, the CEO and board members have the legal responsibility for ensuring the future of an arts organization and thus must take the lead in developing and shaping a culture of philanthropy. In most jurisdictions, the duties and legal obligations of board members are embedded in the law. Fiduciaries approve and amend institutional bylaws, they hire the CEO and possibly the artistic director, they approve annual and capital budgets, they review and approve major strategic and mission related plans, and they nominate other fiduciaries. However, in the not-for-profit arts world, perhaps the most important role they play is providing philanthropic leadership, so the support necessary for arts institutions to fulfil their purposes can be secured. Consequently, leadership plays a key role in developing and shaping a culture of philanthropy. Board leaders should be willing to share their own philanthropic stories and to make fundraising a central topic in their meetings.

To further encourage board members to participate in advancing a culture of philanthropy, CEOs and development directors should provide opportunities for board members, artistic leadership and artists to connect. While the motivations for committing their "time, treasure and talent" to the boards of cultural institutions vary, most board members value this kind of interaction. Board chairs and the institution's CEOs are well advised to foster an environment in which staff, members of the board, musicians and artists get to know and respect each other. If this is done well, each group will gain a better understanding of their respective roles in supporting fundraising activities. Over time, influential artists, staff and donors can provide each other with support and inspiration as their institution transitions to a culture of philanthropy.

In engaging board leaders, one of the issues that occurs most frequently is when even the most experienced members cross the line from governance to management. Conversely, some CEOs are perfectly willing to let the board or its chair make management decisions. This can lead to territoriality issues, and these can sometimes cause further problems. Boards tend to fill management voids when policies are non-existent or not enforced. Building an open conversation with the entire board or with individual board members might help to overcome role confusion (Cornforth, 1999; Ostrower and Stone, 2006). It is only in the mutual awareness and respect of their specific roles that these leaders can find a balance in their duties.

As an arts organization commits itself to initiating and sustaining a culture of philanthropy, the nominating processes play a vital role in keeping the institution's board dynamic and vibrant. When recruiting new board members, nominating committees and board chairs should consider several factors beyond the financial capacity and suitability of prospective candidates. First, they should be suspicious of individuals who are inclined to put their own interests over those of the institution; a well-selected board of directors contributes to the unity of purpose (Dubini and Monti, 2018). Investment in time and resources related to board recruitment and training, as well as the strengthening of overall governance, should improve medium- and long-term returns in thoughtful arts organizations. Secondly, boards should mirror the community they serve, rather than being populated with too many staff members as this can weaken the effectiveness of board leadership. This tends not to be an issue in large cultural institutions in the United States, but fledgling smaller arts organizations occasionally fill their board with staff rather than building a board with expertise, community connections and fund-raising prowess. Thirdly, arts institutions should recruit individuals who can help address equity, diversity, inclusion and accessibility issues, not only with respect to governance, but also throughout the entire organization (Azmat and Rentschler, 2017).[7] Finally, what should be obvious, nominating committees should only recruit individuals who are committed to the mission and goals of the organization and are willing to work to accomplish them (Fanelli et al., 2020). This is fundamental, as, with the exception of paid staff who might serve on the board, board members – with rare exceptions – do not receive a salary. To sustain their commitment to the organization, board members need to feel that their active participation is impactful and consistent with the organization's mission.

---

[7] See also Section 2.4.

Several recent studies have highlighted that board nominating committees focus on prospective members of high professional caliber who have stature in the community. Moreover, financial capacity has been the primary requirement for service on the board of a cultural institution, at least in the United States. Board members who fit this profile are in the best position to raise the funds needed to ensure the long-term financial health of an arts organization. However, as mentioned earlier, desirable and inspired board members can also provide connections, both in social and business contexts; have professional expertise in one or more business disciplines (such as accounting, investments, advertising, finance, law, management, marketing or public relations); and are keen to support the organization's mission and help shape its future (Hopkins and Friedman, 1997).

Nominating the right board members is not enough. Each board must also organize itself and conduct its affairs in such a way that it can attract, retain, motivate, evaluate, reward and, if necessary, change a CEO (who is the top paid administrative individual and, with the board's support, leads the institution to actuate its mission) or the board members themselves. To fulfil these aims, Hopkins and Friedman (1997) note that a typical board includes a chairperson or president, a secretary and a treasurer who oversees financial operations. In large institutions, committees can divide the board's tasks among themselves, each focusing on a specific area. Frequently, an arts organization's bylaws provide for a number of standing committees and a mechanism for the appointment of ad hoc committees. Standing committees typically include an executive committee, which creates/reviews policies; a nominating committee, which recruits board members as well as assessing existing members' performance; a finance committee, which reviews and/or approves operating and capital budgets, as well as long-term financial projections; a development or philanthropy committee, which formulates fundraising strategies with the CEO and development director; an audit committee, which oversees audits and risk management issues; an investment committee, which oversees endowments, as well as pensions and other assets controlled by the institution; a compensation committee, which reviews and approves any adjustments in pay for the senior management team; an education committee, which oversees educational programs; and a buildings and grounds committee, which oversees physical assets. Ad hoc committees typically focus on matters that are not in the regular cycle of business; these include search committees for CEO or artistic director positions (Hopkins and Friedman, 1997; Chait et al., 2011; Wolf, 2014).

The composition of the board of directors (which is typically the largest source of philanthropic support) is vital: it should be the primary force that motivates a culture of philanthropy. Clearly, as arts institutions become more reliant on contributed income (and this is also a trend in Europe, where public funding is still the most relevant subsidy and where the board is primarily made up of representatives from public institutions), the fundraising responsibilities of boards of directors will become ever more important. A typical example of this trend is that of the Italian Fondazioni Lirico-Sinfoniche (opera houses) where the president must be by law the Mayor of the city where the opera house is located. The law further stipulates that two out of the three (or five) members of the board must be members of the Ministry of Culture and of the region. The admission of further private members to the boards depends on their financial capacity, usually estimated as a minimum percentage of that of public partners. Owing to the restrictive and huge leadership influence of the public bodies' representatives, it is becoming harder to recruit individuals to the board because these private members have a limited ability to make an impact. A good exception of this from Italy is that of Teatro alla Scala (see Box 2.4).

---

**Box 2.4 Board composition and structure in Europe: the board of Teatro alla Scala**

Teatro alla Scala is renowned worldwide as a benchmark of opera tradition. Founded in Milan in 1778, the theatre is facing the challenging task of preserving its great tradition and, at the same time, of transitioning into the future. In order to achieve this goal, Teatro alla Scala has invested in its internal governance, focusing on the strategic role of the board. Teatro alla Scala's board composition includes ex-officio members belonging to public institutions, as public support still represents one of the main sources of income for the organization (one-third, as mentioned earlier). La Scala also welcomes a relevant representation of private entities to its board, relevant not only for their financial capacity, but also for their role in the economic and social contexts where the theatre operates.
The statute of Teatro alla Scala clearly states that the board should comprise between nine and fifteen members, half from public institutions and half from the private sector. The president of the board, appointed ex-officio, is the mayor of the city of Milan, which is also among the main public funders. The other public mem-

bers are representatives of the Ministry of Culture and Regione Lombardia. Private board members can be appointed only when a private member of the theatre assembly (a "Founder") suggests them. There are two different levels of support within the assembly: Permanent Founders, who have supported the theatre with at least €6 million in total, and the Supporting Founders, who give a minimum of €600,000 annually. The assembly votes for board members who may be suggested only by those Founders who commit to support the theatre with €3 million per year for three consecutive years. Such a clear definition of private involvement in the theatre's activities is almost unique in the Italian opera landscape.

*Source*: Lanfranco Li Cauli personal communication

### 2.3.2 *The role of development staff in building a culture for philanthropy in arts organizations*

As an arts institution transitions to a culture of philanthropy, the role of the development department should be reconsidered: the skills necessary for the successful implementation of such a culture go beyond merely soliciting gifts. In particular, there should be a move from a tactical to a strategical and relational perspective when raising funds. In donor-centered arts organizations, development staff serve as facilitators, catalysts, advocates and stewards (Burk, 2003).

While there are many ways in which the skills that effective fundraisers should possess can be summarized, it might be informative to highlight just some of them:[8]

- *Art form knowledge*. Fundraisers are most effective when they are conversant not only with their arts institution's mission or a particular program, but also with the art form and other institutions within the same field: a fundraiser for an opera house should know something about singers and other relevant opera companies. Many arts donors are often interested in the broader field, not just the company they are supporting: being able to discuss and even share a mutual passion for the arts can be a very effective way of connecting with a donor.
- *Relationship building skills*. As we discuss when dealing with major donor fundraising, building and cultivating relationships over a

[8] See also Chapter 1.

long period is key to not-for-profit arts fundraising efforts. Indeed, winning a donor's trust and confidence can frequently lead to consistent contributions over time. Relationship-building means the creation of a sense of shared purpose with donors and identifying motivations that may create a sense of urgency. Basic elements of emotional intelligence such as self-awareness, self-regulation, discipline, motivation and empathy often really help in understanding donors and partnering with them.

- *Leadership skills.* These may be summarized as the ability to create and communicate a vision, promote and initiate change, build partnerships both internally and externally and value diversity and inclusion. A leader guides the department and inspires others to follow. Leadership skills also relate to supervising the department and planning and executing its fundraising tasks so that they are aligned with the arts institution's goals. Finally, these skills relate to strategic thinking: effective development leaders do not spend much time or energy on matters they cannot influence, such as those relating to macro socio-economic developments; rather, they focus on areas they can influence, such as stakeholders' behavior that impacts fundraising.
- *Management skills.* Good managers are not always good leaders and vice versa. Above all, development directors in the arts are called upon to make things happen in addition to inspiring donors and staff. These traditional management skills and competencies are seldom emphasized, Furthermore, the advent of artificial intelligence and the increase in competition for funds require the full mastery of more process-oriented/administrative competencies, such as the three that follow here.
- *Analytical skills.* These involve both the examination and assessment of internal and external resources and obstacles. The measurement of resources available for fundraising is particularly germane in gauging the ability of an arts organization to support fundraising activities.
- *Planning skills.* While planning is critical if goals are to be accomplished, arts executives should understand that the amount of time allocated to planning does matter. Too little planning leads to missed opportunities and unanticipated disruptions, but too much planning can bring about paralysis.

- *Implementation skills.* Executing and monitoring fundraising plans requires the capacity to delegate and to support staff and colleagues. Success is also based on the awareness that benchmarks may be modified if the external environment changes.

Effective development directors should therefore nurture a shared awareness of a culture of philanthropy, emphasizing the set of skills and roles that development professionals find fulfilling and meaningful. If this awareness permeates an institution, philanthropy will become a strategic asset and fundraising will be able to play its vital role in the organization's growth. Box 2.5 describes the development of a culture of philanthropy at Tanglewood Music Festival and Music Center.

**Box 2.5 Developing a culture of philanthropy at Tanglewood Music Festival and Music Center (1997–2019)**

Tanglewood is the summer home of the Boston Symphony Orchestra (BSO), located on 530 acres in the Berkshire mountains, approximately 130 miles north of New York City and 125 miles west of Boston. The annual festival attracts over 350,000 people, who attend BSO concerts, Boston Pops concerts, recitals and popular artist concerts. Concurrent with the summer festival, the BSO runs a summer professional training program, which has helped to train Leonard Bernstein, Zubin Mehta, Claudio Abbado, Seiji Ozawa, Wynton Marsalis and thousands of other fellows (students). For decades, annual fundraising was in most cases transactional. Donors were given access to tickets, supper clubs on the grounds and parking based on their giving levels. In other words, the more you gave, the closer you could park to the entrance and the more priority you would have when purchasing tickets for concerts that were destined to sell out quickly (Yo-Yo Ma cello recitals, Beethoven's Ninth Symphony performances, John Williams film nights, Lady Gaga singing with Tony Bennett, for example). Also transactional was the manner in which fellows were sponsored, with regular high end donors getting priority in the assignment of fellows. Furthermore, the BSO had no presence in the Berkshire community beyond the summer season, which was a source of irritation for local towns. Although millions of dollars were raised each year, this was what one development officer termed retail fundraising.

Moreover, while the various incentives worked well to secure annual giving to support annual programming, many of the 100 buildings on the site, a couple of which dated back to the 1840s, were falling into significant disrepair, and it became clear that tens of millions of dollars would be needed to restore them. What's more, the

Tanglewood Music Center lacked sufficient rehearsal and practice space for the 155 fellows who spent the summer there. From 2000 to approximately 2012, various mini-campaigns were initiated to address problems with the physical estate with only incremental success. The donors had been conditioned to treat their giving to Tanglewood like a club membership, and were reluctant to contribute more than their annual gift, so the various efforts to repair the buildings limped along. At this point, the senior management team and the board leadership agreed that the giving culture had to change, and convened a large committee of Tanglewood donors and other stakeholders including local leaders, board members, artistic leaders and musicians. Recognizing that the desired shift to a culture of philanthropy would take time, perseverance and patience, the committee spent the next couple of years imagining what Tanglewood could be, working with master planners, building architects and landscape architects.

All the stakeholders had input, and a master plan evolved that included a new Tanglewood Learning Institute concentrating on adult cultural education; this was highly valued by the donor cohort. With everyone's full endorsement, a comprehensive campaign was launched that resulted in the construction of four new buildings (all available for off season use by local arts and educational organizations), a deferred maintenance fund, a significant investment in landscaping, a programming fund for the new Tanglewood Learning Institute and an endowment to support ongoing maintenance for the new buildings. This campaign would have been unthinkable without the concerted effort to build a culture of philanthropy that was embraced by everyone.

***Figure 2.3*** **Linde Center at Tanglewood (Opened 2019)**

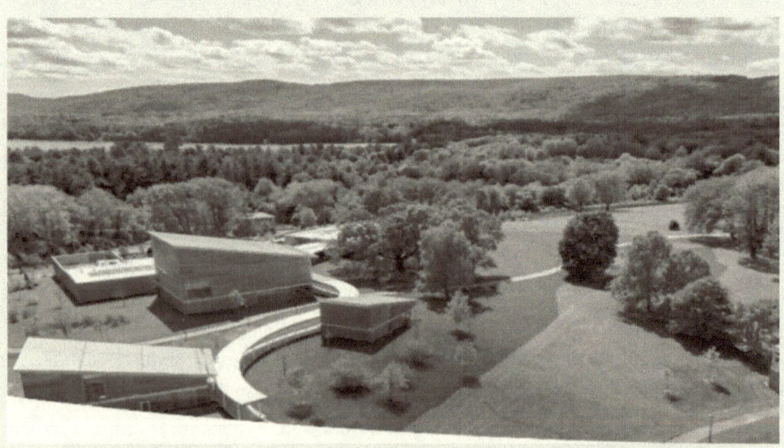

*Credit:* Sam Sorrentino | Boston Symphony Orchestra

This fundamental change in the philanthropic culture was affirmed when the campaign more than achieved its goal in record time. In all, $72 million was committed to transform Tanglewood, and to further solidify its position as the pre-eminent summer music festival in the United States.

*Source:* Mark Volpe personal communication

## 2.4 Challenges in developing a culture of philanthropy in arts organizations

The focus of this chapter has been to highlight how a culture of philanthropy might be introduced in arts organizations and how the strategic apex (board, CEO and development staff) might contribute to advancing this culture among internal and external stakeholders. In this final section, we focus on the challenges that arts institutions face in developing this culture.

As already mentioned, one of the main challenges that arts organizations should be prepared to address is the increasing competitiveness in the fundraising market. The environment has become much more competitive for a variety of reasons. First, there has been a proliferation of not-for-profit institutions during the past several decades, all of which are seeking philanthropic support. Second, there has been an expansion of professional sports teams and commercial music concerns that compete with not-for-profit arts institutions for corporate sponsorship, media attention and, in some instances, paid attendance. Third, the arts are competing with not-for-profits in sectors such as social services, healthcare, environmental and education. These sectors have proven to be especially attractive to individuals who have generated enormous wealth through investments in technology, life sciences, venture capital, private equity and hedge funds. Finding approaches that link cultural institutions with educational and social services or even healthcare institutions can open access to donors who are not inclined to support institutions that are perceived to focus on arts for their own sake.

A second challenge to address is related to audiences that are looking for authenticity in their cultural experience. Given the extremely competitive marketplace for culture and entertainment and the sensibilities and values of younger generations, audiences are more and more interest-

*Figure 2.4* Challenges in developing a culture of philanthropy in arts organizations

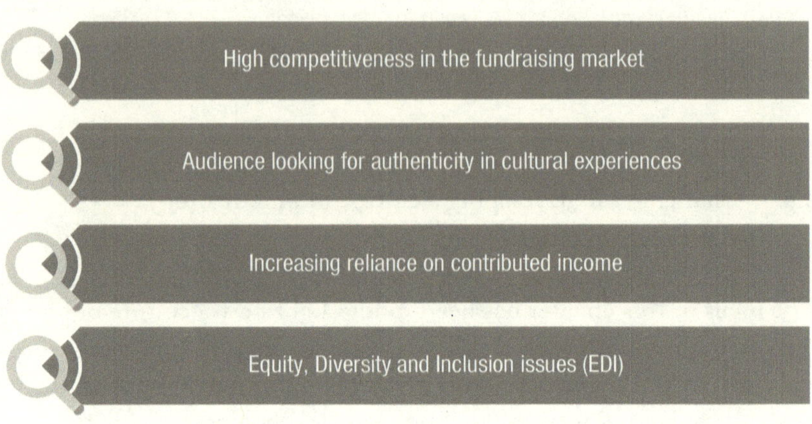


ed in authentic and relevant experiences. While prior generations were more inclined to think of participating in culture as a way of enhancing status, contemporary audiences want art that is relatable and pertinent to their life experience. Both in the United States and in Europe, this shift is becoming more and more prevalent (Radbourne et al., 2009). This trend forces boards and managers to focus on authenticity and accountability when developing and executing their strategies: as a direct consequence, this becomes relevant in terms of securing philanthropic support. A third consideration relates to the increasing reliance of arts institutions on contributed income. The COVID-19 pandemic has dramatically accelerated a trend that has been developing for years in the sector in which earned income (especially subscription revenue) and public funding subsidies are decreasing or are flat. Accordingly, arts institutions are becoming increasingly reliant on contributed income. In particular, especially in the United States, the continuing concentration of wealth among a relatively small number of people can result in such individuals exerting an outsized influence in artistic and other institutional matters because they are able to make very large tax-deductible contributions.

Finally, the advent of the social justice and #MeToo movements in the United States, Europe and other parts of the world has greatly accelerated the process by which cultural institutions are evolving to address equity, diversity and inclusion (EDI) in all areas of operation including governance, staff, artists and programming.[9] Cultural institutions are now expected to be a truer reflection of the communities in which they exist. Given the relevance of this challenge to the development of a culture of philanthropy, the following paragraph outlines how EDI should permeate the philanthropic strategy and attitude of arts organizations.

### 2.4.1 *How EDI impact on a culture of philanthropy in arts organizations*

Until recently, most cultural institutions gave scant attention to EDI when considering fundraising. Of course, museums focused on the African American experience such as the College Museum in Hampton, Virginia (founded in 1868) and the African American Museum in Cleveland, Ohio (established in 1957) have depended on philanthropy for decades. In addition, the Dance Theatre of Harlem has existed since 1969 and has had an active fundraising program However, the large "establishment" art, science and natural history museums as well as orchestras, opera and ballet companies have been slow to address various social justice matters in all areas of their operation, including fundraising. Certainly, the brutal murder of George Floyd in Minneapolis in 2020 has resulted in a realization that most of the large cultural institutions in United States and throughout much of the world have not done enough to address EDI issues. In Europe, EDI is now becoming more of a focus as demographic shifts and immigration have precipitated rethinking of the role of cultural institutions.

It is impossible to address how EDI concepts can be integrated into fundraising without a broader understanding of how they fit into the entire arts organization. As we have argued, development departments do not exist in a vacuum. Rather, they are part of a complex set of depart-

---

[9] For the purposes of this section, diversity is defined as the practice of including individuals from a range of ethnic, racial and social backgrounds. Although different generations have various conceptions of diversity, it is generally understood that it is the embodiment of a group's composition. Equity is about providing fair access and opportunity for everyone. This requires the recognition and eradication of all barriers that prevent the full participation of all demographics. Inclusion addresses the extent to which individuals have a sense of belonging. Within an inclusive culture, differences in backgrounds are embraced and celebrated.

ments and groups that have varying levels of intersection and co-dependency. In other words, the fundraising team can implement EDI practices and philosophy successfully only if they are also incorporated into almost every aspect of the cultural institution.

EDI must start with the board, as it sets an example for the entire institution. The fiduciary dimension of board membership includes five key areas of organizational oversight (strategy, governance, talent, integrity and performance), all of which are relevant with respect to EDI. While these areas do not all lend themselves to metric evaluations, the board should certainly be aware of its demographics (e.g., age, race, gender) and the nominating process through which it is replenished. Metrics should also be used to evaluate the composition of all standing committees and agenda development. Boards that address EDI in meetings and mandate training are much more likely to be sensitive to how EDI influences all aspects of the institution, including strategy, programming and management.

Second, the development department is part of a much larger management staff. Many cultural institutions are now mandating training for all staff, including development personnel, on EDI topics such as unconscious bias. Beyond this training, many larger and mid-sized cultural institutions have taken a significant additional step by creating a senior management position (titled the Chief Diversity Officer or something similar) to oversee EDI efforts across the entire institution.

Third, it would be arduous and probably impossible for a development department to embrace the notions of EDI if the programming/content of the arts organization did not reflect some awareness of and attentiveness to its importance. For more than a century, the programming of most major American performing arts companies has been informed by European traditions. As the demographics of the United States becomes less European and male-centric, programming generated by American cultural institutions has been incrementally shifting to be a little more inclusive. The previously mentioned murder of George Floyd greatly accelerated the progression towards programming in the United States that better reflects communities in which the cultural institutions are situated. Approaches vary, with some institutions embedding more diverse programming into pre-existing templates and others creating festivals and exhibits with inclusive thematic programming. Not all audiences embrace the unfamiliar, so arts organizations are investing in various communication channels and performance formatting to address this challenge. Performing arts institutions are also engaging more diverse artists to better reflect the demographics of their respective communities. Part of the rationale for doing this is to attract a more diverse audience that wants to see itself reflected on stage.

If we focus on the narrower impact of the EDI issue on fundraising, we might observe that most cultural institutions lack diversity in their donor bases, board membership and development staff, and have no clear route to addressing EDI issues. The record suggests that even when there have been efforts to focus on EDI matters in fundraising, they are treated as separate initiatives and are not fully integrated into the department's work. There is so much pressure on development staffs to meet or exceed fundraising goals (especially as they are evaluated in these terms) that development professionals tend to have little time and few incentives to focus on challenges such as creating a more diverse donor base. Furthermore, arts organizations have as a matter of course developed strong relationships with their existing donor base, and tend to add to it by focusing on prospects that have similar demographic characteristics.

In this situation, the criteria by which development staff are evaluated will have to be revised if EDI considerations are to be addressed. This can manifest itself in leadership that provides inspiration and direction to take the necessary steps to attract a more diverse set of funders and development staff. Moreover, current funders can influence the situation by applying pressure on cultural institutions to implement EDI concepts into all aspects of the operations (including fundraising). Either way, the value of a diverse donor base and development operation must be understood and conveyed to all.

As has been noted earlier in this chapter, the culture of philanthropy is a subset of the organizational culture. Likewise, assimilating EDI principles in the fundraising department will only be successful if such principles are embraced at the macro-organizational level. It will require an audit of sorts, involving data collection and assessment of the current environment so that areas that need attention can be identified. Policies and practices that influence EDI will have to be revisited. Objectives will have to be identified, and buy-in and endorsement will be needed at every level and every stage of the process. Implementation will have to be rigorous, with responsibility clearly delineated and timeframes established that are not too lax but also not too forced. Communication throughout the process across all internal and external groups will have to be carefully considered, recognizing that there has to be a public accounting of sorts. And, of course, what matters is results that will be measured when tangible (e.g., the demographics of the board) and understood when intangible (e.g., trust). This is all a formidable challenge, but a necessary one if arts institutions are to be relevant now and for generations to come.

## Keywords for arts fundraisers

Fundraising, philanthropy, development, culture of philanthropy, shared objectives, case for giving, mission statement, inside out approach, metrics, chief advancement officer, communications style, appreciation to donors, transparency, CEO, board chair, board nominating committee, standing committee, ad hoc committee, development or philanthropy committee, board of directors, Equity, Diversity and Inclusion (EDI), chief diversity officer

## Suggested questions for meetings and discussion

- How can arts organizations assess their culture of philanthropy?
- What is the role of the internal culture of philanthropy in shaping an arts organization's fundraising strategy?
- How can people (artists, managers, collaborators) become ambassadors and fundraisers) of their arts organization? What main differences/similarities can you see between American and European arts organizations in respect to this?
- In your experience, are there some case histories in the arts sector that set as a benchmark in the way they have created a culture of philanthropy?
- How do different constituencies become involved in the governance processes of arts organizations? How does this work in your organization or in organizations you are familiar with?
- What are funders looking for when deciding to support an arts organization?
- How and how deep should funders be involved in governance processes? Are there any limits to be aware of or basic rules to follow?

- When managing boards, how can organizations keep the balance between public and private funders?
- From your perspective, are there any cultural and organizational prejudices, pressures or even taboos that can affect funders' involvement in governance processes?
- Are skilled fundraisers also great managers? What are the main examples of success or mistakes to avoid? Can you describe some cases from your direct experience?
- How can the style of leadership or managers' personalities be a driver? In your experience, what main differences/similarities can you see between American and European arts organizations in respect to this?
- From your perspective, what will be the future trends of the role played by philanthropy in arts organizations?
- How are arts institutions analyzing these trends?
- What role has EDI in the culture and procedures of arts organizations you know?

## References

Azmat, F. and Rentschler, R. (2017). "Gender and ethnic diversity on boards and corporate responsibility: The case of the arts sector," *Journal of Business Ethics*, 141 (2): 317–336.

Bell J. and Cornelius, M (2013). *Underdeveloped: A national study of challenges facing nonprofit fundraising.* Evelyn & Walter Haas, Jr. Fund, San Francisco, CA.

Burk, P. (2003). *Donor-centered fundraising: How to hold on to your donors and raise much more money.* Chicago: Cygnus Applied Research,

Chait, R. P., Ryan, W. P. and Taylor, B. E. (2011). *Governance as leadership: Reframing the work of nonprofit boards.* Hoboken, NJ: John Wiley and Sons.

Cornforth, C. and Edwards, C. (1999). "Board roles in the strategic management of non-profit organizations: Theory and practice," *Corporate Governance: An International Review*, 7 (4): 346–362.

Dubini, P. and Monti, A. (2018). "Board composition and organizational performance in the cultural sector: The case of Italian opera houses," *International Journal of Arts Management*, 20 (2): 56–70.

Fanelli, S., Donelli, C. C., Zangrandi, A. and Mozzoni, I. (2020). "Balancing artistic and financial performance: is collaborative governance the answer?," *International Journal of Public Sector Management*, 33 (1): 78–93.

Gibson C. M. (2016) *Beyond fundraising: What does it mean to build a culture of philanthropy?* Evelyn and Walter Haas Jr Fund, San Francisco, CA.

Hopkins, K. B and, Friedman, C. S., (1997). *Successful fundraising for arts and cultural organizations*, second edition. Phoenix, AZ: Greenwood.

Ostrower, F. and Stone, M. M. (2006). "Governance: Research trends, gaps, and future prospects," in Powell, W. W. and Steinberg, R. (eds), *The nonprofit sector*, 612–628. New Haven, CT: Yale University Press.

Payton, R. L. and Moody, M. P. (2008). *Understanding Philanthropy. Its meaning and mission.* Bloomington: Indiana University Press.

Radbourne, J., Johanson, K., Glow, H. and White, T. (2009). "The audience experience: Measuring quality in the performing arts," *International Journal of Arts Management*, 11 (3): 16–29.

Schein, E. H. (2004). *Organizational culture and leadership*, third edition. San Francisco: Jossey-Bass.

Whitchurch, J. and Comer, A. (2016). "Creating a culture of philanthropy," *The Bottom Line*, 29 (2): 114–122.

Wolf, T. (2014). *Effective leadership for nonprofit organizations: How executive directors and boards work together.* New York: Simon and Schuster.

Worth M. J. (2016). *Fundraising: Principles and practice*, Los Angeles, CA: SAGE Publications, Inc.

Yoon, C. (2014). "Developing a culture of philanthropy to support your mission," *Nursing Administration Quarterly*, 38 (4): 299–302.

Zirkle, K. W. (2017). *Creating a culture of philanthropy: Three things to keep in mind.* Richmond: Virginia Commonwealth University.

# Part II
# Actors

# 3 Annual Giving and Membership Programs in the Arts

with *James Ryan Jillson* and *Alessandro Borchini*

## 3.1 Annual giving and membership programs in the arts: concepts and definitions

Even if arts organizations sometimes rely heavily on the contributions of a few major donors for their most significant financial needs, the involvement of members or small donors in their development activities is useful for three main reasons.[1] First, at the beginning of their relationship with an arts institution, some donors might prefer to start giving at a lower level and increase their future giving as their relationship with the institution evolves. Second, the sum of all small donations can have a substantial impact on the total contributed income. Third, broad support that includes gifts from individuals with modest financial capacity reinforces the institution's positioning as being accessible to all.

The best way to achieve this goal is by developing individual giving programs. Regularly scheduled solicitations are often part of an annual giving program. This usually includes a range of fundraising activities that are implemented throughout the year with the purpose of raising restricted or unrestricted funds to support special projects or specific needs, or to fund general operations (Worth, 2016). Small gifts are typically made in an annual giving program; they usually range from less than $/€/£100 to a few thousand dollars, euros or pounds and often cover short-term needs (Sargeant, 2001). However, annual gifts to large Amer-

---

[1] According to Hopkins and Friedman (1997), we can distinguish between major donors (often characterized as large givers with the ability to contribute $/€/£1000 to $/€/£100,000 or more) and smaller donors (those who provide relatively smaller support as their gifts are usually less than $/€/£1000).

ican cultural institutions can be measured in the tens or even hundreds of thousands of dollars.

Membership programs are focused on regular solicitation, and their main objective is to engage modest givers in a more stable and constant relationship with the arts institution. These programs boost people's willingness to contribute, and arts organizations benefit from the support of modest contributors at different levels. They can also create a path for the evolution of the donor's giving profile. Through the structure of benefit systems, membership programs can be an effective tool that incrementally engage smaller donors and build up a long-term donor base.

In order to achieve these incremental goals, arts organizations generally offer donors the choice of a range of different contribution levels, each corresponding to an applicable package of benefits. These benefits are the central element of membership programs and have the specific objective of advancing lower-level donors further within the institution, by relating a donor's contribution to specific donor perks. The rationale is that the higher the level of support, the more exclusive the rewards. A typical membership program scheme couples different levels of benefits with various ranges of required contributions (Sargeant, 2001; Worth, 2016).

Relying on an escalating benefits system, membership programs can also have a beneficial indirect effect on earned income, as they can positively influence attendance levels, tickets sales and the results of the organization's other commercial activities such as merchandizing. Moreover, a broad-based membership program is an entry-point for first-time donors to cultural institutions, a few of which might become major donors over time. Arts organizations can work on their membership programs to retain the commitment of their smaller donors, and also to persuade them to increase their gift every time they renew their membership.

Membership and annual giving programs include a broad range of activities that help to keep modest givers consistently engaged. These activities usually range from online and mailed solicitations (e.g., via web tools, social media sharing or regular newsletters), to "in-person" touchpoints, such as offline meetings and welcoming or large fundraising events. Despite the digital revolution, live events still play an important role in fundraising.[2] Stronger personal contact in soliciting donors

[2] See also Chapter 5.

is recommended in particular at the upper end of the annual gifts scale defined by the organization (Worth, 2016).

Summarizing the points discussed here, we can state that annual giving and membership programs play a very important role in arts organizations because they can do the following:

- *Provide a source of unrestricted revenue*: There are ongoing, necessary expenses of every arts organization such as utilities, maintenance and staff expenses that typically do not attract major donor interest. Annual fund or membership gifts can offset these expenses.
- *Broaden the base of support*: these programs typically have multiple giving tiers and are accessible to donors with a wide range of giving capacities. Arts organizations that rely on just a small number of major donors run the risk of excessive reliance on those supporters and not sufficiently diversifying their sources of funding.
- *Engage donors*: this deepens the relationship and encourages continued contributions. Extensive one-on-one interaction with hundreds or thousands of donors may be impractical, so annual giving and membership programs typically offer special benefits or exclusive events to donors that can serve to keep them engaged at scale.
- *Create built-in audiences for programming*: when building an audience for a special initiative, it can be effective to promote it first to existing members and annual donors. Arts institutions with robust membership and annual donor bases therefore begin with a meaningful audience when introducing a new offering.
- *Feed pipelines to other types of giving*: members have already shown interest in the organization and also have an ability to give. Through further engagement, cultivation and solicitation, these donors may contribute to additional initiatives.

When addressing new or existing individual donors, arts organizations often use marketing principles and approaches: the level of connection between marketing and fundraising depends on the competitive environment in which the organization operates, on its size, type and its balance between earned and contributed income. In particular, annual giving and membership programs often benefit from the use of direct-response marketing tools, including direct mail and email as well as phone and text solicitation (Worth, 2016). These methods usually include, for example, the requirement for a response or immediate reaction from the solicited person (a call-to-action) that can also be a request for a payment (donation). Direct marketing applied to fundraising activities also gives arts organizations effective tools to measure and evaluate their efforts, thereby representing the most scientific component of their fundraising strategy (Sargeant et Shang, 2010). Finally, thanks to the abundance of new web tools at their disposal, arts institutions can also cut related costs and become more efficient. This is, for example, the case for web-based acquisition annual campaigns that are addressed to specific segments of the donor pool (defined by their demographics and behavioral profile) and for communication campaigns that need scope.

## 3.2 Understanding small donors and their motivations to give

As many factors can influence their behavior, the motivations of donors are complex and multifaceted, and nowhere is this truer than in annual giving and membership programs, where rational and emotional drivers usually interact. Analyzing donors' motivations therefore helps a fundraising manager understand the specific drivers that can influence people in their giving choices. The classification of motivational drivers we outline or recommend in this book, being the best representation for the arts industry, focuses on people's orientation and expected benefits when making giving decisions. This scheme divides donors' motivational drivers into three: altruistic orientation, needs orientation and value orientation. As Figure 3.1 summarizes, these orientations can sometimes overlap.

### 3.2.1 *Altruistic orientation*

Altruistic donors are those who are motivated in their giving by the desire to fulfil the needs of other people. The main benefit they look for is the creation, thanks to their contribution, of a connection with those members of the community whom they perceive as in need or underserved in respect to a specific good or service. When altruistic donors support a cause or give to produce a public good, such as the arts, they also want to be involved in something that is clearly meaningful for the community. If pure altruism were the only driver motivating this seg-

*Figure 3.1* The main individual donor motivational drivers

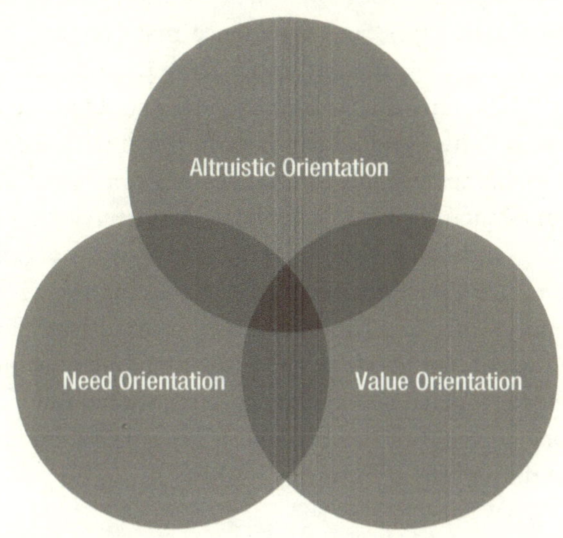


ment of donors, they would interrupt their giving as soon as they realized that the supported organization's needs had been satisfied (by the contribution of other donors, including public funders). However, research has demonstrated that when this crowding-out effect occurs – especially in the arts and in education – there is "not a one-to-one reduction of donors' gifts in response to a matched contribution from other sources" (Worth, 2016: 66). This may help to explain why some donors continue to give to well-funded institutions. Consequently, altruistic donors probably take into consideration further motivators for giving, an example being the visibility they gain from belonging to the list of the donors associated with worldwide renowned arts organizations, such as the Metropolitan Opera or the Louvre Museum. This is where the motivational interest that focuses on other people's needs leads to an improvement in donors' self-esteem and pride.

When people perceive that those they know personally or with whom they are connected are in need, the relevance (or the perceived urgency) of that need increases in their view. In other words, empathy and identification with others can often be at the root of an altruistic giving choice. We can argue that this principle is key in the fundraising strategies of many arts organizations, as they focus on building-up valuable relationships with people. Moreover, identification grows proportionately with the amount of time and experience that potential donors share with those to whom their philanthropic actions are directed (Schervish and Havens, 2002). This is why organizations should invite their donors to attend their activities and be regularly in touch with them, including involvement in higher visibility initiatives (e.g., enlisting some donors as committee, council, or board members, volunteers or spokesmen). In addition, when cultivating these members, a cultural organization can nurture donors' altruistic motivations by enhancing their interest in the institution and its mission. Moreover, they can cultivate donors' desire to influence the context in which the institution operates; they can help to align supporters' personal values with institutional ones; they can reinforce donors' personal connections with the cultural organization and their sense of duty to the community it serves.

### 3.2.2 *Needs orientation*

The motivation to give can depend on the thoughtful desire of people to fulfil some personal needs. Usually, this focuses on two main groups of motivators: internal/ psychological and external/ social (Sargeant and Shang, 2010).

Broadly speaking, the generation of warm feelings, the alleviation of negative feelings and the sense of the human joy of giving are examples of a donor's internal and psychological needs (Bekkers and Wiepking, 2010). Arts organizations can therefore steer individuals in their giving choices by helping them to anticipate or to figure out the fulfilment of those emotional and psychological prerequisites.

Donors looking to fulfil social and external needs are influenced, by factors such as social pressure and recognition, or by the desire to gain a good reputation in the community (Bekkers and Wiepking, 2010). When social aspects are a relevant factor in giving, people look (more or less thoughtfully) for a benchmark or a "giving norm" (Bekkers and Wiepking, 2010) that they should respect when making their choices. Consequently, the influence of peers, of family, of their personal contacts or socially prominent personalities with whom they would like to be identified can be very powerful in influencing social needs-oriented donors at different levels. This may indeed prompt the choice of the cause to support in the first place, and even the size of a contribution and how it is made. Taking this into account, arts organizations should therefore pay particular attention to who solicits donations (e.g., fundraisers, executives, artists, members of the artistic staff, volunteers or even the CEO). The development of peer-to-peer relations are crucial when volunteers are involved in fundraising programs. Volunteers are actually more credible and effective than any development professional can be when influencing the giving decisions of social needs-oriented donors. These trends may have interesting implications in social media fundraising strategies, especially with the development of digital membership programs. For instance, we can consider digital peer-to-peer fundraising and the impact of online reputation and influencers on the size and frequency of each donation. However, arts organizations should always favor face-to-face solicitations when asking for more generous contributions.[3]

The fulfilment of social recognition needs can have a mutual benefit, both for the donor and for the institution. Donors can gain social recognition by being among the generous supporters of a renowned institution, while the enhancing of their social standing endorses the organization's activities and programs in the eyes of the community. As Worth (2016) argues, the donor's reputation helps to validate the institution's worthiness, and this might explain why anonymous giving is a rarity.

Altruistic and need orientations in individual giving highlight the importance of intangible benefits for arts donors. This implies that, in addition to tangible rewards for different levels of contributions (which appeal to the rational element in donors' motivations), arts organizations can engage individual donors by helping them fulfil their emotional, psychological and social needs.

### 3.2.3 *Value orientation*

Some individuals will donate to cultural institutions in return for very tangible benefits. Broadly speaking, they are motivated to give because they associate their contribution with specific, material and quantifiable advantages (e.g., special discounts, invitations to exclusive events, tax incentives). These motivational drivers are usually transactional, and the

---

[3] See also Chapter 4.

decision process is based on calculation: donors contribute after quantifying what the organization will give them in return. According to this orientation, donors behave as rational decision makers, considering different alternatives before deciding how much and to which cause they should give (Sargeant, 2014). However, as mentioned earlier, even when they approach value-motivated donors, arts organizations should always maintain an appropriate balance between offering tangible benefits (thus fulfilling extrinsic motivations) and appealing to donors' intrinsic motivations. When focusing on tangible benefits only, they can affect the philanthropic nature of donations and convert them into a mere commercial exchange. This risks disempowering relationships with donors and giving the fundraising process a very narrow and short-term perspective (Worth, 2016).

Tangible benefits might offset the cost of attendance, such as free parking or discounts on entrance fees. Other drivers might include specific benefits, such free tickets for guests, discounts at the gift shop, or tax benefits. The influence of charitable deductibility is one of the main topics at the heart of research into value orientation in individual giving, and as it is essential to understand how donors can be incentivized to give by the opportunity to reduce their taxes. The economic rationale of tax benefits as an incentive to donate is that they reduce the overall cost of gifts for donors. From an economic perspective, if donors can benefit from proportional tax savings or credits related to the amount of their contribution and their tax brackets, they have a further motivation to give to an arts organization. Consequently, the response of donors to the level of tax deductibility can also be a parameter that helps to evaluate the amount of elasticity in charitable giving (Worth, 2016). As changes in tax policy can affect these choices, tax planning can also influence how much donors are able to give, the timing of and the methods by which they pay their gifts. It is noteworthy, as Worth (2016) argues, that when directly asked, donors tend to minimize the relevance that charitable deduction has for them, even if tax benefits play a role in orienting their giving choices. Broadly speaking, it seems that tax deduction policies influence donors' giving vehicles[4] more than they motivate their giving

[4] In the United States, donors giving appreciated stock are able to deduct the value of the stock at the time of the gift as well as avoid any capital gains tax on the increase of value the donor experienced holding the stock.

decisions. Consequently, some philanthropic intent and a clear focus on the organization's mission, values and impacts are always essential in soliciting donors, as tax avoidance itself is not always a primary motivation.

## 3.3 Subscribers or members? Membership programs as bridges between marketing and fundraising

In arts organizations, the function of marketers and fundraisers is deeply connected as they are both responsible for building a consistent (and valuable) relationship with a community of individuals, either as audiences or as members.

Although both marketing and development departments aim to establish long-term relationships, they have different functions. Marketing helps to connect the right targets with the right arts products, engaging audiences in the organization's activities. Fundraising departments begin by assessing potential donors and subscribers, and then design the tools that are intended to activate donor–organization relationships.

In a wider perspective, we can consider membership programs to be a functional bridge between marketing and development, as they can convert an initial transactional exchange between an organization and an individual into philanthropic giving. Indeed, regular attendees can be the ideal starting point upon which to build a broad-based community of members.

Interest in an arts organization's activity can be the first motivator for individual donations. To support this assertion, we can note that about 90 per cent of the regular individual donors to Western arts institutions are also among their subscribers (ABA, 2021). However, especially in Europe, it is also true that people tend to see subscriptions as the most appropriate way to support arts institutions at an individual level, in particular when organizations are receiving public funding. Therefore, they often do not consider other forms of support.

Even if there is a strong connection between the two, it is important to clarify the distinction between membership and subscription models. In the case of subscriptions, attendees have access to a product or a service in exchange for the payment of a (usually reduced) fee, as a reward for regular attendance. In other words, subscribers are mainly interested in what the arts organization offers. On the other hand, becoming a member or an annual donor implies a deeper connection with an institution, and that attending performances or exhibitions is just one aspect of this connection.

When arts institutions work to develop membership programs, factors such as community impact, shared values, emotional connections and personal relationships with the organization are all relevant. Therefore, the biggest challenge that they face is designing a consistent path that converts passionate subscribers into engaged members. A lever that encourages arts devotees to become members is loyalty. For the purpose of this book, we can define loyalty as an indicator of the value of the relationship between the arts organization and its attendees. Loyal consumers are not only likely to repeat their purchase over time, but also have a high willingness to recommend the experience to other people, as well as self-identifying with the brand to which they are loyal. Arts marketers evaluate loyalty as one of the most desirable kinds of connection with individuals, as it often means regular attendance at arts venues, greater willingness to pay and a higher average price paid. Box 3.1 describes the loyalty program of Piccolo Teatro in Milan.

**Box 3.1 Piccolo Card: a loyalty program for the performing arts in Milan**

Piccolo Card is the loyalty program for the Piccolo Teatro in Milan. It is an initiative that works in a similar way to loyalty cards from shops and other retail organizations. The purpose of the program is to involve audiences more intensely, stimulating them to attend a higher number of performances per year. Once people buy a ticket or a subscription online or at the box office, they automatically receive a Piccolo Card and begin to accumulate points. The number of points gained at each purchase depends on whether the show is hosted, if it is a production or an international performance, and the type of subscription chosen by the buyer. For every fifteen points gained, members may purchase a ticket of their choice for €5. There are three membership levels, defined according to the number of gained points: *foyer* (1–34 points); *platea* (stall) (35–69 points); *palcoscenico* (stage) (70+ points).

*Source:* Alessandro Borchini personal communication; www.piccoloteatro.org

Loyalty also is at the basis of any kind of membership. Moreover, by sharing values, subscribers often are inclined to convert into members, working together with a cultural institution to reach a higher purpose.

This progression towards something else (which goes beyond a mere transactional exchange) indicates a search for values that attendees and the arts institution share. For some people, recognizing these shared values can be even more important than the cultural experience (or art form) itself. Those arts organizations that are aware of this and begin to focus their strategies on sharing their values, rather than simply selling something, can differentiate themselves emotionally, positioning their brand more effectively and boosting the loyalty of their audience (ABA, 2020). A shared values strategy is all about making sure that audiences – loyal or not – are aware of what an organization stands for, what it believes in and what it fights for. Having a cultural experience while looking for something else means searching for experiential attributes that can be social, relational, educational, even spiritual: they convert the arts into something more personal and consequently more valuable for the engaged public. It follows that, in order to increase the engagement of their audience (and hopefully to convert attendees into members), arts organizations have to encourage a shift from a value perception perspective to one of value sharing. Sharing values with the donors means building up a stronger relationship, as the institution and donors are linked by something they both stand for, not just a commercial exchange. Therefore, a valuable, long-lasting relationship in fundraising is guaranteed when people who are likely to consider themselves philanthropists find the ideal partner in an organization that satisfies their needs, as it stands for values that are relevant to the community it serves and works every day to align its activities with those values. In Chapter 2, we discuss the relevance of culture, purpose and mission in arts organizations as a driver for successful development. The combination of a strong culture of philanthropy and of an effective shared values strategy can boost fund development results significantly. Box 3.2 describes the shared values strategy of the American Ballet Theatre.

Loyalty is also an indicator of the emotional connection between attendees and an arts organization. As mentioned previously, loyal attendees tend to repeat their purchases over time, and they are the first to react (both positively and negatively) to programming or policy positions the arts organization articulates. They are so involved in the organization's life that they are not only passionate in "advertising" what the cultural institution does (the word-of-mouth effect), but also engaged ambassadors of the values for which it stands. They can help the organization to fos-

**Box 3.2 American Ballet Theater for social justice and inclusion as shared values**

Since its foundation in 1939, the American Ballet Theatre (ABT) has promoted American ballet, "developing a repertoire of the best ballets from the past, and the creation of new works by gifted choreographers, wherever they might be found."

Though located in New York City, ABT annually tours the United States – performing for 300,000 people annually – and is the only major American cultural institution to do so. The company has undertaken more than thirty international tours to forty-five countries in order to share American ballet with the world, and on many of these engagements ABT has received sponsorship from the State Department. On 27 April 2006, by an act of Congress, ABT was designated America's National Ballet Company®. Owing to its national relevance and its international stance, ABT has assessed its position in respect to the social debate in the United States by declaring itself to be against any kind of racism and social discrimination and to believe in inclusion, thus sustaining excellence in the arts. This is the core message of the ABT RISE (Representation and Inclusion Sustain Excellence) Statement.

This value proposition is pursued in terms not only of artists and staff, but also in programs, initiatives and activities embedded across all aspects of America's National Ballet Company®. It includes education programs and artistic and administrative endeavours, being embedded in the fabric of ABT's corporate culture – and also in specific projects such as the Project Plié in 2013, which was ABT's industry-leading initiative to advance diversity in the training pipeline for ballet students, teachers and administrative interns.

*Source:* https://www.abt.org/

ter new relationships with the community they both serve, because they already experience a meaningful and emotionally relevant attachment with it. As already emphasized, this is the most solid base for successful fundraising development. It is therefore possible to consider subscribers as being at the entry level of membership programs.

The key strategic factor that determines this behavioral change in the arts audience is a focus on the emotional connection with these people. This drives people's loyalty and helps them to move from the status of not-yet-loyal attendees (e.g., occasional ticket buyers, lapsed subscribers or frequent single ticket buyers) to the status of loyal attendees (e.g., subscribers, donors, even large donors or supe- loyal audience members).

Loyal audiences therefore usually have a deep emotional relationship with the institution they attend. Subscribers have often been attending a venue for years, perhaps after an introduction to the arts by a relative or a close friend, or because of an interest or a passion that has been nurtured since childhood. Because of this background, in addition to a sensitivity to the functional aspects of the artistic offering (let us say the arts product), they are driven in their loyal behavior by factors that speak about family memories, or the desire for personal development. This means that for loyal attendees, functional attributes of the arts product can also have an emotional relevance. In other words, what brings people to develop a strong connection with and become loyal to an arts organization is that – starting from the functional characteristic of the art form with which they have become familiar – the institution is able to represent something meaningful in their everyday lives.

*Figure 3.2* A BSO All Beethoven Program couple on Tanglewood lawn, 10 July 2021

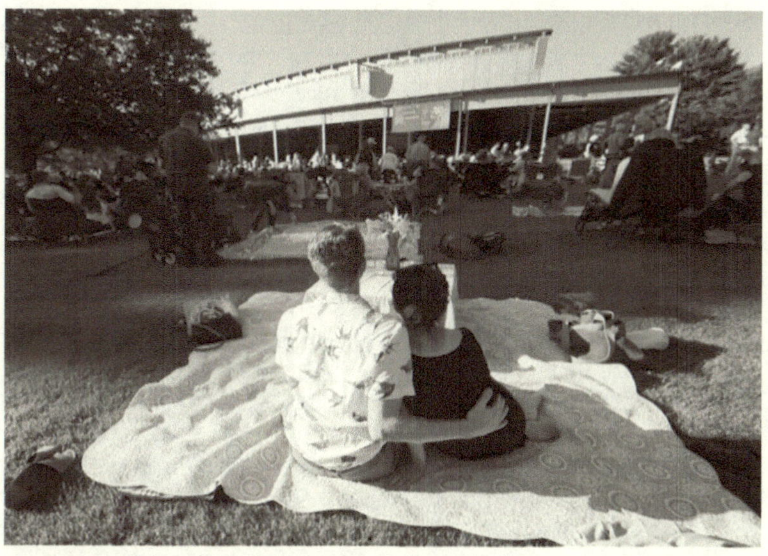

*Credit*: Hillary Scott | Boston Symphony Orchestra

## 3.4 Structuring a membership program for arts organizations

Both in the United States and in Europe, many cultural institutions rely on membership programs. Despite the great variety of the available options, memberships usually grant access to benefits such as priority booking, advanced information or to exclusive events and activities in return for a contribution. The most common in cultural and creative organizations include patron and member (or friend) programs.

Patron programs focus on the higher end of the annual giving spectrum. For the larger arts institutions, patron annual giving can range from $1000 to over $100,000 in the United States. Typically, patrons are philanthropists with interests in multiple institutions and are motivated by many of the same factors that inspire more modest givers. However, social visibility and recognition are typically more important to patrons. Patrons benefit from a set of basic functional benefits (such as discounted access to the venue, performances and exhibitions) and a set of "exclusive" advantages (such as access to special events, lectures and behind-the-scenes activities). In addition, they are often involved in bigger development projects that can better fulfil their desire for social recognition such as the restoration, the acquisition or the exhibition of a specific artwork, for example.

Contrasted with patron giving, joining a friends program is usually less expensive and a more broad-based program. Broadly speaking, friends are a bigger group of smaller donors who make modest and unrestricted contributions and in return receive functional benefits (e.g., free entry to exhibitions, discounted tickets for performances and retail discounts). Sometimes, friends also support more substantial fundraising efforts (restricted to special projects) as well as being a source of volunteers and advocates.

---

**Box 3.3 The Louvre's friends and patron schemes**

The Louvre is one of the most renowned arts museums in the world, hosting some of the greatest masterpieces ever created, such as Da Vinci's "Mona Lisa." The Louvre has developed a very structured support system, tailored to different kinds of supporters according to the level of their contributions:

- *Members*: the membership fee goes from €15 to a maximum of €140 according to the option that is selected (young visitors, solo or duo cardholders, families). Members receive benefits such as free entrances or discount for tickets and merchandising. By moving up the "giving ladder," they can receive special invitations to a limited set of events.

- *Companies and benefactors*: in return for a membership fee from €190 to a maximum of €1200, these donors get the same benefits as the previous categories, but in addition get access to some more exclusive advantages, (including invitations to international events, even abroad (e.g., to FAI (Italian National Trust) sites.
- *Membres d'honneur*: those who contribute a minimum of €4000 are classified as members d'honneur. In addition to the previous benefits, such members enter a more exclusive group, the Cercle des Mécènes du Louvre, which finances new projects for the museum.
- *Patrons*: this last group is involved in specific and larger fundraising campaigns. The Louvre Patrons Circle provides funding for conservation, publication and exhibition projects, alongside the Amis du Louvre projects.

In addition to the various support groups described here, the Louvre relies on the support of the Decorative Arts Circle, which brings together people and collectors who wish to share their passion for objets d'art and the Louvre's Department of Decorative Arts. In addition, the International Council brings together art lovers from around the world who are eager to share their interest in culture and enthusiasm for the Louvre. The circle supports ambitious international projects headed by the Louvre; Finally, the American Friends of the Louvre actively contributes to shining a spotlight on the Louvre from across the Atlantic. US-based and foreign donors can make contributions and benefit from tax advantages specific to the United States, as the group has been granted tax exempt status by the US Internal Revenue Service.

*Source:* https://www.louvre.fr/en/support-the-louvre

### 3.4.1 *Defining benefits*

Benefits have a central role in the design of a well-structured patrons or friends program. As previously mentioned, the general rule in defining benefit packages is that there should be a proper match between each package and the related level of required contribution. This design is conceived in order to create a correlation between the donors' and the arts organization's needs. Effective membership programs usually include a defined set of various levels of benefits serving the purpose of offering members "something unique" that cannot be found elsewhere (e.g., exclusive access or experiences). To understand this rationale, a discount on the entrance fee or in the gift shop is of general interest and corresponds to a lower level of contribution. More exclusive privileges, such as a dedicated ticket booking service or admission to cocktails with the artistic staff, fit better with a higher-level contribution. However, although each donor category has different needs, it is also not viable for organizations to build extremely personalized benefit packages: as well as not being feasible, these are also counterproductive, since audiences experience choice fatigue if there are too many alternatives. Box 3.4 gives an overview of the benefit system adopted at Nasher Sculpture Center.

**Box 3.4 Increasing benefit system in the membership program of the Nasher Sculpture Center**

With a gift of $85, a supporter can become a member of the Nasher Sculpture Center and be entitled to free admission for two adults, free parking, discounts at the museum restaurant and shop, and invitations to member-exclusive events such as exhibition previews. At higher levels of giving, a supporter is offered premiums of a more exclusive nature, such as free reciprocal admission at other partner museums, invitations to behind-the-scenes tours and gallery talks with curators, complimentary exhibition catalogues and invitations to join excursions led by the museum director.

*Source:* James Ryan Jillson personal communication

The main purpose of a well-structured benefit system is to motivate members to move up the "giving ladder." However, as noted, it is important to understand that donors make a decision to give more not only in return for benefits, but also because they have become more closely connected with the organization's mission. In other words, benefits should be a tool to reinforce the relationship between the institution and its donors. Higher levels of engagement and involvement usually correspond to higher levels of giving.

Benefits should be convenient and easy to access for members, and they should be communicated clearly to donors. One of the problems identified is that members often do not take advantage of benefits because they are not aware of them, thus highlighting an institutional communication issue. In addition to establishing a direct link with donors, benefits should also be regarded as symbolic recognition of the donors' support.

*Figure 3.3* A classification of benefits for arts organizations members

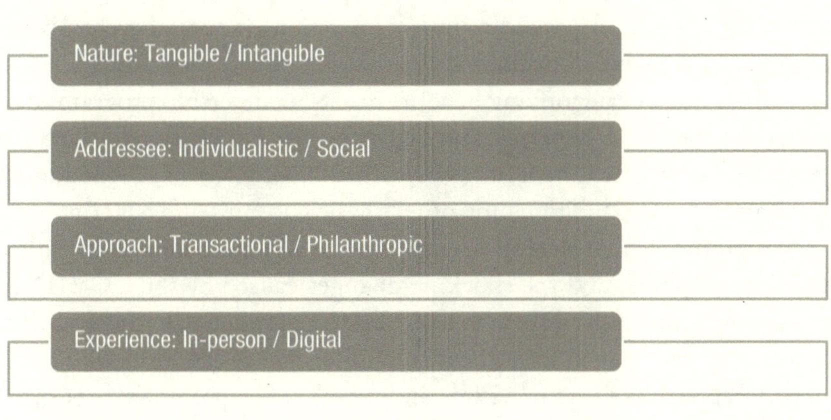


Figure 3.3 outlines a possible classification of benefits (or ways of thinking about benefits) in an arts organization membership program.

The first classification is based on the nature of the benefits, dividing them into tangible and intangible. Tangible benefits are material advantages that donors receive in return for their donations (e.g., discounts, free parking, special admissions); intangible benefits are personal, indirect gratifications (e.g., emotional satisfaction, doing a good thing for other people).

Another way to analyze benefits is by dividing them into individualistic and social. In the first category are those benefits that give donors a direct, personal advantage in return for a donation. A discount or a dedicated service or perk when attending a venue (e.g., reserved seats, free parking, promotional newsletters) are typical examples. Social benefits refer to a desire for social connection and recognition. These include the opportunity of meeting noteworthy people at a gala or special event, the guarantee of regular access to VIP seats at a venue and being included on official lists of donors.

Benefits can also be transactional or philanthropic. Transactional benefits appeal to those supporters who are motivated by economic incentives and comfort. They refer to quantifiable advantages related to the membership fees, such as free parking, free admissions to events and discounts (e.g., in the gift shop or restaurant). Philanthropic advantages, on the other hand, connect the donor with the institution in an exclusive relationship that is based on the common goal of providing a public good. They are based on the status of members, and can involve invitations to special events, backstage tours, previews of exhibitions/seasons and open rehearsals.

A final way of categorizing benefits in arts membership programs distinguishes between in-person and digital benefits. Traditionally, arts organizations offer their benefits as in-person experiences (e.g., free admissions, preview of exhibitions and other physical in-museum benefits, etc.). However, the current state of the arts is more and more immersed within the digital sphere, and the shocking changes caused by the COVID-19 pandemic have required them to make benefits attractive to those visitors who are more engaged with the virtual offerings of the institution. The need to appeal to a virtual visitor and member has prompted arts institutions to create new benefits such as exclusive original digital content, online previews and talks. For example, the digital Member Lounge is a digital membership initiative launched by the Museum of Modern Art in New York (MoMA) that aims at engaging online visitors and attracting them to become members. In Box 3.5 we describe the membership program developed by Piccolo Teatro in Milan.

**Box 3.5 The Albo d'Oro of the Piccolo Teatro in Milan**

The Albo d'Oro is the official "golden circle" of supporters of the Piccolo Teatro in Milan. It aims at gathering friends of the theatre, supporters and patrons. Members contribute to the programming, subsidize prices so the theatre is accessible and generally support its activities so its mission as an ambassador of Italian culture worldwide can grow. For individuals, levels of annual membership are friend (from €500), supporter (from €1000) and patron (from €2500). For organizations (companies, corporations, foundations, etc.), levels of annual membership are friend (from €5000), supporter (from €15,000) and patron (from €30,000). The benefits of being a member of the golden circle include invitations to exclusive events, international trips accompanying tours, previews of the season, backstage meetings with artists and the chance to associate one's name with a specific seat. The creation of the "circle" fosters personal relationships with donors so that their habits and needs can be better understood. These supporters are not necessarily regular attendees at performances, so they have a different type of connection with the institution.

*Source:* Alessandro Borchini personal communication and www.piccoloteatro.org

### 3.4.2 *Deciding contribution levels*

When asking for contributions, arts organizations can appeal to donors in different ways. Usually, development staff define the specific contribution tiers that give access to related packages of benefits and membership status. This is the rational strategy, based on fixed contribution targets and on structured paths so donors can be upgraded. However, as emotional drivers strongly motivate donations in the arts, it is possible for arts institutions to involve donors in a more engaging way when they organize and communicate categories of giving. In other words, they may require donors to reflect more thoughtfully about the connections between the level of contribution and the worth of the organization's content and mission. In this way, the connection and the proximity of donors to the needs of the arts organization become more significant, as does their awareness of the institution and its mission.

The core idea of this "thoughtful asking" is that donors are required to suggest voluntary contributions. This approach leaves donors with a choice, the main advantage being that there is no limit. However, it is important to find the right balance in this voluntary definition: the potential risk is that donors might misunderstand the meaning of "no limit" and interpret it as "no value," and therefore reduce (or even discontinue) their donations. Arts organizations can forego a "pure" voluntarist approach in favor of an "impure" one by suggesting to donors how much extra they could give. The logic behind this is that it matches funding, aligning what the organization is asking for and what the donor thinks is a worthy level of support. This mixed approach can be useful in that an organization can orient donors' choices without losing the spontaneity of their actions. Marketing offers an interesting example of how to achieve this goal with the development of a sort of dynamic pricing technique. Arts organizations can ask purchasers of their products (however defined) to reflect on the extended value of what the institution offers (i.e., not just what they are buying in that precise moment) and to add an extra to the fixed price in return for that. This is the so-called pay what you want (PWYW) model that usually combines a price suggested by the organization with an extra fee, added by the customer. This goal can be achieved not only through the use of sales techniques (e.g., by anchoring), but also by directly asking for donations or suggesting matching donations given by sponsors or larger donors.

The COVID-19 pandemic has offered organizations the chance to experiment with pricing techniques to increase donations, with the goal of covering the income gap that all institutions are experiencing. When launching digital offerings during the shutdowns, many arts organizations began to suggest a different price from the basic one in order to enhance donations. Consequently, some organizations have involved individuals in understanding and defining the right price, soliciting a donation in addition to a fixed price. These extra exchanges, boosted by digital tools, have given them the opportunity to engage customers (both regular and occasional) in fundraising activities. As these techniques rely on donors' awareness about how their contribution can make a difference, arts organizations should advertise and communicate the effects of these extra efforts. Through social media, for instance, they can make this asking for extra more impactful, giving purchasers the opportunity to discover how their peers (or other influential members of their community) have behaved and to let them share their experience with other potential contributors.[5]

### 3.4.3 *Recognizing, recognizing, recognizing*

Even the most altruistic donor expects thanks in return for a contribution. Moreover, it is at the moment of acknowledgement that the connection between the arts organization and its donors can be tightened, as it becomes more personal and sets the path for future contributions. The stewardship process is delicate and therefore requires the regular maintenance of contact and communication with donors. This communication also provides donors with information about how their gifts are used. It usually includes acknowledgement of receipt of the gift and a more personal note of thanks – often from a top representative of the organization – in order to balance the functional and emotional aspects of the giving process.

Recognition is the key concept here. Most donors look for recognition of their generosity from the wider community and also from arts organizations. An inadequate level of recognition can negatively influence future donations. Contributors might wrongly perceive that their

[5] We discuss this topic in Chapter 10.

support is useless or unappreciated, or even that the organization has just pocketed the money received. Consequently, the process of thanking donors is extremely important and requires a formal structure. Prompt acknowledgement is a top priority, and fundraising practitioners recommend that a week is a good average time frame when thanking modest donors. Adopting a personal approach is important as well. Donors generally appreciate it if they are recognized throughout an organization, especially when the institution underlines how important it is that they are on board by specifically using their name when recording the gift. Emphasizing the emotional bond between the organization and its donors is another key step in effective acknowledgements. In addition, donors appreciate it when an organization stresses how impactful donations have been in helping to fulfil its mission. Finally, as modest donors can contribute in many different ways, arts organizations should have a sense of the most appropriate way in which their gratitude can be expressed and donors can be made aware of the impact of their gifts.

### 3.4.4 *Acquiring, retaining and upgrading*

Membership programs can offer an "entry level" for first-time donors. Furthermore, through the careful design of an appropriate set of benefits, these programs can help lower-level donors move up the giving ladder. Finally, by empowering the donors' relationship with the arts organization thanks to the cultivation process, membership programs also play a key role in retaining donors.

As previously stated, donors are more likely to be acquired from within the organization's attendance base. Moreover, the conversion cost of loyal attendees (especially subscribers) into donors is lower than those prospects who only have a more general interest in the arts organization's activities. During the acquisition process, institutions can adopt several different and sophisticated techniques. We suggest focusing on four key factors in analyzing prospects (Tempel et al., 2011):

- *Interest*: the strongest prospects are those who are committed to the institution's cause and the art form. Most loyal supporters have a strong passion for the art form beyond a specific institution.
- *Capacity*: arts organizations should undertake research to assess how much prospects can give. However, they should always look

at financial capacity in relative terms. If, for example, someone is capable of providing a gift of $/€1000, it may be wise to ask for initial support at a lower level. Capacity should not be confused with propensity.

- *Connection*: even if an individual has an interest in an organization and an ability to give, this is not sufficient if there is no clear connection with the cultural institution. In these instances, organizations might explore if there are any mutual connections (e.g., with a board member or event chair who could make an introduction) so they can be included in the donor cultivation/acquisition process.
- *Personalization*: as individual giving might be motivated by a combination of different triggers, arts organizations should define the level of personalization when addressing their prospects.

To retain existing members, cultural institutions should pay constant attention to the evolution of the relationship they have with donors over time. In particular, they should be aware of the fact that donors' needs do not remain the same throughout relationship timeline. Moreover, arts organizations should nurture donors' attention and interest in the institution, and attempt to maintain their connection over time. A detailed segmentation of the donor base can be the first step to take when working on donor retention. There are no general rules, as each organization should adopt the segmentation technique that best allows for matching donor profiles with fundraising actions. However, the longer the relationship with the donors, the richer and more sophisticated this segmentation can be. In addition, organizations can improve donor retention by being aware of the lifetime value of each donor; long-term support is a good indicator of loyalty. Research into donors' behavior can be particularly useful here (e.g., understanding donors' motivations for supporting a specific organization, what factors are the most important for them and the reasons why they withdraw from membership programs). Arts institutions can improve donor retention by involving donors in activities that increase their perception of specialness (e.g., inviting them to exclusive events, such as meetings with creative staff, invitations to rehearsals and other behind-the-scenes occasions) and through communicating awareness of different ways in which support can be offered (e.g., in-kind contributions, volunteering and bequests). Of course, cultural institutions should also enhance their donors' wish to have a relevant impact on the organization's existence and activity (e.g., by asking for their help in solving specific problems or informing them directly about specific issues before such matters are disclosed to the press or via social media). Finally, as emphasized earlier, individuals' emotional and personal connections with the arts institution they are supporting improves their loyalty to it.

Another relevant phase of the retention process is the implementation of regular communication with members. Soliciting annual donations usually involves direct methods such as mail, telephone, email and personal contact (although this is not practical when attempting to reach a large number of modest givers). When working on members' retention, arts organizations should communicate a strong and persuasive case for support. In other words, donors must always understand exactly why the institution still needs their support and why their contributions will make an important difference. As Hopkins and Friedman (1997) suggest, in designing a message aimed at retaining members, it is important not to assume that they all know what an arts organization's unique qualities are. What's more, perfecting both the clarity and the effectiveness of an organization's core message to its members (the reasons for support) can be extremely important, because even the most informed supporters can benefit from a regular reinforcement of this information – *Repetita iuvant.* A compelling case for support is made if donors perceive the urgency and relevance of their contribution. In other words, donors should trust that, by the intermediation of the cultural institution, their gift satisfies a higher, shared purpose, increasing the common good. In order to boost the relationship with them, communication with donors must always stress the fact that contributing is more than a simple transactional exchange in return for benefits. Of course, this is not to downplay the usefulness of benefits, but arts organizations should focus on making members understand that they are being asked to deepen their connection so they are part of the future of the institution and the community it serves. Consequently, institutions should clarify that what they are promising is not just privileges, but a lifetime of treasured service. Furthermore, as noted earlier, if they over-emphasize the role of benefits in their fundraising campaigns and these are not properly valued or used, donors will be left with no further motivation to contribute.

By developing a good donor retention strategy, arts organizations can also benefit from some practical advantages: stability of contributions over time and reductions in donor management costs, including marketing expenditure. It is more costly to attract new donors than to retain and upgrade existing ones. Moreover, retaining strategies can relate to the development of cross- and up-selling activities that can appeal to acquired regular donors, in order to increase their level of support.

As noted, in respect to financial results, membership programs can be an effective way to make donors move towards the top of the giving ladder. The upgrading process of gift levels is possible not only vertically (i.e., by boosting the donations level of existing members), but also horizontally (i.e., matching upper-level donors with some cross-actions). Some techniques of vertical upgrading are:

- *Upgrading lower-level members and donors*: Arts organizations should identify those individuals who are currently giving at lower levels but have signaled an increasing interest (e.g., some museums target members who visit the museum frequently for upgrade solicitations) and have a higher estimated capacity for giving. Moreover, Burk (2003) argues that the value of the gift may increase if donors are given the opportunity to designate a specific purpose for their contribution. Although restricted revenue may create resistance among managers, some donors may have difficulties in making unrestricted contributions, missing the ability to see the tangible impact of their gift.
- *Contacting former upper-level members and donors*: Maximizing these donors' propensity to give can be more cost-effective than looking for new prospects. However, understanding why such donors suspended or discontinued giving is important to know before initiating a solicitation. Such cognizance might suggest that other charitable vehicles might be of more interest (e.g., bequest intentions, frequency, cumulative lifetime giving) (Warwick, 2013).
- *Working on post-event engagement*: Individuals who attend one-time fundraising events could be approached with regard to providing annual support as annual fund donors or members.

Horizontal upgrading can be pursued by:

- *Developing more transactional programs*: some arts organizations offer transactional opportunities to attract upper-level annual fund donors. Arts organizations with an appealing venue, for example, can rent out spaces for weddings, receptions or other special events, and require that those who rent the facility be annual fund donors or members at a certain level. Transactional donors are not as invested as those moved by philanthropic values, and are therefore less likely to renew their support throughout the years.

- *Making peer-to-peer efforts*: some donors may be engaged in the organization, willing to spontaneously donate more and introduce other prospects. Peer-to-peer connections can be fostered if donors are engaged as volunteers, serve on a volunteer committee or help with a special fundraising campaign or initiative. This is also possible if dedicated peer-to-peer programs are developed, an example being bring-a-friend initiatives.

Being able to measure the results of acquiring, retaining or upgrading donors is also crucial. This should include assessing the quality of services offered – in order to identify weaknesses as well as the overall strategy. Measuring donors' input should not just focus on immediate returns, but should also include the lifetime value of the relationship. In other words, measurements should highlight the total giving estimated for a single donor throughout the course of their relationship with the organization. Metrics that measure successful membership programs will vary according to the institution because of the variety of goals that cultural organizations have. In arts fundraising, the most common metrics are:

- *Acquisition metrics*: these measure at what level an organization is able to acquire donors, not only in terms of the number of donors, but also in terms of costs for activities and the lifetime value of contributors. These metrics are:
  - *Response rate*: $\dfrac{\textit{New membership sold via specific channel}}{\textit{Total membership asks via specific channel}}$
  - *Return on investment (ROI)*: $\dfrac{\textit{Net revenue from new members}}{\textit{Cost of acquiring new members}}$
  - *Cost of sale*: $\dfrac{\textit{Cost of acquiring new members}}{\textit{Revenue from new members}}$
  - *Customer lifetime value*: *Average annual contribution* × *Average length of membership*

- *Renewal metrics*: these quantify the "regularity index" of members' donations, not only in terms of number of members, but also, again, in terms of costs and level of donation per year. These rates are useful in helping to understand the retention and loyalty of members; however, they should be coupled with the evaluation of customer lifetime value. These metrics are:
  - *Renewal rate*: $\dfrac{\textit{Number of members who gave in Year 1 and Year 2}}{\textit{Number of members who gave in Year 1}}$
  - *Cost of sale*: $\dfrac{\textit{Cost of renewing members}}{\textit{Gross revenue from renewing members}}$
  - *Upgraded renewal rate*:
    $\dfrac{\textit{Number of members who gave in Year 1 and at higher level in Year 2}}{\textit{Number of members who gave in Year 1 and 2 at any level}}$
- *Rejoining metrics*: these measure how amenable donors are to rejoining the organization after their relationship has been interrupted. This metric is:
  - *Reactivation rate*: $\dfrac{\textit{Memberships sold to former members}}{\textit{Total rejoin membership asks}}$

## 3.5 Attracting individual donors through digital memberships

In this chapter we have discussed how small donors represent an important contributor base for arts organizations. This is because they are often frequent attendees and are interested in what the institution does; as a consequence, they typically provide consistent support while increasing their financial involvement on many occasions over time.

Membership programs can help arts organizations to effectively engage with their modest donors. By spelling out the set of benefits that fulfils donors' different needs, these programs can attract new donors. By ensuring consistent and appropriate benefits and by working on community management and communication techniques, membership programs allow arts organizations to retain their modest donors more easily. By structuring an incremental giving ladder (with calibrated and proportional benefits) in their programs, they can also secure upgrades in giving levels over time.

Relationship boosting and regular communication with small donors are at the heart of any effective membership program, as the large community of small donors must be carefully managed and engaged in order not to lose their enthusiasm and support.

Enhancing the most traditional community management strategies undertaken by cultural institutions, digital systems offer interesting opportunities to build community and relationships. Thanks to the familiarity that everybody has with devices such as smartphones and tablets, and the pervasive impact of the internet on everyday life, arts organizations can exploit new interactive ways in which they can gather contributions and stay in touch with their supporters.

When membership goes digital, the benefits can be both functional and relational. Functionally, organizations benefit from technical advances (e.g., automatic registration processes) or economic efficiencies (e.g., savings in management and marketing costs). Because of digital solutions, they can automate some phases of the member acquisition and retention processes, while at the same time maintain an acceptable level of personalization. For example, it is now very common to find membership or donation pages on arts organization websites, where small donors can find information about the membership program, make donations online (paying with a credit card or via a payment app) and officially become signed-up members. It is very easy to send automatic (but personalized) follow-up email replies from the very first moment of contact with new donors. In addition, the existing database can be contacted (and eventually solicited) in one shot, thanks to accessible email programs that allow personalized and targeted messages that can be customized with special content. Finally, taking membership solicitations online means that potential donors have access to an organization's fundraising activities twenty-four hours a day, seven days a week.

An incredible strategic opportunity for fundraising is provided by social media. Facebook, Twitter and Instagram are all virtual platforms where people meet, exchange ideas and participate in the life of the communities to which they belong. These tools allow arts organizations to reconsider their community management strategies because they have the opportunity to interact directly with the members of their virtual community on pertinent topics (whether they are asking for comments and endorsement or for concrete actions, such as a donation). Furthermore, social media platforms give members the feeling that they are always connected with the organization they support: they can join and participate – in a way that is complementary to the in-person-experience – whenever they want and wherever they are. In addition, the peer-to-peer nature of web communication can result in other web users following an organization's supporters (and hopefully its account), and this may stimulate membership applications. Online, active members can become passionate and motivated spokespersons for a particular institution. And of course, we should remember how social media impacts our society at different levels.[6]

### Keywords for arts fundraisers

Members, small donors, individual giving programs, annual giving program, restricted or unrestricted funds, small gifts, membership programs, benefit system, contribution levels (tiers), earned income, first time donors, direct-response marketing tools, altruism, social pressure, recognition, face-to-face solicitations, intrinsic and extrinsic motivations, disempowering the relationship, tax benefits, subscriptions, loyalty, emotional connection, shared value strategy, patron or friend program, non-transferable membership, giving ladder, tangible or intangible benefits, individualistic and social benefits, transactional or philanthropic benefits, in-person or digital benefits, voluntary contributions, pay what you want (PWYW) model, donors' awareness, acknowledgement, recognition, donor acquisition, lifetime value, case for support, donors' retention, donors' vertical or horizontal upgrading, acquisition, or renewal or rejoining metrics

### Suggested questions for meetings and discussion

- What are the main motivations for individual giving to the arts?
- How can arts institutions classify the motivations of individual givers? What clusters are adopted in arts organizations you know?
- Why do people become members? Why do they stay members?

[6] Chapter 10 provides a wider discussion of this topic.

- How can arts organizations attract new members?
- What are the elements and characteristics of a well-structured benefit system? What makes a membership benefit effective?
- What is the correct balance between philanthropic and transactional intents in arts membership programs?
- What are some examples of values that arts organizations can share with their constituencies?
- How can a cultural institution establish its own shared value strategy?
- What are the processes to follow in developing a membership program for an arts organization?
- What challenges do arts organizations face in developing a membership program?
- What differences/similarities are there between membership programs in visual arts and those in performing arts?
- In your perspective, what are the trends and the possible evolution of membership programs for the arts?
- What is the difference between loyalty and membership programs?
- Given the different roles that membership plays in arts organizations, how is it possible to measure success?
- In your experience, how helpful can membership programs be in enhancing the relationship between arts organizations and members of the community?
- What role can marketing play in enhancing the effectiveness of a membership program for the arts? What is your experience?
- What should arts organizations do to convert their subscribers into members or into major donors?
- What is the relationship between marketing and fundraising?
- Are you aware of any case histories of successful membership programs for the arts that can be set as benchmarks?

## References

ABA (Advisory Board of the Arts) (2020). *Coming back stronger summit.* Available at: https://www.advisoryBoardArts.com/coming-back-stronger-session-1-recap-and-recording.

ABA (Advisory Board of the Arts.) (2021). *Individual Arts Donor Survey*, July 2021.

Bekkers, R. and Wiepking, P. (2011). "A literature review of empirical studies of philanthropy: Eight mechanisms that drive charitable giving," *Nonprofit and Voluntary Sector Quarterly*, 40 (5): 924–973.

Burk, P. (2003). *Donor-centered fundraising: How to hold on to your donors and raise much more money*. Chicago: Cygnus Applied Research.

Hopkins, K. B. and Friedman, C. S. (1997). *Successful fundraising for arts and cultural organizations*, 2nd Edition, Phoenix, AZ: Greenwood.

Sargeant, A. (2001). "Relationship fundraising: How to keep donors loyal," *Nonprofit Management and Leadership*, 12 (2): 177–192.

Sargeant, A. (2014). "A retrospective – charitable giving: Towards a model of donor behavior," *Social Business*, 4 (4): 293–323.

Sargeant, A. and Shang, J. (2010). *Fundraising principles and practice*. Hoboken, NJ: John Wiley and Sons.

Schervish, P. G. and Havens, J. J. (2002). "The Boston area diary study and the moral citizenship of care," *Voluntas: International Journal of Voluntary and Nonprofit Organizations*, 13 (1): 47–71.

Tempel, E. R., Seiler, T. L. and Aldrich, E. E. (eds) (2011). *Achieving excellence in fundraising*, third edition. San Francisco: Jossey-Bass.

Warwick, M. (2013). *How to write successful fundraising appeals*, third edition. San Francisco: Jossey-Bass.

Worth, M. J. (2016). *Fundraising: Principles and practice*. Los Angeles: SAGE Publications, Inc.

# 4 The Role of Major Donors in Arts Fundraising

with *Piergiacomo Mion Dalle Carbonare* and *Marek Prokupek*

## 4.1 Major donors and arts philanthropists: who are they?

Philanthropists have always played a significant role in supporting arts and cultural organizations. Individual generosity has historically benefited these institutions, especially in the United States, where private arts philanthropy is prevalent. In Europe, with the recent decreasing trends in public subsidies to the arts, cultural institutions are looking with growing interest at philanthropists and collectors as important partners and sources of support. In the last three decades, public arts funding schemes have changed in many European countries, with governments encouraging arts organizations to use some tools from the British or American arts funding model to gather resources.

By definition, arts philanthropists and major donors are individuals who make significant gifts to arts institutions. These major donations can be both financial and in kind, including assets, artworks and other resources. Given the variety and scale of arts institutions, the definition of "major donor" and the gift amount required may vary.[1]

Major donations frequently reflect the donor's interest in supporting cultural ideals or their desire for social recognition: economic return is not their primary motivator. Arts philanthropists can also be interested in the visibility that comes from naming opportunities. Offering these is a tried and tested way to raise money and to cultivate enduring relationships with major benefactors. Donations required for them are typically high, as benefactors receive public acclaim in return (e.g., the donor's

---

[1] See also Chapter 3.

name posted in a prominent location). Naming benefits are often one of the highest levels of donation acknowledgement, with examples being a wing in a museum or a rehearsal room in an opera house named after donors who significantly contributed to the building or restoration of facilities. Box 4.1 provides the example of an entire building that is named after a major donor, the Blavatnik Building of London's Tate Modern.

**Box 4.1 Example of a naming opportunity: the Blavatnik Building, Tate Modern, London**

In honor of the USSR-born billionaire oligarch Len Blavatnik, who gave one of the greatest donations in Tate Modern's history, the arts organization named its newest building the Blavatnik Building. Blavatnik donated to the Tate in 2011. The government and local authority granted the museum a total of £58 million for the new galleries, while the Blavatnik Family Foundation's donation accounted for a sizable portion of the $260 million needed to finish it.

*Source*: Author's elaboration from https://www.tate.org.uk/

Major donors are among the most sought-after sources of funding for arts organizations for several reasons. First, major contributors usually make long-term financial commitments, providing a dependable source of annual financing. Second, unlike businesses or foundations, major donors can make their donations in some instances without the constraint of stringent giving guidelines or committee decisions. As a result, many arts development departments can even ask these donors to fund particularly ambitious projects that other kinds of givers might be reluctant to support. Third, major donors can be a crucial link to other funding sources (e.g., other people, businesses and foundations), because many of them have broad connections in the corporate, political and social spheres (Hopkins and Friedman, 1997) that can be converted into effective advocacy for support of the arts. However, receiving support from major donors can also have some negative effects, especially in terms of internal governance. A common example of this – especially when major donors are board members – is that they can exert excessive pressure on decision-making (e.g., on programming, potential projects) and undermine strategic objectives. However, these side effects do not affect the relevance and importance of major contributions to an organization's fundraising structure.

Kotler and Scheff (1997) argue that major donors are the goal of any fundraising effort, and that any arts organization should nurture effective relationships with them. Case histories and research highlight how – on average – 20 per cent of donors account for 80 per cent of the total donations to arts organizations. Because of this, arts fundraisers often choose to focus on potential major donors. However, a balance should be achieved: depending too heavily on a relatively small number of major supporters can risk financial fragility when even just one of them decides not to confirm future support. Many arts organizations have put themselves at risk by relying overwhelmingly on the generosity of a small group of benefactors. Heetland (1992) argues that in the United States, the traditional 80/20 ratio is underestimated: it is common among American arts institutions to rely on 10 per cent of their donors for 90 per cent of their philanthropic funds. Arts fundraisers should take this polarization of donations into account when planning their fundraising budgets and the gifts pyramid. Case histories suggest that in the most successful fundraising initiatives, the largest two gifts represent 10–15 per cent of the goal, while the top ten gifts are equivalent to roughly 40 per cent and the top 100 gifts are 90 per cent of the amount raised (Brock, 1989; Sargeant, et al. 2002).

Research has confirmed, both in the United States and in Europe, that major donations are positively influenced by incentives (e.g., tax benefits). Major donors are wealthy people who typically own a range of different assets including cash, real estate, retirement assets, insurance and securities. As they are hesitant about parting with their possessions and protective of them, in some cases they expect a return on their gift-giving investment. Concerning these expected benefits, Fredricks (2001) argues that major donors can range from someone seeking the maximum amount of celebrity that money can buy to an anonymous gift. Like other individual givers, major donors often support a variety of not-for-profits. Historically, major donors have been over fifty-five years old, male, married, conservative, religious, on the verge of retirement, with a history of involvement and giving, and possess a mix of assets, such as a family foundation, a business or inherited wealth (Williams, 1991). The corporate executive, the affluent widow, the high-net self-made person and those with inherited money are typical major arts donors (Lawson 1995). In 2022, however, such descriptions are outdated: major donors now come from a much wider variety of backgrounds. As we outline later in this chapter, involving these major donors in fundraising for an arts organization may take years, and often involves attorneys and accountants.

In the United States, where major donor fundraising is paramount, arts managers are familiar with a series of generational stereotypes (Strauss et al., 1991). Scholars have segmented major philanthropists into four different generational clusters:

- *Idealists*: a dominating generation that sets new objectives, seeks innovation and advancement, and frequently establishes the philosophical foundation for succeeding generations.
- *Reactives*: a recessive generation that responds pragmatically to being made the scapegoat for society's problems.
- *Civics*: a dominating generation that creates social institutions, wins wars and overcomes social challenges.
- *Adaptives*: civic generation successes who are refined and improved upon by the reactives.

Considering how they have expressed their philanthropy over the centuries, each of these clusters can be split into generational sub-groups:

- *The Lost Generation*, born between 1883 and 1900, was of the reactive type. Donors belonging to this generation frequently bequeathed their fortunes to the arts organizations or institutions that "raised" them (e.g., their profession, the church or their local school system).
- *The GI Generation*, born between 1901 and 1924, was a civic-type generation. The group is collectivist, supporting social institutions and challenges.
- *The Silent Generation*, born between 1925 and 1942, belongs to the adaptive cluster: this generation is expected to leave the majority of their wealth to the next comers.
- *The Boomer Generation*, born between 1942 and 1960, belongs to the idealistic cluster and attracts the greatest attention of arts fundraisers, as its members are sensitive to the possibility of giving moral capital to a grand moral movement (Eastman, 1995).

- *Generation X*, born between 1961 and 1980, belongs to the reactive cluster.
- *The Millennials*, born from 1982, belong to the civic cluster as they are concerned with community donations.

Although the experiences of earlier generations in Europe have undoubtedly been different from those of their counterparts in the United States, the same generational archetypes are also applicable there (Sargeant et al., 2002).

### 4.1.1 *The new philanthropists*

Philanthropic sensitiveness is being expressed earlier than ever before: students at many top business schools are incorporating philanthropy into their education from a relatively early age, and wealthy donors frequently start to give significant amounts of money many years before they have accumulated great wealth. In addition, the dot-com boom in the 1990s (Grace and Wendroff, 2001) and the rise of the so-called new wealth industries represent a great driver of change in arts philanthropy. These major donors are changing the conventional definition of charity, as they are tackling massive problems with greater ambition than past generations. With a more global outlook, they demand that funded organizations perform in accordance with their expectations, and want to get more involved in the life of the arts institution they are supporting. Recipients are often uneasy in responding to these expectations (Grace and Wendroff, 2001). According to a research paper by Briscoe and Marion (2001), entrepreneurs, venture capitalists and stock option millionaires are those bringing new and interesting dynamics to major giving. When properly engaged, they can be the ideal supporters of arts organizations' fundraising efforts. However, their attitudes and approaches are so specific that they can be referred to as new philanthropists.

Unlike the traditional major donors, new philanthropists have typically not inherited their wealth (Briscoe and Marion, 2001), and have seen it increase since the COVID-19 pandemic. These "new wealthy" acquired their fortunes from businesses that have been spawned mainly by technology and the internet. Briscoe and Marion (2001) refer to them as "new investors" because they think of philanthropy not as giving but rather as investing. New philanthropists are often very well trained and highly educated (with a technological background) and form tight friendships and networks. Even if their job is the core of their everyday life, when looking for philanthropic initiatives they search for opportunities to spread their energy and knowledge. Consequently, new philanthropists want better not-for-profits in their communities and want to be involved in their work.

Many new philanthropists have a middle-class upbringing that has left them unprepared for their sudden fortunes, and they do not rely on family role models when giving (Briscoe and Marion, 2001). This means that when they step into the not-for-profit world, counselling services and stewardship are fundamental in order to shift their venture capitalist approach to one of social entrepreneurship and to soften potential discomfort and distrust (Briscoe and Marion, 2001).

New philanthropy exhibits a number of recurrent traits. First, the size of gifts is substantial. This can be the result of new major donors' commitment to rapid action. The traditional giving methods (in which contributors are closely assessed for their ability to make sizable gifts), may be too "slow" for this new generation of givers. In other words, new philanthropists follow the same approach that has helped them thrive in business, and they use their donations strategically, rather than just treating symptoms. Second, as a direct consequence of such a pragmatic approach to giving, new philanthropists are more focused on a cause rather than an organization. This implies a third feature of these new givers: they look for values-driven arts organizations to support. Consequently, not-for-profit cultural institutions should clearly promote their values in order to profit from the new philanthropy market. Fourth, when accepting new philanthropists' donations, arts organizations should also embrace their ideas and values, as accepting money is often the equivalent of an endorsement. Fifth, new philanthropists are significantly result-oriented. They need feedback about the impact of their donations very fast, and often find the not-for-profits arts sectors overly slow. Thoughtful and careful communication with these new philanthropists (e.g., by keeping them up to date with all relevant happenings) is the only way in which arts organizations can manage these compelling needs. As they are so time-sensitive, new philanthropists should not be forced to wait for their requests. They expect to conduct business swiftly and are used to rapidly obtaining information whenever they need it, often informally by phone or email. In order to meet these expectations, not-for-profit institutions should be ready to modify their approaches and procedures, by internalizing or removing phases that may not seem crucial to these donors. Finally, new philanthropists tend to exercise authority or control and want to be an active part of the program or the arts organization they support. A way in which organizations can fulfil this is by offering them a position on the board, inviting them to join a committee or advisory board or asking them to head a task force in the department that is responsible for the use of their gift (Grace and Wendroff, 2001).

## 4.2 Motivations for major gifts to arts organizations

As major arts philanthropists are of increasing importance for arts and cultural organizations, these institutions have to monitor this segment of donors and adjust their fundraising techniques to the new tastes and needs of these contributors. To do this, they should carefully analyze major donors' motivations to donate. The growing economic uncertainty and the increasing competitiveness in the philanthropy market are among the hardest challenges that arts managers are facing today. Consequently, in order to implement their fundraising strategies successfully, arts organizations have to persuade donors to give, especially those with the greatest capacity to offer large donations. In this section, we cover the main motivational drivers that push major donors to give. In particular, we discuss the connections that exist between participation in the arts and the level of contribution.

The main drivers for individual participation in the arts include factors such as age, gender, education level and income (Hager and Winkler, 2012). These traits are common to the average arts attender, who is identified as an individual with higher levels of formal education and income and is likely to be older, Caucasian and female (Clopton et al., 2006). In addition, if people work in a field related to culture and education, they are likely to attend performing arts venues more frequently (Borgonovi, 2004).

Wiggins (2004) defines motivation as the desire to participate. According to Stokmans (2003), there are correlations between an individual's motivation and his or her beliefs about philanthropic support for arts and culture. Moreover, donors may have hedonic as well as utilitarian expectations for their philanthropic actions (Batra and Athola, 1991).

These expectations can relate to the expected value or utility of the donation. Donors' personal habits and vision of the world can also have an impact on their level of motivation.

In respect of major donations in particular, the social motivators of giving are extremely powerful. The individual sense of social responsibility is among the most relevant justifications for arts philanthropy. Researchers define this social responsibility as all the actions that are carried on by individuals who feel called to action because they perceive they are responsible for the safety and well-being of other people. Donors themselves often state that a sense of duty towards the institution or the wider community drives their commitment to an arts organization or a cause (Barnes, 2010). Other researchers have argued that making donations is a norm in some cases, with some donors making the assumption that giving is a part of normal life and that all individuals with a social conscience are expected to contribute to the common well-being (Neumayr and Handy, 2019). This social norm is particularly relevant among the wealthiest or socially involved individuals, who perceive giving as an obligation that is related to their privileged status or position in society (Ostrower, 1995). Furthermore, such philanthropists strongly believe that if they suspend their financial contributions to the common well-being, all society will suffer. This brings about a sense of obligation and facilitates their continuous support (Barnes, 2011).

Empathy and social emulation can also motivate charitable giving at the highest levels. Individuals become more likely to give and to repeatedly do so after they observe other people doing the same, especially if they are friends or family, or those they refer to as social models.[2] Familial influence is particularly relevant for major donations. Families that have traditionally been philanthropically active often encourage the following generations to engage in charitable giving in the same way (Prince and File, 1996).

Social norms are very powerful as predictors of major gifts; however, personal interest can also play an important role in motivating donors (Barnes, 2011). Donors can decide to give for personal enjoyment because beauty and pleasure are stimulated by the arts; they consider that aesthetic preferences are a fundamental driver of cultural support.

---

[2] See also Chapter 3.

### 4.2.1 *Major donors' motivational clusters and profiles*

In their seminal study about major donors, Prince and File (1994) group philanthropists according to their motivations to give, their attitudes and their beliefs. The study also outlines donors' expectations in terms of communication, involvement, decision-making and recognition. Despite the different characteristics of new philanthropists, this study still represents a reference point for fundraising practices, and we briefly summarize its main findings here. Figure 4.1 outlines the seven clusters that Price and File (1994) list, based on the data they collected.

The social norm is particularly relevant to the devout donors, who are driven by moral obligation more than civic choice. This is often an outcome of religious culture, in which supporting the common good is linked to the implementation of God's will. Consequently, devout donors do not look for any type of public recognition in return of their donations

*Figure 4.1* The seven faces of philanthropy

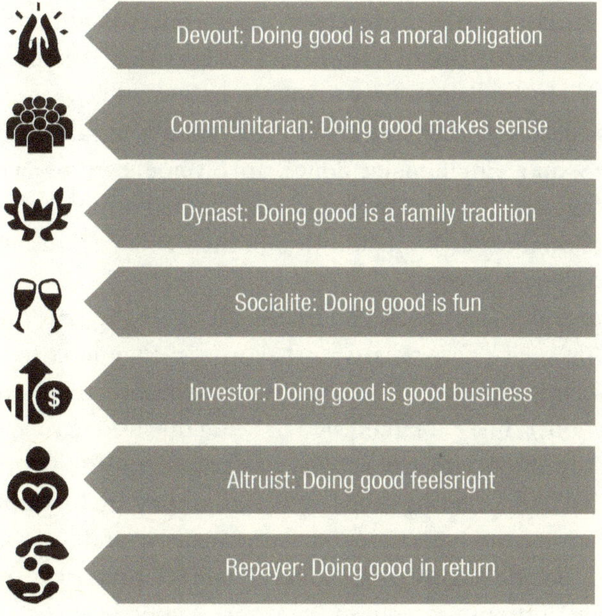


*Source*: Author's elaboration from Prince and File (1994)

and have a strong faith in the organization they support. No personal interests, passions or tastes influence them in their choices.

Communitarian donors believe in active community involvement, and they donate to local arts organizations in order to help their communities prosper. These donors typically own local businesses and often sit on the boards and committees of the not-for-profits they support. The network of relationships they have can be particularly useful for the organization they fund. Communitarian donors strongly believe that not-for-profit institutions can be more effective in solving problems related to the community they serve than local government. Consequently, they are interested in influencing an arts organization's decision-making process through their role in the board or by earmarking their donations. Public acknowledgement is a relevant benefit for them as well.

Dynast donors perceive the family tradition of giving as a relevant motivator for their donation choices. They often belong to families that have been philanthropic for generations. Consequently, donations are a means by which to increase the breadth of their impact on the well-being of the society over many decades, leaving a legacy that extends far beyond a single lifetime. Moreover, they conceive philanthropy as a family value and distinctive trait, and believe that it is everyone's responsibility. In addition, they strongly believe that, thanks to their continuous support, they can ensure that an arts organization will not have to rely on a single major donor. Involvement in managerial decision-making, serving on the board and contributing with their time and professional expertise in addition to their financial resources are all relevant to dynast donors.

Socialite donors are motivated by the idea that the not-for-profits are benefited by social networks. In other words, they look to serve good causes by being involved in social activities (whether these are events or specific actions). They are interested in being involved in social initiatives rather than in the day-to-day activity of a not-for-profit. They are particularly skilled in developing social networks as they are interested in gaining recognition from both the funded organization and their social peers.

Investors decide to contribute to not-for-profit arts organizations only when the institutions are value-driven, have a good business strategy and are able to provide tax benefits for donors. The new philanthropists mentioned earlier belong to this category of donors. They see their donation as an investment, looking at pros and cons as well as different opportunities that are available. When making their giving decisions, investors apply a win-win strategy, with the aim of satisfying a mutually beneficial interest: theirs and that of the organization. Consequently, these donors carefully plan their giving and are particularly likely to support arts organizations with a strong strategy. Fiscal advantages related to giving are a plus for investors.

Altruist donors base their behavior on a sense of generosity and empathy, typically directing their gifts towards urgent causes. They make their funding decisions without the support of any advisors, do not look for any active role in the not-for-profit they support and often wish to remain anonymous. What motivates altruist donors is the sense of urgency of the specific need that is expressed by the not-for-profit. They donate in a selfless manner, inspired by true philanthropy (i.e., love for humankind). They strongly believe in the role of not-for-profits in society, and they are positive about the potential for their actions.

Finally, repayers are connected with the institutions they support either because they have accessed their services or because they have benefited from their activities. Repayers are initially consumers and become donors. The benefit they have received reinforces their sense of obligation and it is a strong motivation to give. Perhaps the most obvious example of repayers are grateful patients who upon being cured begin to make donations to the hospital that cared for them and/or the not-for-profit that funds research on the specific disease from which the repayer has recovered. In addition, they believe that those who are more fortunate (i.e., with more money or facilities) should contribute to the common good by supporting not-for-profits.

Arts organizations may have relationships with some or all these categories of major donors. Consequently, they should develop strategies that make sense for each donor target. This should turn into a cultivation process and a donation–reward system that is based on the most relevant motivators for each donor group. Careful analysis and deep knowledge of the various categories of major donor and their motivations can also help arts fundraisers to find and attract major prospects, and to build long-lasting relationships with them based on mutual trust and understanding. In the following section, we outline the main tools that might activate and strengthen relationships with major donors.

## 4.3 How to engage major donors and arts philanthropists

Engaging major donors and philanthropists is a delicate and key process in arts fundraising. As previously mentioned, the financial stability of many arts organizations – as for many not-for-profit organizations – depends on the contributions of a few major donors. Figure 4.2 helps us to better understand this structure by outlining the donor pyramid as it is relevant to not-for-profit fundraising.

This traditional model further demonstrates how these organizations rely on a multitude of small or first-time modest donors who populate the base of the pyramid, while at the top of the pyramid there is a small pool of major donors, whose large gifts provide most of the institution's financial support.

As underscored in Chapter 3, arts fundraisers cultivate smaller donors with the aim of enticing them to upgrade their level of donation. However, this is often unrealistic because of the limited giving capacity of smaller donors. In respect to major donors, arts fundraisers should frequently be in touch with the aim of keeping/building a relationship with them,

*Figure 4.2* The donor pyramid

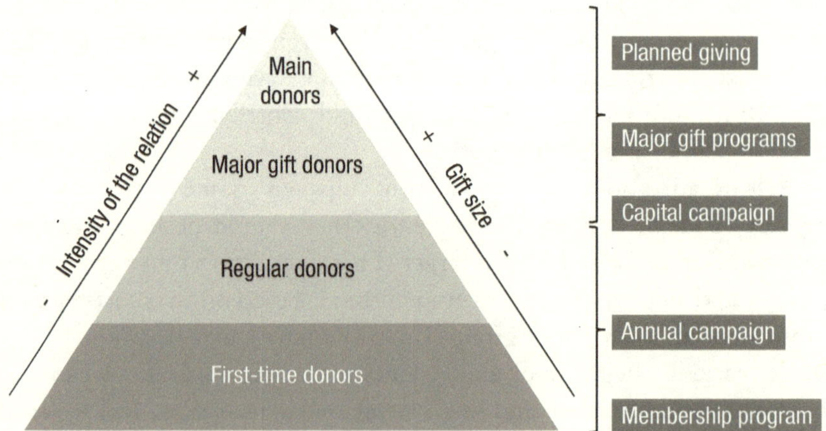


*Source*: Authors' elaboration from Worth (2016)

rather than simply seeking contributions. Understandably, this process is highly time-consuming because the needs, interests and expectations of major donors have to be addressed by the arts institution in detail, and this is a labor-intensive activity. Consequently, personal solicitation is very important as this increases donors' feelings of being personally involved in the life of the cultural institution.

Major donors therefore end up playing a prominent role in the day-by-day activity of the funded arts organization, acting as its ambassadors, board members, committee members or chairs of fundraising events or ceremonies. Engaging major donors and arts philanthropists is therefore not only about friendly public relations or casual socializing, but also about developing a relation-building process, and this is at the core of the professionalism of major gifts officers. This process is fully aligned with the fundraising strategy and goals of the development department, and with the annual target that major gifts officers have.

We can outline five different stages in the major donors fundraising process, and these are summarized in Figure 4.3. Each stage – and even every move within each stage – implies a high level of preparedness and

*Figure 4.3* The five-stage major donor fundraising process

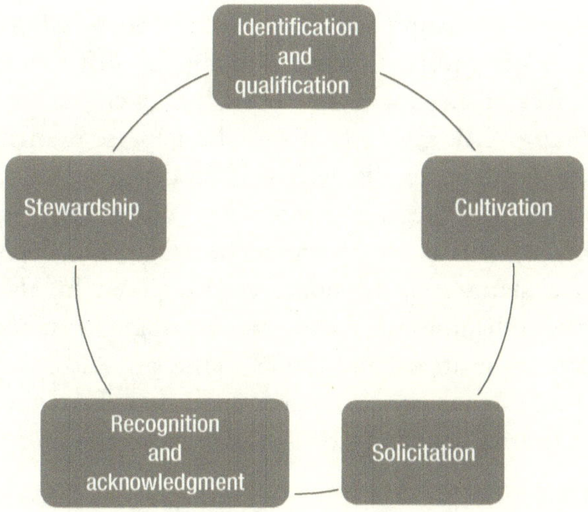

planning, together with a willingness to learn when it might be appropriate to move from one stage to the next.

The first stage concerns the identification and qualification (i.e., profiling) of prospects. Time and money are scarce resources. Consequently, arts fundraisers know that it is better to invest them in enhancing the quality of their programs, rather than wasting them in soliciting unlikely prospects. For this reason, prospect identification and qualification are key steps: the likelihood of success increases dramatically if the arts organization makes a proper preliminary check about who is a likely donor and if he or she might be willing to donate consistent gifts. Therefore, this first stage is devoted to gathering information about prospects and to create a list of targets. To this end, development directors have many tools at their disposal – and with the advent of various technologies, significant information about prospective donors is easily available online. Of course, this abundance of information requires clarification about how much of it is actually relevant and useful.

Also in the case of major donors,[3] Tempel et al. (2010) suggest that information should be collected relating to three main attributes of the target donor: the type of link the donor has with the organization (e.g., giving history, frequency of attendance, other donors he or she knows); the capacity to give (i.e., in terms of estimated wealth) and the type of his or her current philanthropic and other interests. Information about major donors and their contacts should be gathered in a donor profile record which should be shared and become part of the organization's data base.

Targeting major prospects requires a slightly different approach to broad-based fundraising appeals. While creating clusters of regular donors according to their giving habits might help, for example, to model solicitation tactics (i.e.: emails, letters) or to design surveys that gather information, thereby integrating secondary sources (e.g., social media, the ticket office), this is not recommended for major donors. Because of their special status, major donors always require a highly customized approach even in the research stage. Practices might be standardized, but customization of the appeal and actions is the key. Also, for this reason, arts organizations can gather better information about their donors if they rely on "warm" sources, such as the inner circles of existing major

---

[3] See also Chapter 3.

donors or the board. Built-in databases are a valuable source of data about major gift prospects: these contain contact information that are captured in different ways – for example, from market research carried out by an organization among its existing customers or attendees; from personal talks or surveys circulated during events or receptions; from personal meetings and visits; from internal data mining; and from peer-screening (i.e., consulting volunteers or staff, asking them either to name possible new contacts or to rate a list of individuals that the development unit might contact).

After collecting information about their prospects, major gifts officers can more easily prioritize their efforts and select their targets in consultation with the chief development officer. They usually create their own donor profile folder; that is, a list of prospect relationships for which they are responsible. The gift officer's portfolio (ranging from 75 to 150 prospects) includes major gift prospects in various stages of the pipeline. In some cases, the arts organization has identified them, but many aspects of their life or giving record are still unknown. Other prospects are already at more advanced stages in the fundraising process. Information collecting is a never-ending activity, and must not be confined to the first stage of the relationship-building cycle.

The second stage of the major donors fundraising process is prospect cultivation. At this stage, the development officer has identified target donors and has decided to invest time and money in approaching them. The cultivation of major donors is another core task of every major gift officer, but this process often involves the development director and, in some cases, even the CEO or artistic director. During the cultivation, fundraisers can complement discovery visits (whose aim is to collect more information about the prospect and his family) with the provision of details about the organization's activities, projects and programs. This is fundamental because it confirms whether or not the institutional needs fit a prospective donor's expectations, and it can therefore help the arts organization in advancing the relationship and exploring common interests. Typically, at this stage, development directors also try to involve prospects as members of internal committees, taskforces or even the board. The objective being to increase the psychological identification and personal commitment of the prospect with the organization and its mission. Broadly speaking, institutional involvement can often effectively meet the expectations of those major donors who are interested in active participation in the life of the arts organization, such as investors or dynasts.[4] In other cases, organizations can use tactics that require "investment" to cultivate their prospective major donors. Typical examples of these are exclusive tours, invitations to events, dinners with the CEO and exclusive meetings with artists.

Moving from the cultivation stage to gift solicitation might take a long time, and each donor portfolio can be completed with a move record (Worth, 2016) that highlights the status of the cultivation process by recording target sizes of major gifts and the various actions that have been undertaken, together with the related outcomes. We can compare the cultivation process to the moves in tango dancing, which work only if dancers' actions and reactions are well calibrated. The key point of successful donor cultivation is regarding the ongoing conversation as a learning process, which clarifies what the institution can do for the donors and vice versa.

A third step in the fundraising process when it involves high net worth donors is the "ask," or in other words the solicitation of the gift. After an average of twelve to eighteen months, identification and cultivation processes end and solicitation can begin. Even though there are statistics about the typical time that these preliminary phases take, there is no golden rule about the perfect time to ask. Indeed, when the various conversations during the cultivation have been successful, some donors tend to anticipate the proposal by directly asking to support a given project or the arts organization itself. However, this does not always happen, and arts fundraisers should remember that in order to receive gifts they need to ask.

Panas (2002) highlights some key factors that increase the likelihood of a 'yes' from a major donor. First, personal meetings can be particularly effective in increasing the connection between an arts organization and a prospective donor. It behooves major gift officers to carefully prepare and plan for each meeting, especially the one during which the "ask" will be made. They should decide well in advance who from the organization should be involved, who should speak and when, where the meeting should take place (e.g., the prospect's office or house or some other private space) and, of course, the size of the suggested gift and which cause it will support. Even the invitation phone call to the donor requires proper preparation (Panas, 2002), and a script for this can be very help-

[4] See Section 4.2.

ful. During the solicitation visit, it is also very important to keep the plan in mind, without relinquishing its goals or simply accepting promises of future gifts (Panas, 2002).

Fundraising professionals agree that successful fundraising is possible when the right person targets the right donor, proposing the right gift size to support the right project at the right time and in the right way. This is a deliberative process, and for this reason, it is crucial to be aware whether or not it is the "right" moment to ask. Sometimes small talk and informal questions help to test whether the ongoing meeting is the right time to solicit a gift.

This "testing assumptions" rule makes particular sense if prospects turn down the proposal and refuse to give. Even when arts fundraisers get a "no" from a prospect, testing donors' concerns might be very helpful when attempting to understand what has gone wrong, and asking directly has its merits. Panas (2002) suggests that typically donors' concerns revolve around the type of project, the amount of money requested or the timing of the request. In order to understand how to change their approach and prepare the path for future requests for support, fundraisers should listen rather than talk. A salesman knows that after the "ask," the first who speaks will lose. In fundraising, transactional or cajoling approaches should be limited, but staying silent after the "ask" is consistent with the idea that major gifts officers should partner with major donors – and that they also are interested in the prospect's motivations and ideas rather than just their pockets.

The fourth fundraising step concerns acknowledgement and recognition after a successful solicitation. In Chapter 3, we highlight how thanking donors for their support and indicating that the value of their contribution has been recognized is a crucial follow-up action after a gift has been secured. Arts organizations should be careful in choosing what kind of recognition to offer a major donor, and also be properly reactive in showing their gratitude. According to many fundraising practitioners, organizations should address their thank-you notes to their major donors within forty-eight hours of receiving a commitment. Later recognition might make the donor perceive a lack of timeliness or efficiency, or – even worse – that the donation is not needed or appreciated. There are different ways of expressing gratitude: after a successful solicitation visit, typical examples are a phone call or a formal letter from the CEO. Finally, naming opportunities can be an interesting tool to honor donor contributions, as previously mentioned.

The final stage in the major donor fundraising process pertains to stewardship. From what we have described so far, it is evident that identification, cultivation and solicitation of a major donor can be expensive. Moreover, if not properly engaged, a past donor is likely to behave like a new donor after some time has passed. This is why successful arts institutions always nurture relationships with their major donors, providing regular reports about how they have used particular gifts and their impacts. This is made possible by designing a regular program of communications (e.g., annual reports and newsletters, and invitations to participate in a range of events).[5]

### 4.3.1 *Building relationships with major donors*

Fundraising from major donors stands at the heart of development professionals' practice as it revolves around the building of philanthropic relationships. We can trace three main ingredients at the core of the fundraising profession that represent milestones for building meaningful relationships with major donors (Panas, 2002, Tempel et al. 2010).

The first element in addressing and bonding with donors is integrity. This does not just mean honesty and earnestness. In an encounter with the arts organization's fundraising staff, donors should not feel manipulated. On the contrary, it is important that the major gifts officer shows a true interest in them and in the ways in which they can satisfactorily invest their wealth for the well-being of a broader community. This means showing true empathy, a capacity for listening, caring and genuinely expressing interest in donors' desires and expectations. In short, major donors rely on fundraisers who are trustworthy – and who actually care about them as people more than they do about their bank accounts.

The second ingredient for a successful philanthropic relationship is personal enthusiasm. People give when they are good humored. Consequently, fundraisers' passion for the art form that the organization provides or for the mission or project for which support is needed helps in creating a positive environment in the relationship. We know that wealthy donors are not likely to give to organizations that appear to be

---

[5] We discuss how the impact of arts fundraising is communicated in Chapter 8.

losers or beggars, but support those that are proud and self-confident about the quality of the content they deliver.

The third ingredient for success is groundwork. Before starting cultivation, fundraisers should get all the information they require (e.g., about the prospective donor, the project that needs support, the arts organization's general financial condition). They should commit to a consistent strategy, and even anticipate the donor's reactions and expectations (i.e., what might be the donor's concerns or how the meeting should transpire). In order to do this, many arts fundraisers practice their opening few statements and even rehearse before meetings. And after every encounter, professional major gifts officers enter into the organization's data base all germane information that has been gleamed from the meeting so that future meetings can build on prior sessions.

## 4.4 Tailoring planned giving to major donors and arts philanthropists

Planned giving offers generous people the possibility of supporting not-for-profit arts organizations beyond their lifetime with gifts that can be many times larger than those previously provided. A planned gift indicates the donor's intent to contribute a significant gift from the donor's estate that benefits the arts institution beyond the donor's lifetime. Such gifts are labelled planned giving because they typically involve estate planning, which needs to be carefully considered with the advice of legal counsel. These gifts can be in the form of real estate, life insurance, personal property, cash or virtually any other type of financial asset. Some types of planned donations provide the donor with a lifetime income. In other gift plans, organizations attempt to maximize the donation and/or lessen its effect on the donor's estate. This can be done by relying on tools such as estate and tax planning. Funding a planned gift can make this kind of giving very alluring both to the donor and the recipient organization, regardless of whether a donor uses cash, appreciated securities/stock, real estate, artworks, partnership interests, personal property, life insurance or a retirement plan. Consequently, planned gifts are key tools in major arts philanthropy. As mentioned, when major donors choose planned giving, they can provide their gifts over time with fairly immediate tax benefits. Moreover, planned giving offers donors enticing, cutting-edge and imaginative contribution possibilities. Arts organizations also benefit by gaining additional ways to connect with more contributors, increase donations and produce new gift revenue.

According to Jordan and Quynn (2009), there are four main planned gifts categories: outright gifts, bequests, life income gifts and endowment funds. Outright gifts include cash, stocks, tangible personal property and some real estate. They typically provide the beneficiary organization with direct access to the given assets. Bequests are arrangements in which the donor uses the planned-to-be-given asset during his or her lifetime leaving it to the not-for-profit after death. Life income gifts allow a donor to make a contribution in exchange for a lifetime income stream, with the arts organization receiving the remaining value of the gift after the donor's passing. Endowment funds – as permanent gift arrangements – work by following the principle that the fund is preserved and its related incomes (e.g., profit or active interests) are distributed according to the provisions established when the endowment is created. When endowments are used as planned gifts, the donor's original fund (i.e., money or other assets) is known as the principal capital. Income made from that capital goes to the beneficiary organization from a draw on the assets. More sophisticated arts institutions have drawn policies that specify a specific percentage of the assets that can be taken from the endowment instead of just distributing income or profits, which can be extremely variable year to year. Endowment funds are very common among arts and cultural organizations in the United States and have a strong tradition there. In Europe, they are still relatively new in the arts industry, but we can find several examples of their use such as the Louvre Endowment Fund, described in Box 4.2.

Donors are drawn to planned giving for a variety of reasons. For some of them, a planned gift is the only way they are able to make a sizable donation to a not-for-profit-organization. Planned giving frequently helps donors to give greater amounts and sooner than they initially thought possible. Donors can be motivated to make a gift when they learn they can get a stream of income for life, increase the yield they might currently receive from investments, receive a charitable income tax deduction and/or reduce or eliminate capital gains taxes or estate taxes. For example, the planned giving of real estate or other tangible personal property (such as a donor's advised funds) to a not-for-profit arts organization can provide the donor with a stream of in-

**Box 4.2 The Louvre Endowment Fund**

The Louvre was the first museum in France to establish an endowment fund in 2009, following the American model. The money for the long-term investments made by the fund comes from donations, bequests and income from the collaboration between the Louvre and Abu Dhabi. The donations themselves remain intact and annually produce a reliable income. The only source of funding used to support public interest museum projects is this fund revenue. Bequests and donations are unaltered and preserve the contributors' names for future generations. Donors now have the opportunity to establish links with future generations while also leaving their mark on the history of the Louvre thanks to this fund. In addition to direct patronage, the fund enables contributors to give the Louvre ongoing support.

come and several tax benefits. A life income gift can be made using conservative blue-chip securities, earning a yield of 1 to 2 per cent and giving the donor access to a greater income stream. Most of these life income plans, including charitable gift annuities and charitable remainder trusts, provide a donor with an income for the rest of his or her lifetime. This means that until the donor passes away, the organization cannot spend the gift capital, since it must invest it to generate a yearly income stream for the donor (see Box 4.3).

**Box 4.3 Arts institutions and planned giving vehicles: an array of opportunities**

Arts organizations are exponentially increasing their involvement with planned giving vehicles, above all in the United States. The Public Theater in New York, for example, suggests donors make a grant through their donor's advised fund (DAF). The donor completes a DAF online form by simply entering the amount and designation (i.e., the Public), and he or she is directed to the DAF sponsor portal login page.

Traditionally, DAF sponsors have been community foundations, but in the past two decades, charitable branches of many financial services providers have created DAFs adding to "the fastest-growing vehicle in philanthropy" (National Philanthropic Trust, 2017). Individuals who want to give through this means put money or other assets into a DAF account, which is held by a 501(c)(3) not-for-

profit organization. This way, the contribution into the account is considered a tax-deductible donation, and the donor directs the sponsor to make a gift to an arts institution or other charity or indeed do nothing at all.
What is attractive about this tool is that donors usually qualify for a tax deduction when they contribute to the DAF, without needing to decide where or when the money will be transferred to an arts organization or any other charity. Money or assets placed in DAF could hypothetically stay in the account forever without reaching charities that need support. However, once an individual places assets into a DAF account, those funds can only be directed to other charities so unallocated funds cannot be returned to the original donor.
Beside bequests and DAF requests, other life income plans and planned giving vehicles have started to be included in arts institutions' giving strategies. The Metropolitan Museum of Art in New York has been one of the more proactive institutions in this regard, and offers the following options:

- Charitable gift annuities: donors can irrevocably confer cash or securities to the Metropolitan Museum of Arts (minimum gift: $25,000) and have in return an annuity (i.e., an annual fixed payment for life) whose amount depends on the size of the gift and the age of the donor. The tax advantage for the donor resides both in the deduction receivable in the year of the gift and in the lessened annual tax burden, as a portion of the annuity is not taxable.
- Retirement assets or life insurance: donors might designate the Metropolitan Museum of Arts as recipient of the benefits from individual retirement accounts (IRA) or as a beneficiary of the life insurance policies, these having tax benefits.
- Retained life estate: donors might donate their property, keeping the right to live in or use it for life.
- Charitable remainder trusts: donors might confer for life or up to twenty years cash or securities or properties to a trustee. On the basis of the size of the gift, donors might receive an annual fixed income or a variable sum until the end of the trust. At the termination of the trust, the remaining assets (i.e., the remaining principal) pass to the Metropolitan Museum of Arts. Donors benefit from a charitable deduction for a portion of the gift devoted to the trust.
- Pooled income funds: the Metropolitan Museum of Arts accepts irrevocable gifts (i.e., cash or marketable securities) from many donors, manages them as a mutual fund and then distributes the income proportionately to the beneficiaries. Also in this case, upon the death of the beneficiary, the remaining principal passes to the Metropolitan Museum of Arts and donors might receive a tax charitable deduction for a portion of the gift.
- Charitable lead trusts: in this case, a donor might decide to elect the Metropolitan Museum of Arts as beneficiary of the income from a trust composed

of assets expected to gain in value. The museum receives income from the trust for a specified number of years, after which the property in the trust is transferred to the donor's heirs without the imposition of any additional taxes, thus reducing or even eliminating the estate tax that would normally be payable by heirs. An immediate charitable deduction is also available for the income streams the Metropolitan Museum of Arts receives during the trust term.

The planned giving vehicles listed above are available to all arts institutions and other charities which is why many cultural institutions are investing in planned giving programs. In fact, the larger, more sophisticated cultural institutions have created staff positions for lawyers who specialize in planned giving and have marketed such programs. To that end, the Metropolitan Museum of Art has created an online calculator, designed to provide prospects with an illustration of the income and tax benefits to which they may be entitled if they make a planned gift. Moreover, all the donors committing to one or more of these gifts are eligible to join the William Society, a membership program that is named after the nickname of a small faience hippopotamus that was made in Egypt about 4000 years ago and placed in a tomb to magically guarantee the rebirth of the deceased (Fig. 4.4).

*Figure 4.4* William the Hippo

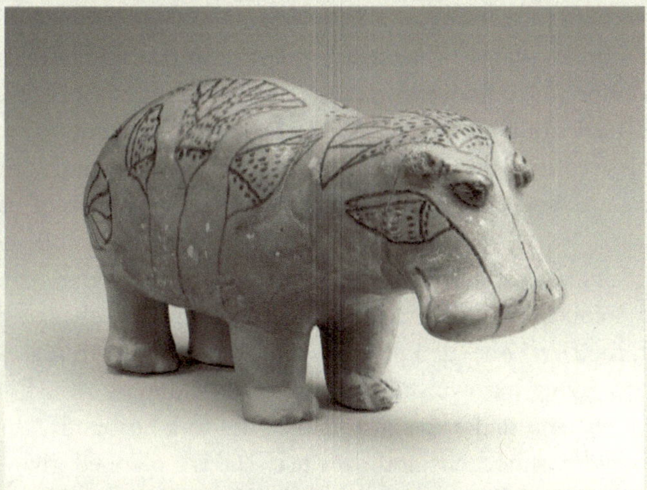

*Credit*: CC0 1.0, via Wikimedia Commons

*Source*: Author's elaboration on www.publictheater.org and https://www.metmuseum.org

By providing a full range of giving alternatives, including numerous planned giving vehicles, an arts organization can attract more donors and donations. With the help of its contributors, an organization can strengthen its endowments and future thanks to this special commitment (Jordan and Quynn, 2009).

Bequests in particular are an opportunity to make a gift that appeals to those who would like to donate but are unable to give up their current possessions. For example, while most Americans use bequests as part of their estate planning, childless couples or those who see the organization as a replacement for their heirs are especially good bequest prospects for arts institutions. Bequests from such donors can be sizable. Even organizations without a formal bequest or planned giving program receive bequests. A planned giving program can be begun by simply marketing and promoting bequests as the first step. However, arts institutions should be mindful that bequests come in different structures. The Museum of Fine Arts, Boston, for instance, distinguishes between outright bequests, residual bequests, contingent bequests and restricted bequests. In the case of an outright bequest, a donor designates in his or her will a specific asset or amount of money that he or she wishes to bequeath, usually for general purposes. If a donor wants to make a residual bequest, he or she designates in his or her will a percentage of the remaining value of his or her estate to come to an organization after all outright bequests have been made. If a donor wants to make a bequest with conditions that must be satisfied before the organization can receive the bequest, it is a contingent bequest. If a donor wants to designate a bequest for a particular purpose – which is less common – then it is a *restricted bequest*. Bequests are important for all arts and cultural organizations, but in the case of visual arts organizations such as museums, they play a significant role, especially in respect to art collections. Museums should nourish relationships with private art collectors and art patrons, since there is a chance they may bequeath their art collection to a museum. In respect of this, see Box 4.4.

Planned giving has evolved over time. Most donors are no longer elderly widows who make the customary gifts to a husband's alma mater and the neighborhood hospital over tea. Today's planned giving donors might include middle-aged executives who fund charitable remainder trusts with company stock. Donors of planned gifts are now much more astute and informed, and today's planned giving officer frequently interacts with a donor's attorney (e.g., a financial advisor, broker, trust officer

**Box 4.4 An example of a bequest to the Metropolitan Museum of Art in New York**

A significant benefactor of the Metropolitan Museum of Art in New York left tens of millions of dollars in her will. The museum assumed ownership of Jayne Wrightsman's collection of over 375 works of art when she passed away in April 2019. This gift also provided the board of directors with a cash contribution valued at $80 million. The millionaire, who was born in Michigan, had long been recognized as one of the museum's most significant donors. Few, though, were aware that she had in mind such a significant bequest. Wrightsman had already donated a number of significant and priceless works of art to the museum before she passed away at the ripe old age of ninety-nine. For instance, the well-known Eugene Delacroix painting, *Portrait of Madame Henri François Riesener*, was among her collection that had already made it to the museum. These enormous gifts, however, were dwarfed by the directive in her will to leave the museum hundreds of pieces of art. In total, Wrightsman donated well over 1200 pieces of art throughout her lifetime. Her final magnificent contribution was, according to Max Hollein, director of the Metropolitan Museum of Art, the crowning achievement of more than fifty years of charity.

and/or accountant) on a regular basis. Historically, donors involved with planned giving were more established, older and wealthy. This is still the case, although some younger planned givers have emerged to support arts organizations.

Planned giving is a complex process, which begins when donors decide to give a considerable amount of money to an organization or when they begin the estate planning process. Staff members responsible for planned giving operations must be knowledgeable about a wide range of planned gift vehicles and should possess or learn skills that other fundraising professionals might not have (Jordan and Quynn, 2009). However, owing to the variety and complexity of gift alternatives accessible to donors of different ages with varying personal and financial goals, external consultants are often involved in the planned giving solicitation process, also because of the numerous legal and tax options that can optimize the impact of the donation. The goal and financial situation of the donor should determine the appropriate structure of the planned gift, so the help of a attorney is advisable. People frequently begin the process of planned giving when they create an estate plan, since this is the ideal time to make asset distribution decisions. The drafting of a bequest is certainly such an occasion. A bequest stipulation can be included in a last will and testament or be incorporated as a component of a trust. Donors can also plan a gift to an arts organization while preparing for retirement, using deferred gift annuities.

What are the main skills required for planned giving officers? First, they must keep up to date with the latest developments in tax law, estate planning and financial planning. Second, they need to have skills typical of the for-profit corporate world, so they can bring its vigor and knowledge to the not-for-profit sector. Third, even if planned giving has evolved over time, it will always be rooted in relationships with people. Consequently, building strong working connections (e.g., with donors, donors' advisers, donors' families and colleagues in fundraising) is another key aspect of planned giving. Fourth, owing to the complexity of the industry, problem-solving skills across multiple disciplines are also essential. Teaching management about the distinctions between planned giving and general development is a further part of a planned giving officer's job description.

The benefits of a structured giving program can be significant, but they come with time and patience. Programs for long-term planned contributions can provide an arts organization with significant and stable financial rewards over time as planned gifts are a desirable choice for many donors. Many not-for-profit organizations can benefit from collaboration and a shared understanding of the responsibilities of planned giving and growth. The gift option of planned giving is timeless and resilient in the face of a struggling economy or a volatile housing market. It is clearly natural for donors to be reluctant to make philanthropic contributions when they are experiencing financial uncertainty, as surplus assets and discretionary income are used to fund a major portion of charitable contributions. But when economic conditions are not good or are uncertain, there is still plenty that can be done to prepare for the future when favorable circumstances return. So, when donors delay choices about their philanthropy, or space out their offerings, it may very well be productive to raise the mutual advantages of planned giving. It is also crucial to continue to add prospects to the not-for-profit's pipeline. Replenishing donor networks, starting regional, national or even international visitation programs, and spreading awareness of the vital job that charities do for the common good are all necessary at any time. Now is always the perfect moment to establish new relationships that could lead to gifts in the future.

### Keywords for arts fundraisers

Arts philanthropists, major donors, naming opportunities, generational sub-groups, new philanthropist, venture capitalist approach, social responsibility, sense of duty, social emulation, donor pyramid, personal solicitation, relation-building process, prospects' identification and qualification, donor profile, built-in databases, peer-screening, prospects cultivation, institutional involvement, discovery visit, move record, learning process, the "ask," solicitation visit, testing donors' concerns, listen to the gift, acknowledgement and recognition, stewardship, integrity, enthusiasm, groundwork, planned giving, estate and tax planning, outright gift, bequest, life income gifts, endowment funds, principal capital, donor's advised funds, charitable gift annuities, pooled income funds, charitable remainder trusts, community foundations, retirement assets, life insurance, retained life estate, charitable lead trusts

### Suggested questions for meetings and discussion

- How can arts institutions attract major donors and philanthropists?
- What is the profile of an ideal major donor to the arts?
- What motivates major donors for the arts?
- How can arts organizations best manage their donor pyramid?
- How can arts organizations engage their major donors effectively? How can they attract new major prospects?
- How would you cultivate a major donor for the arts?
- What is the role of planned giving in the fundraising strategy of arts organizations? What are main the differences/similarities between American and European arts organizations in respect to this?
- How can arts organization recognize and acknowledge their major donors?
- How do naming opportunities work in the engagement and recognition of major donors?

- Is it possible to upgrade smaller donors to the status of major donor? How?
- How can arts organizations balance their reliance on major donors with other funding sources?
- Is there a desirable percentage of total contributed income from major donors for which arts institutions should strive?

## References


Barnes, M. L. (2011). "'Music to our ears': understanding why Canadians donate to arts and cultural organizations," *International Journal of Nonprofit and Voluntary Sector Marketing*, 16 (1): 115–126.

Batra, R. and Ahtola, O. T. (1991). "Measuring the hedonic and utilitarian sources of consumer attitudes," *Marketing Letters*, 2 (2): 159–170.

Borgonovi, F. (2004). "Performing arts attendance: an economic approach," *Applied Economics*, 36 (17): 1871–1885.

Briscoe, M. G. and Marion, B. H. (2001). "Capital campaigns and the new charitable investors," *New Directions for Philanthropic Fundraising*, 32: 25–46.

Brock, G. J. (1989). *Effective Major Gift Negotiations: The Basis for Success*. New York: Impact Books.

Clopton, S. W., Stoddard, J. E. and Dave, D. (2006). "Event preferences among arts patrons: Implications for market segmentation and arts management," *International Journal of Arts Management*, 9 (1): 48–59.

Eastman, C. L. (1995). "Philanthropic cultures of generational archetypes," *New Directions for Philanthropic Fundraising*, 8: 137–149.

Fredricks, L. (2001). *Developing major gifts: Turning small donors into big contributors*. Burlington, MA: Jones and Bartlett Learning.

Hopkins, K. B. and Friedman, C. S. (1997). *Successful fundraising for arts and cultural organizations*. Phoenix, AZ: Greenwood Publishing Group.

Grace, K. S. and Wendroff, A. L. (2001). *High impact philanthropy: How donors, boards, and nonprofit organizations can transform communities*. Hoboken, NJ: John Wiley and Sons.

Hager, M. A. and Winkler, M. K. (2012). "Motivational and Demographic Factors for Performing Arts Attendance Across Place and Form," *Nonprofit and Voluntary Sector Quarterly*, 41 (3): 474–496.

Heetland, D. (1992). "How to build a major gifts program," *Fund Raising Management*, 23 (7): 35.

Jordan, R. R. and Quynn, K. L. (2009). *Planned Giving: A Guide to Fundraising and Philanthropy*. Hoboken, NJ: John Wiley and Sons.

Kotler, P. and Scheff, J. (1997). *Standing room only: Strategies for marketing the performing arts*. Cambridge, MA: Harvard Business School Press.

Lawson, M, (1995) "Major gift development in your organization," *Fund Raising Management*, 25 (5): 18–21.

McCarthy, K. F., Ondaatje, E. H., Zakaras, L. and Brooks, A. (2001). *Gifts of the muse: Reframing the debate about the benefits of the arts*. Santa Monica, CA: Rand Corporation.

National Philanthropic Trust (2017). *2017 Donor-advised fund report*. Jenkintown, PA: National Philanthropic Trust.

Neumayr, M. and Handy, F. (2019). "Charitable giving: What influences donors' choice among different causes?," *VOLUNTAS: International Journal of Voluntary and Nonprofit Organizations*, 30 (4): 783–799.

Ostrower, F. (2002). *Trustees of culture: Power, wealth, and status on elite arts boards*. Chicago: University of Chicago Press.

Panas, J. (2002). *Asking: A 59-minute guide to everything board members, volunteers, and staff must know to secure the gift*. Medfield, MA: Emerson and Church, Publishers.

Panas, J. (2005). *Mega gifts: Who gives them, who gets them*. Medfield, MA: Emerson and Church, Publishers.

Prince, R. A. and File, K. M. (1994). *The seven faces of philanthropy: A new approach to cultivating major donors*. San Francisco: Jossey-Bass.

Sargeant, A., Lee, S. and Jay, E. (2002). *Major gift philanthropy: Individual giving to the arts*. Henley-on-Thames: Centre for Voluntary Sector Management, Henley Management College.

Stokmans, M. J. (2003). "How heterogeneity in cultural tastes is captured by psychological factors: a study of reading fiction," *Poetics*, 31 (5–6): 423–439.

Strauss, B., Strauss, W. and Howe, N. (1991). *Generations: The history of America's future, 1584 to 2069*. William Morrow and Company.

Tempel, E. R., Seiler, T. L. and Burlingam, D. F. (2016). *Achieving Excellence in Fundraising*, fourth edition. Hoboken, NJ: Jossey-Bass.

Wiggins, J. (2004). "Motivation, ability and opportunity to participate: a reconceptualization of the RAND model of audience development," *International Journal of Arts Management*, (7) 1: 22–33.

Williams, M. J. (1991). *Big gifts*. Farmington Hills, MI: The Taft Group.

# 5 Corporate Fundraising and Sponsorship for the Arts

with *Kim Noltemy*

## 5.1 Corporate fundraising and sponsorship: concepts and definitions

Corporate philanthropy (or corporate giving) is defined as "an unconditional transfer of cash or other assets to an entity or a settlement or the cancellation of its liabilities in a voluntary non-reciprocal transfer by another entity acting other than as an owner" (FASB, 1993). Schwartz (1968: 480) further considers corporate giving as a "one way flow of resources from a donor to an addressee, a flow voluntarily generated by the donor and based upon no expectation that a return flow, or economic quid pro quo, will reward the act." During the 1980s, Fry et al. (1982: 95) defined corporate philanthropy as a "transfer, of a charitable nature, of corporate resources to recipients at below market prices." Some years later, Godfrey (2005: 778) argued that corporate giving is a "discretionary manifestation of Corporate Social Responsibility." More recently, some scholars have given an interesting definition of corporate philanthropy, talking about a long-term corporate investment in favor of the community (Gautier and Pache, 2015).

To understand the nature of corporate giving for the arts, it can be useful to compare it with individual support of cultural institutions, discussed in Chapters 3 and 4. The main difference relates to the process and the strong guidelines in today's corporate structure, along with the priorities of the people who make the decision to donate or sponsor. As mentioned before, personal factors (both emotional and rational) are the main drivers of individual giving; companies, instead, usually work with a more complex set of processes when formulating their giving decisions. In fact, firms' decision-making usually involves numerous people, with a consequent set of different – and often unpredictable – motivations and needs. In particular, factors like business interests (such as brand association) play a crucial role in making the final decision. Consequently, choosing the process for soliciting corporate philanthropy depends on how the corporation has organized its giving program.

Gathering appropriate information about how the company manages its giving policies is the first step for an effective approach. Aspects such as the size of the company, its structure, the degree of complexity in its business relations and the philanthropic role of managers and employees are all relevant (Worth, 2016). For example, a small museum or theatre serving a single local community may consider the local or regional manager of a national corporation (who may or may not have a budget for contributions) as the most promising source for corporate support. Conversely, if the arts institution is seeking a major grant, it will more likely need to approach the corporation's national headquarters. The fundraising efforts required to secure a major grant from a company can be highly demanding and time consuming: corporate fundraising requires an arts organization to find alignment with the company's approach to philanthropy, marketing and even public relations across multiple levels of management.

Some corporations may decide to establish a corporate foundation to manage their cash gifts. This trend has increased in recent years. In the United States there were 2700 corporate foundations in 2011, which gave an estimated $5.2 billion (Worth, 2016: 253). In Europe, one study by the European Research Network on Philanthropy has listed 6115 corporate foundations, whose contributions to charitable purpose in 2013 is included in the €21 billion and 729 million overall amount of European corporate giving for that year (Gehringer and von Schnurbein, 2017). If a corporate foundation manages a company's philanthropy, the process for soliciting support will be more structured. A corporate foundation is a charitable vehicle created and financially supported by a corporation, but it is a separate legal entity from it regardless of the close ties with its funding business. Corporate foundations act primarily as grant-making entities and are likely to have clearly articulated priorities, guidelines and application procedures. In other words, large corporate foundations operate exactly like any other large private foundation. Therefore, organizations should address them properly in order to achieve their fundraising goals.

When approaching corporate foundations, arts organizations should carefully tailor their proposal for funding so it is compliant with the corporate foundation's statement of purpose and guidelines. Moreover, they must fully understand that the foundation is a separate entity and be respectful of the boundaries between the corporation and its corporate foundation (see Box 5.1). This means that they have to focus carefully on whom they are addressing. As a general rule, when the connection is between an arts organization and the corporation, the proposal's business relevance can supersede philanthropic purposes. When the approach is directly to a corporate foundation, the approach must focus on a philanthropic purpose, rather than on business interests.

**Box 5.1 The Ford Foundation**

The Ford Foundation evolved into a very liberal and progressive foundation totally independent from the Ford Motor Company highlighting the founding family's loss of control with respect to the foundation's activities.

*Source*: Mark Volpe personal communication

## 5.2 Key motivators triggering corporate donations

As noted, different factors can affect the way firms make their philanthropic decisions regarding arts organizations. Both personal and business reasons can influence CEOs and others in the corporate decision-making chain. On their side, when developing their strategies, arts organizations have to analyze all potentially useful elements that may influence this decision-making. When considering the key motivation factors to be focused on in corporate fundraising, it is possible to group these drivers into two main categories: altruism and business interests. These are not mutually exclusive, as some business goals can be enhanced even if the corporate decision was made on the basis of emotion and desire of the company's CEO to do "good." Consequently, different factors can coexist when a firm decides to support a cultural institution. This is another example of the complexity that institutional development departments have to address when working on corporate fundraising proposals.

Altruism in corporate giving has to do with the declared attitude of firms towards helping not-for-profit institutions, so that they can play a visible and useful social role in the community they serve. Pure altruism aims to further the well-being of others in a selfless way, but, as for individual donors, pure altruism by corporate givers is more theoretical than practical. As an example of this, we can mention the great "robber barons" of American history (e.g., Carnegie, Mellon, Rockefeller, Ford, Vanderbilt) who, after exploiting the working classes in their business enterprises and accumulating great wealth, paid for the building of medical, educational and cultural institutions that benefited the masses. Andrew Carnegie even argued, in his book *The Gospel of Wealth* (1889), that founders of corporate fortunes were somehow obliged to redistribute their resources by supporting charities, including the arts. A further example of a family foundation is provided in Box 5.2.

Altruism as a driver for corporate giving is extremely powerful, as it is deeply connected to the emotions and personal history of funders, and for the same reason it can be extremely volatile, especially if there is management turnover. According to research by Dang and Nguyen (2021), there are also interesting managerial implications if the corporations' shareholders are positively involved emotionally when altruistic decisions are made regarding a charitable cause. Researchers' findings suggest that it can be beneficial for managers to explicitly share their

**Box 5.2 The altruistic approach to corporate giving of the Dayton family**

The Dayton family – creators of Target, the seventh largest retail company in the United States – owned major department stores in Chicago, Detroit and Minneapolis. The family was led by four brothers who each supported various cultural institutions in Minneapolis, including the Minneapolis Institute of Art, the Guthrie Theater, the Minnesota Orchestra and the Walker Art Gallery.

Together, the brothers donated hundreds of millions of dollars to build a cultural infrastructure that was the envy of similar sized cities across the United States. The brothers also created an informal club of Minneapolis-based companies that were asked to give 5 per cent of their pre-tax profits to Minneapolis charities. However, as non-family member professional executives with noticeably less commitment to Minneapolis succeeded the founding brothers, donations have been significantly reduced.

*Source*: Mark Volpe personal communication

thoughts and emotions about the cause or institution they support, because this helps to increase the firm's public credibility. Social media can help managers to effectively share this emotional sentiment as they amplify investors' attention, which in turn determines market reactions (Dang and Nguyen, 2021).

Eventually, the notion of corporate citizenship takes hold, with corporations playing an active role in their respective communities. In a sense, their giving back by investing in the community – beyond employing people and paying taxes – improves corporations' "active citizenship." Moreover, corporate fundraisers argue that supporting the arts and creating cultural infrastructure in a city improves the city's living conditions of the city itself and also of the broader community, including those who work at that corporation (see Box 5.3 for an example).

**Box 5.3 Adriano Olivetti and his commitment to arts and culture**

In the north of Italy, at Ivrea, the complex of industrial buildings that was developed for Olivetti, one of the most innovative firms ever, has been recently added to the UNESCO World Heritage List. The site includes twenty-seven buildings that were enlarged by Adriano Olivetti between 1939 and 1962, showcasing the work of illustrious architects and Italian city planners. Olivetti had a humanistic vision of work, taking care of workers' personal, social and cultural conditions while always improving the competitiveness and financial health of his company. Olivetti was also one of the first companies to embody the concept of corporate citizenship that leveraged arts and culture. "We deeply believe in the revolutionary power of culture," said Adriano Olivetti. "The culture plays a pre-eminent role and when we look at the men, we know that every sacrifice is useless if we don't elevate the human spirit." On these grounds, he gathered intellectuals from different disciplines in Ivrea and created a cultural hub at Olivetti headquarters, as he thought that a factory should be a place where material and spiritual culture could live together. He also opened a library of more than 150,000 books and a venue where concerts and exhibitions were hosted regularly. His attention to architecture and city-planning is evidenced by the design of the Olivetti factory in Ivrea, where he called upon Italian architects Figini and Pollini (1934–1935), and the same philosophy inspired the building of the Guarulhos factory in Brazil (1956–1961), the American headquarters by Louis Kahn (1966–1970) and laboratories and stores in Japan by Kenzo Tange. The Olivetti factory in Pozzuoli, with its offices overlooking the beautiful Gulf of Naples, represents a perfect union of nature and architecture. Olivetti always focused on beauty and aesthetics, even in the design of its products: the famous Lettera 22 and Valentine by Ettore Sottsass (Fig. 5.1), for example, soon became design icons, today exhibited in the most renowned museums around the world.

*Figure 5.1* Valentine typewriting machine

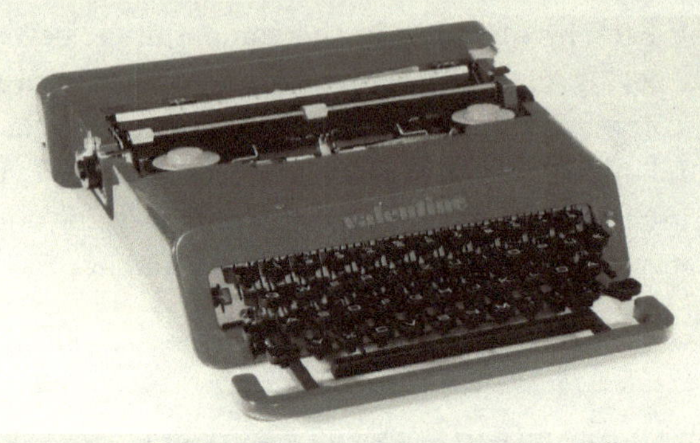


*Credit*: Peter Mitterhofer, CC BY-SA 4.0, via Wikimedia Commons

*Source*: https://www.levelofficelandscape.com/en/olivetti-beyond-the-company/

The massive consolidation of most industries both in the United States and in Europe and the globalization of the world economy have further shifted the thinking regarding corporate giving and, in particular, support for the arts. Moreover, as the business model of many corporations has evolved over years, many practitioners have observed an increasing shift from altruism to business interests as motivating corporate giving. The business implications of firms' funding decisions are a second group of motivators for corporate support of the arts. One can argue that when corporations fund not-for-profits, including arts organizations, their ultimate purpose is to increase their sales, to improve their image and reputation or to increase their visibility in a particular market (Worth, 2016). Corporate managers can certainly be driven in their philanthropic activities by altruism, a particular set of values and involvement in a specific cause or interest in an art form, but their giving is typically purposeful and consistent with the corporation's business strategy.

Whatever the business interest is for corporate giving, arts organizations should have a thorough understanding of a company's business model and the motivations that might encourage it to support a specific cultural cause. For cultural institutions, this means deepening their intelligence in observing the firms they intend to approach and the environment in which they operate, and also producing metrics about their own activity that indicate funding requests are worthwhile in business terms.

*Figure 5.2* Altruism and business interest levers as motivators of corporate giving

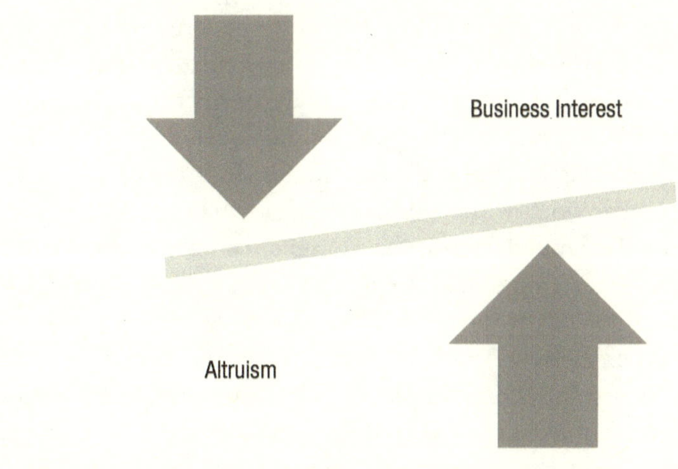


## 5.3 How corporations support arts institutions

Corporations and other businesses can provide philanthropic support for cultural institutions in various ways. The type of support depends on the purpose of the donations and on how they can be developed.

A corporation can decide to give a cultural institution general financial support. This is an example of unrestricted contribution, which helps arts organizations to cover their operating expenses. General support is typically paid out of an annual contribution budget. Case histories highlight how – owing to its unrestricted nature – this kind of support usually goes up to $/€/£25,000 as an average. Of course, the resource availability of the funding company, as well as the specific needs of the recipient organization will determine the final amount. Cultural institutions should be aware that approaching corporations for this kind of grant is not easy. However, if a business has given once, it can be easier to secure its support in subsequent years. As a general rule, it is wise to make a grant request every year, even if a line item regarding the arts organization has been included in the corporation's annual contribution budget (Hopkins and Friedman, 1997).

Beyond contributing general operating support, some companies can be persuaded to provide special project funding or sponsorship. As these are restricted contributions, such grants tend to be larger than general support, going up even to several million dollars/euros/pounds. In the case of sponsorships (e.g., of an event, a play, an opera production or an art exhibition), corporations may pay (in part or in total) from their marketing, advertising or public affairs budgets. In some cases, corporations can receive worthwhile tax advantages when sponsoring arts institutions. In the United States, for example, companies can deduct advertising and marketing dollars spent, as they can when they make a gift funded by their contributions budget, so the deductibility issue is moot. On another matter, American arts institutions should be aware that some sponsorship income might be subject to unrelated business income tax treatment from the Internal Revenue Service (UBIT) issue.[1] In Europe, taxes related to arts sponsorships are managed according to the different fiscal policies of individual member states. However, in most European countries, no extensive tax deduction schemes for arts sponsorship exists.

Corporations may look at sponsorship as a more concrete giving action, as this support can enhance their brand image and/or direct income. When acting as primary sponsor of an event or of a special project, a company (and its brand or product) can acquire some positioning and public relation benefits. Its brand can be directly associated with those

[1] UBIT in the US Internal Revenue Code is the tax on unrelated business income, which comes from activities engaged in by a tax-exempt 26 USC 501 organization that are not related to the tax-exempt purpose of that organization.

of renowned arts organizations and publicized through offline materials, websites and social media accounts (e.g., prestigious fashion brands such as Giorgio Armani and Rolex regularly sponsor Teatro alla Scala in Milan). When sponsoring arts institutions, corporations may ask to sponsor a venue or part of a venue. Research via a panel of sixty-five representatives of American and European arts institutions has revealed, for example, that corporations focusing on sponsoring a part of a building (instead of the whole venue) for a perpetual naming right (44 per cent of cases) have a range of expenditure between $25,000 and $6 million (ABA, 2022).

When corporate investment in the arts shifts from general support to sponsorship, the boundaries between business and philanthropy are blurred. The brand identities of the sponsor and the entity that is sponsored are in fact deeply connected in such projects. As previously emphasized, sponsorship support is typically funded through large marketing or advertising budgets and can be significant. Moreover, owing to a constant decrease in government grants, business sponsorships often represent the best opportunity for arts organizations to leverage large sums of money in a fundraising operation. Moreover, consistent with the trend towards adopting business approaches to corporate giving, sponsorships are now fully recorded in written agreements that have defined business purposes and frequently include metrics to measure a project's results.

When underwriting a sponsorship, companies aim to secure maximum visibility and improve their positioning thanks to identification with the sponsored organization. However, it should be clarified that sponsorship works differently from advertising. Advertising is often linked to the promotion of one or more of a corporation's products, while sponsorship advances the company's name or logo and is intended to enhance the company's brand and image, without specifically promoting the sale of a product (Worth, 2016). Furthermore, sponsorships and advertising have different fiscal treatments, both for a corporation and the arts organization. In spite of all the related benefits, arts organizations should always consider the compatibility of the corporation and its products with their own mission and values before concluding a sponsorship agreement.

In addition or in lieu of a monetary gift, a corporation can express its generosity with an in-kind contribution, where the donation of business services or products is provided as an alternative to money. Gifts of this nature often have little actual cost to the corporation, while the value of the donated services to the recipient can be greater than an equivalent cash gift (Hopkins and Friedman, 1997). To allow the arts organization to fully benefit from in-kind support, the development director should review the organization's entire annual operating and capital expense budgets, and carefully consider items that could be contributed in kind, thereby saving the institution the expense of purchasing them. Donations may include anything that fulfils the interests of both the business and the organization – from furniture and equipment (including computers and other technology products) to spaces (e.g., offices, rehearsal rooms, halls) to professional services (such as accounting or counselling). Examples of in-kind donations also include free space or time provided by media companies that act as official "media partners" for an event or season and free or heavily discounted fares on airlines, railroads or shipping companies that offset the costs of touring performing arts groups or exhibits. In-kind supporters usually ask for ticket packages for their special customers in return, as well as visibility on related communication materials. It is noteworthy that not every company has policies that support in-kind gifts (for some of them it is even prohibited), so it is important that arts institutions understand company policies before asking. In-kind contributions can be an interesting alternative to cash gifts, especially for small local companies that can provide specific support for the local community. However, even if it is often easier for local businesses to provide in-kind support rather than monetary donations, arts organizations should ask them to consider both kinds of gifts when making their giving decisions (Hopkins and Friedman, 1997).

Despite the reduction in in-person activities owing to the COVID-19 crisis, special corporate fundraising events are still attractive. Benefit dinners, opening nights, parties, testimonials and balls are good occasions to increase a corporation's visibility in a community and to raise funds for a specific purpose. International research conducted by the Advisory Board for the Arts in 2022 shows that 85 per cent of arts organizations still rely on galas for one-fifth or less of their overall contributed income. In comparison with the pre-pandemic situation, 80 per cent of the surveyed organizations stated that they plan to organize such events regularly again, beginning in 2022. While special events and galas do not typically generate as much net income as annual funds, they can have the ancillary benefit of providing social access to donors, political leaders and other influencers in the community (ABA, 2022).

Corporate giving driven by business interests can express itself also as a commercial collaboration between an arts organization and a corporation. Examples of this type of giving are cause-related marketing and licensing agreements (Worth, 2016). These are both based on the building of a branding relationship between the two parties, where the main benefit that the corporate funder expects is an enhanced image, deriving from giving to a specific cause or from the connection with the arts brand. This can also stimulate an increase in the corporation's sales. Through these types of collaborations, focused on brand relationships among the parties, the identities of the company and the arts institution are tightly connected. Cause-related marketing associates a brand or a business with a cause or an institution. This approach has become increasingly popular, both as a fundraising tool for the arts institutions and as a promotional and sales strategy for businesses. When adopting this type of collaboration, the corporation contributes a fixed amount (or percentage) of its sales to the not-for-profit during a short-term promotional activity. Licensing agreements focus on brand licensing, in which arts organizations let the licensee corporations use their brand or image in return for royalties. The most relevant concern for an institution that decides to adopt this type of arrangement relates to ethics and reputation, owing to the consequent implied endorsement of the company's activities (see Fig. 5.3)

Companies also support the arts and other worthy causes while incentivizing their employees to become philanthropic by creating matching gift programs. Employee gift-matching and engagement programs match the contribution by a company's employee to an arts institution with a donation from the company itself. Some companies also consider it beneficial to engage their employees and collaborators in matching gift or volunteering programs that involve a specific arts institution, in order to share valuable experiences with them. In respect to matching gift programs, the firm's donation can equal or be greater than the employee's, depending on company policy. Some corporations set restrictions on these programs (e.g., on the kind of organizations eligible to match funds or on the amounts involved). Arts organizations should carefully focus on the follow up from these initiatives in order to avoid incorrect

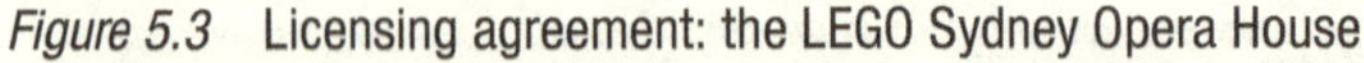

*Figure 5.3* Licensing agreement: the LEGO Sydney Opera House

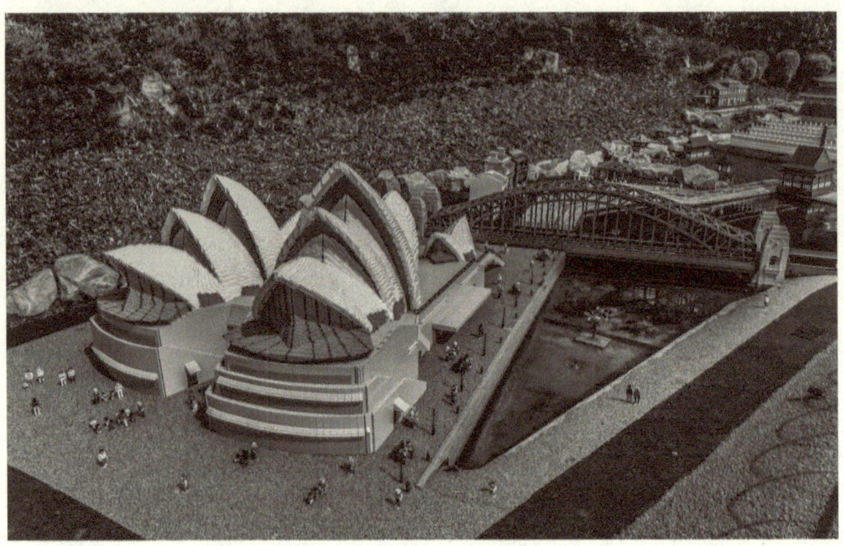

*Credit*: Gareth Milner, CC BY 2.0, via Wikimedia Commons

reporting of employees' contribution to firms' gift-matching programs. Institutions could, for instance, update their communication material with a list of businesses known to have gift-matching programs, consequently helping donors register their gifts with their employers. Public institutions can be helpful in this effort as similar lists can be provided through official information channels (e.g., the lists produced by the Business Committee for the Arts in New York City or the Arts Council in the United Kingdom).

Employee engagement has also become a focus of corporations that want to promote community involvement in socially relevant projects: the drive to attract and retain talented employees has moved many companies to offer meaningful volunteer opportunities, with programs such as employee recognition awards, flexible scheduling and paid-release programs. Because of the restrictions imposed by social distancing during the COVID-19 pandemic, in-person volunteering dropped by 37 per cent between 2018 and 2020. However, in some cases, in-person virtual volunteering programs replaced volunteering.

Virtual volunteering has increased to an unprecedented degree and more than any other volunteer program. It was offered in the United States by only 38 per cent of companies in 2018, and this increased to 87 per cent in 2020 (N=139). Similarly, virtual volunteering offered to international employees increased from 19 per cent of companies in 2018 to 47 per cent in 2020 (CECP, 2021).

Figure 5.4 summarizes the different ways corporations can support the arts.

*Figure 5.4* How corporations can support the arts

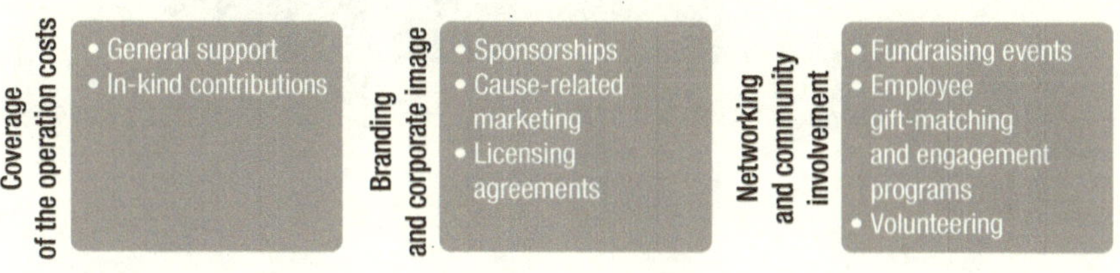


## 5.4 Guidelines for successful corporate fundraising

Corporations and other businesses have a clear idea of how valuable the benefits are that they derive from supporting not-for-profit organizations. Because of this awareness, firms have consistently contributed to numerous causes, including the arts, over time. That being stated, while it is somewhat difficult to predict the full and lasting impact of the COVID-19 pandemic, and of recent economic and political conditions (owing to the energy crisis in Europe and the Russia–Ukraine conflict), the competition for corporate philanthropy among arts not-for-profits is becoming more intense. Arts institutions are "competing" with other causes such as health, education and social services for donors' attention and generosity. In this challenging and ever-changing context, what can arts organizations do to attract corporate interest? In the following paragraphs, we try to answer this question by outlining the most relevant features arts organizations should consider when developing their strategies for asking firms for support. Figure 5.5 outlines the recommended guidelines balance for achieving success in corporate fundraising.

*Figure 5.5* The guidelines balance for achieving success in corporate fundraising

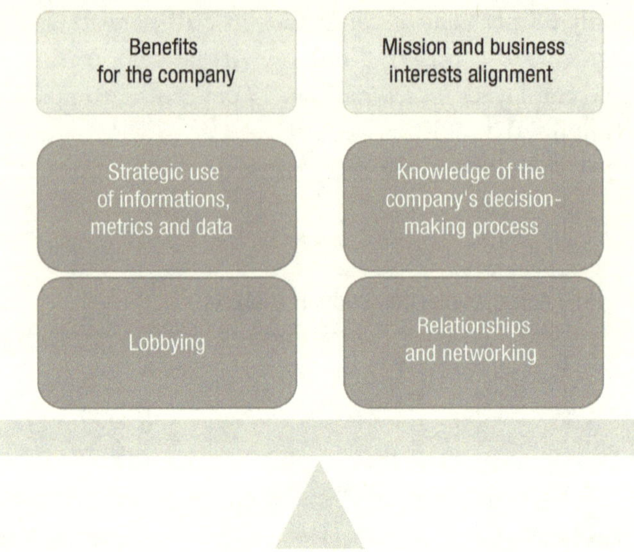


### 5.4.1 *Demonstrating company benefits from corporate giving*

Frequently, a business's first requirement in corporate fundraising is to support a not for-profit, tax-exempt or special tax regime arts organization. However, cultural institutions seeking corporate support should always approach firms with the main purpose of demonstrating the different kinds of benefits a company can gain from giving (Hopkins and Friedman, 1997). For example, they can convey the potential reputational and branding benefits related to an association between the firm's value proposition and the mission of the arts organization. Some businesses also recognize that their support for the arts contributes to a community's sense of well-being and its positive image. Corporate giving of this kind can also potentially connect businesses to new customers who are avid arts consumers. Moreover, a corporation that has a retail or consumer focus may benefit from the additional marketing, branding and visibility its support of an arts organization may provide. Arts institutions can therefore help corporations to become more visible and impactful in the community they both serve. In addition, by supporting social well-being through the arts, a firm becomes actively involved in the life of the community where it operates, with positive effects on its economic results. Corporate giving to the arts can also be motivated by the necessity of the corporation to stimulate the local economy, which can be done by attracting people, both residents and tourists, to theatres, galleries, concert halls, museums and other venues. In addition, stimulating a dynamic cultural environment in the area where they operate allows corporations to attract better educated and talented people as employees and collaborators. Taking a more political perspective, corporate managers recognize the public relations value that relates to supporting culture. Finally, by giving to the arts and by being involved in a cultural institution's life, a firm can link with artistic and cultural excellence and thereby enrich its corporate image.

Corporate giving policies also reflect a company's industry or business model. Industries such as telecommunication or travel businesses, for example, which are dependent on large consumer markets, tend to support a broad range of highly visible arts organizations, such as major opera houses, concert halls and museums. Pharmaceutical or high technology firms might instead allocate their funds to healthcare, education and technological improvements. Earnings objectives can influence corporate giving decisions as well. The size of a company's budget and the level of its profits may be the basis for annual philanthropic decisions. Consequently, even if a firm made favorable funding decisions for an arts organization in the past, a negative shift in its net results can reduce or even suspend future funding.

### 5.4.2 *Alignment between arts organizations' mission and corporate business interests*

To have the best chance of success, fundraisers should look for a strong alignment of their cultural institution's mission and programs with a company's business interests. Data and research can be very helpful in this respect. Arts fundraisers should know all about a potential business sponsor. They should have data about the size of the company, its market (including its local, regional, national or international focus), its products, its corporate culture and cycle, any news coverage involving the business and specific occasions to be leveraged (e.g., company anniversaries/product launch). Moreover, arts fundraisers should be aware of the company's philanthropic funding history and policy regarding support of the arts. Knowing who is responsible for corporate foundation or sponsorships is key when addressing funding requests. To find a fit with their business prospects, arts organizations should review a company's assets and their value. In addition, fundraisers should pitch customization so that it matches branding and reputational necessities. Surveying members of a cultural institution's board of directors for possible corporate contacts and leads can be very helpful when researching connections with business prospects. When working on this alignment, organizations should also explore any business interests that might be compelling for potential funders.

For example, a cultural institution and a prospective business sponsor may both benefit from a marketing and/or promotional collaboration (see Box 5.4) Another alignment might feature an arts institution offering volunteer opportunities to a business that is interested in enhancing personnel engagement and retention by encouraging and setting up inspiring volunteer programs with charities, and thereby nurturing employees' motivation (see Box 5.5).

**Box 5.4 The PNC bank in Dallas: a classic sponsorship case based on visibility objectives**

In its funding strategies, the PNC bank in Dallas has prioritized investments in early education programs (so called pre-k education). The Dallas Symphony Orchestra offered no early education programs, so decided to approach PNC – focusing its solicitation strategy on the role it plays as the biggest performing arts organization in the region. Second, fundraisers collaborated with the PNC team to find potential connections between the two businesses. These were found in technology and digital content distribution. PNC therefore became the Dallas Symphony's sponsor for the Next Stage portal, utilized by the orchestra to distribute more than forty digital concerts produced each season. This effort launched during the COVID-19 pandemic. Thanks to this sponsorship, donors and subscribers could access the Next Stage concerts for free, while the bank could benefit from good visibility in return.

*Source*: Kim Noltemy personal communication

**Box 5.5 Texas Instruments: using culture to attract and retain talented employees**

Texas Instruments (TI) strongly believes in the power of music and arts to attract the best talent from around the world to work for the company. For many decades, there has been a TI representative on the Dallas Symphony Board, and the company has provided Dallas Symphony with significant annual support for decades. The name of one of the founders, Eugene McDermott, is prominent in the building as a result of a major gift by his family that honored this legacy. Mr McDermott and the other TI founders understood the value of the arts. This important and generous gift helped the orchestra to build a new concert hall, which opened in 1989.

*Source*: Kim Noltemy personal communication

### 5.4.3 *Relationships and networking in corporate fundraising*

The increasing professionalization and structuring of corporate giving processes have not reduced the importance of relationships between arts organizations' representatives and individuals within companies. Many corporations decide to support those organizations that have connections with "their people" (an example being if a member of the corporation's management participates on the arts institutions board). Corporate giving to the arts can also depend on the CEO's interest in a specific art form. If we look back on the history of great corporate funders, both in Europe and in the United States, we can note that they gave millions to support charitable causes because of personal involvement with the leadership of particular arts institutions. With respect to the corporate hierarchy, CEOs – at least until approximately thirty years ago – had absolute control over corporate philanthropy strategies and in defining priorities and policies. Good relationships between arts organizations' CEOs and these corporate decision makers have been one of the most effective ways of ensuring that grants are made to cultural activities: the personal involvement of managers in particular causes can really make a difference. The influence of personal relationships with business families such as those behind Chrysler, FIAT, General Motors and Ford has been relevant in securing funds to institutions such as the Detroit Symphony Orchestra or Fondazione Agnelli in Turin. In this regard, relationships with an organization's board may help to enlarge the network of prospects and to create new contacts: as board members with corporate affiliations tend to have strong corporate networks.

An arts organization's development director should have information about business and personal contacts of each board member and senior manager of the business that is being approached, and be able to determine if any of them is in touch with a top official in the firm. After being contacted, the top official, if interested, will make the appropriate staff person aware of the request and his or her endorsement of it. The staff person will then handle the request, including advising the not-for-profit of any documentation that is required. It is important that the fundraiser establishes a relationship with this person and includes him or her in the solicitation process. Events including corporate and political leadership may foster this type of networking, although they should be managed with great care owing to the ethical boundaries that cultural institutions face in the context of lobbying. Although some corporate donors may not prioritize press (if their sales are business to business, for example), it is often true that cultural institutions receiving favorable treatment in the press have an advantage when securing corporate gifts. Corporations may enhance goodwill by associating with highly regarded cultural institutions. In the United States, many corporations sponsor sports teams and even individual athletes. Consequently, the cultural sector is competing in one respect with the sports sector for sponsorship attention. However, as relationships matter, attending major sports events with corporate leaders is an effective way for an arts leader to connect with senior executives. Sharing mutual interests with corporate leaders has resulted in millions of dollars being raised for the Boston and Detroit Symphony Orchestras for instance.

Within this context of networking and relationships, likability may also make the difference (see Boxes 5.6 and 5.7). Both in the case of CEOs and mid-level management, likability increases the predisposition for the listener to pay real attention, and eventually increases the likelihood of donations.

When considering relationships within the company's management, arts organizations should have a comprehensive approach: although decision-making regarding corporate philanthropy and sponsorship has been decentralized in many companies during the last two decades, it is still important to consider the priorities of the CEO and other corporate executives, along with the board of directors. Although the CEO is still the major policymaker within a company, there are many stakeholders to take into consideration given the complex dynamics of the modern corporation. This list includes shareholders, employees, customers and large institutional investors such as mutual funds and pensions that may influence the perception of and motives for philanthropic efforts within a company.

**Box 5.6 Running for the win: Ford sponsorship for the Detroit Symphony Orchestra**

When working at the Detroit Symphony Orchestra, Mark Volpe became extremely knowledgeable about the car industry in order to foster relationships with the influential families involved. (Even David Halberstam, one of the most important historians in America used Volpe, as a source for his books on the car industry.) Volpe developed close working relationships and friendships with senior car industry executives such as Lloyd Reuss, one-time president of General Motors who became the Detroit Symphony's campaign chair at Volpe's request. This attitude to finding important and authentic connections led Volpe to drive with a co-pilot at 140 mph (225 kmh) around a Ford test track, thereby bonding with several Ford executives who shortly thereafter committed to a multi-million grant for the Detroit Symphony.

*Source*: Mark Volpe personal communication

**Box 5.7 The relationship-based fundraising strategy of the Boston Symphony Orchestra (BSO)**

Relationship building is an important part of the presentation of an arts organization's brand and its strengths, and also affects the accountability of their CEO. Between 1997 and 2021, the BSO raised an average of $6–8 million per year from corporate sources that were traditionally not inclined to sponsor cultural institutions or the orchestras' education and outreach programs. Among these, UBS became an important sponsor for the orchestra, so that – when attending the Lucerne Festival – the two CEOs used to spend time after each concert discussing Swiss bank policy more than topics related to the orchestra.

*Source*: Mark Volpe personal communication

If no personal contacts exist between the board members or senior managers of the arts organization and the executives of the targeted firm, the development director should determine which corporate staff person is responsible for contributions through detailed research. He or she should then contact the firm to set up a meeting, in order to find out about the company's priorities and processes and to determine if and when a request for funds is appropriate. Some corporate funders prefer to receive a request for funds before they agree to a meeting with the firm's representative. The proposal should clearly explain why the business and the institution are a good match, and it should include a persuasive presentation of the benefits the business will receive for providing support. These benefits can be stated broadly or specifically, and it should be made clear that they are negotiable within certain parameters. Corporate proposals should be short, persuasive and practical. Generally, these documents focus more on promoting the relationship between the institution and the business rather than on problem-solving. They should be sent with appropriate background and supporting materials.

A firm's decision to fund a cultural organization is based on many criteria, and it often takes several years for plans to come to fruition. Support awarded beyond a token level is typically the result of judgements made by the business about its own interests and needs. A business makes a grant to an organization only after being convinced that its interests are served. Case histories in the arts sector demonstrate that there will be about ten "NOs" before a positive answer to a funding request is received. For these reasons, identifying development talent that can work well with corporate partners is a challenge for all HR departments, and it becomes particularly difficult for smaller arts organizations that decide, owing to the lack of resources for hiring, to look for external professional support. People working for development departments in cultural institutions should understand the organization's business and also have skills that are related to lateral thinking and connection building. This is true not only in terms of hard skills (e.g., business training, knowledge of the art form they represent and the business environment with which they aim to connect), but also soft ones (e.g., the ability to present compelling cases, a positive attitude toward relationships and an ability to connect with people who will deliver on every level). Development staff should also be expected to use their interpersonal skills with their staff colleagues, these including the ability to compromise (especially when presenting a customized proposal), so that the organization can present a united approach to donors.

### 5.4.4 *Strategic use of information, metrics and data*

As the consolidation of many industries has resulted in the loss of corporate headquarters in many cities, as well as a substantial decline in the number of "home grown" executives, the corporate landscape has been dramatically altered. One consequence of this development is that in many cases, CEOs no longer make philanthropic decisions based on personal preferences or social obligations. This means that corporate philanthropy has to be in sync with prescribed corporate objectives, decision-making being flattened and decentralized. Therefore, research and data are key in determining how to approach a corporation when the objective is arts funding.

While relationships still matter, arts organizations should study all information that is relevant and available about a corporation before approaching it for support. In particular, it is critical to learn about branding strategies and the potential connections that can be made between mutual brand identities. In addition, as noted earlier, it is very important to know the areas of philanthropic interest of the potential funder. Gathering this information is cheaper than ever today (even if it is not always easy), and it can make all the difference when preparing a proposal.

Another key element to be used in developing the proposal concerns metrics. Arts organizations have to be well prepared with data about demographics, audiences and visitor statistics, sales figures, media performance (e.g., website visitors, presence on national and international media, social media followers) and other factors that define a sizable and interesting ROI for the prospective funder. In other words, a marketing-driven approach is critical when proposing a fundraising or sponsorship project to potential corporate funders. They should clearly understand what kind of value exchange is possible (see Box 5.8).

In a nutshell, research and technology are critical to the success of any development effort focused on corporate giving (or any other type of giving for that matter). These attitudes not only help to facilitate the gathering and organization of information and knowledge required to develop compelling and sustainable proposals for potential partners, but they can also attract funding. Many practitioners argue that technology companies, in particular, target their philanthropic giving to encourage capacity building through technology and research (see Box 5.9).

**Box 5.8 Knowing the investment area of interest: Dallas Symphony Orchestra and Neiman Marcus**

Neiman Marcus, a Dallas-based international brand, is committed to equity, diversity and inclusion. In order to get support from the company, the Dallas Symphony Orchestra developed a proposal connected to their Southern Dallas Program, which includes funding for after-school programs for children of color, and therefore meets corporate priorities. This has resulted in corporate support, although on a smaller scale than the previous example.

*Source*: Kim Noltemy personal communication

**Box 5.9 Dallas Symphony Orchestra and the Toyota sponsorship: when metrics make a difference**

As Toyota had recently based its US headquarters just outside Dallas, the Dallas Symphony was determined to make a case for the Japanese company to support the orchestra's music education programs in an underserved area of the city. However, the company decided to support the education programs of other arts organizations instead. Toyota was then reproached when the Dallas Symphony formed a partnership with Bloomberg Media; and presented data to Toyota that demonstrated ROI supporting this initiative. Thanks to this data package and defined metrics, Toyota agreed to sponsor some educational initiatives paired with the Bloomberg Media package – which broadcast three programs on their network of TV stations, website, terminals placed in various financial companies and on the Bloomberg app. Dallas Symphony had to assure Toyota that their programming was family friendly and that it would be complete within the fourth quarter of the year, because that was when the marketing dollars were available.

*Source*: Kim Noltemy personal communication

### 5.4.5 *Knowing the structure of corporate funders*

As mentioned earlier, arts organizations should consider a firm's structure and operational scale before approaching it as a business prospect.

Large corporations with multiple departments and regional offices may not have a uniform giving policy, and the discretion of regional managers can impact on how philanthropic money is allocated. Furthermore, companies that give without the intermediation of a corporate foundation may do so through an office of community or public relations, marketing or some other dedicated unit, such as a contribution committee that involves employees from various departments and levels of the organization. In the case of gifts in kind of company products (and the negotiation of commercial partnerships), the central office or a specific department can be in charge.

Understanding the decision-making process regarding corporate charitable gifts and the departmental structure of a business is even more important when arts organizations ask for substantial gifts or sponsorship. As previously stated, when there are major sponsorship requests, the marketing department of the business is usually involved, given that money allocated is most likely coming from the marketing department's general sponsorship budget. Consequently, when making sponsorship requests, the development professional should understand that the arts organization might not only be competing with other not-for- profit entities, but also with a more complex set of for-profit entertainment and sports companies.

Most large companies have charitable donation policies that formalize the process by which philanthropic endeavors are managed. Typically, such policies address who oversees the charitable giving process within the company, criteria for eligibility, areas of focus, procedures, exclusions and possible matching programs. In general, we can assume that, when their funding decisions are made, firms' actions are influenced by the promotion of favorable public relations. Indeed, there are still many for-profit companies with no formalized giving policies or structures for disbursing funds for philanthropic purposes. Often, the CEO's special interests and commitment to social responsibility drive the giving policies of such firms. In businesses where the philanthropic function is well established, contributions are often within the purview of a specific department, such as public affairs, marketing, community relations, personnel or corporate communications. The surest entry into a business is to approach the CEO or another top executive through a personal connection or business colleague. Cultural organization board members are key intermediaries (or referees) when approaching top-level executives.

### 5.4.6 *Lobbying and political collaborations*

Sometimes, corporations give to not-for-profits arts organizations with the goal of affecting the political environment in ways that are beneficial to the company. In other words, funding decisions occasionally take lobbying into account. However, it is not always possible to easily achieve this. Federal law in the United States, for instance, precludes 501(c)(3) cultural institutions from participating in the lobbying of government officials when there is no direct impact on the cultural organization. In response to this, a sort of indirect lobbying can be pursued by businesses and cultural institutions, both in the United States and in Europe, by including corporate and government leaders in their events. This may raise an ethical concern, but sophisticated arts institutions understand where the boundaries are (see Boxes 5.10 and 5.11).

From the corporate standpoint, businesses supporting the arts and education programs are able to improve their reputation and, as a result, may undergo less legislative scrutiny. At the same time, the presence of government and corporate leaders during events provides access to networks and related opportunities. Serving on the board of a cultural institution is also a way for corporate executives to gain access to such networks. This aspect is also significant in European countries, where representatives from national or local government are frequently the most influential and

**Box 5.10 Takeda Pharmaceuticals and the Boston Symphony Orchestra (BSO)**

The BSO decided to approach Takeda Pharmaceuticals for a corporate giving partnership. The pharaceutical industry is heavily regulated and invests significant resources in advocacy. Takeda, the Japanese pharmaceutical company – whose research and development operations are based near Boston – wanted to play a role in the community by leveraging a relationship with an important cultural institution. The BSO is one of the biggest arts organizations in the United States and was able to offer an important and interesting network of influential people (e.g., world famous scientists, political representatives, business leaders) who were of interest to Takeda, thus stimulating Takeda's decision to support the orchestra.

*Source*: Mark Volpe personal communication

**Box 5.11 Fidelity Foundation and the Boston Symphony Orchestra (BSO)**

Fidelity Investments and the Fidelity Foundation have provided tens of millions of dollars of support to the BSO during the past several decades. Over the course of a year, Fidelity held many events with invitees including customers, employees, corporate leadership and occasionally political leaders. Fidelity Charitable is the leader in the fastest growing part of the philanthropic space in the United States through its donor advised funds, which distributed $10.3 billion in 2021. A donor advised fund is a giving account established at a public charity (it can be a charity organized by a mutual fund company, such as Fidelity Charitable, or a community foundation, such as the Boston Foundation). Gifts to such funds receive an immediate tax deduction as they are irrevocable, and the donor can then recommend grants to charitable organizations over time. When the Commonwealth of Massachusetts was considering legislation that would impact donor advised funds, the leadership of the Fidelity Foundation asked the BSO's CEO to support the foundation's case in discussions with the leadership of the Massachusetts legislature. Given that Fidelity has been and continues to be a major supporter of the BSO, and that the BSO derives much benefit from the donor advised funds, the BSO's CEO supported Fidelity's lobbying.

*Source*: Mark Volpe personal communication

relevant members of such boards. For instance, Italian opera houses have to appoint the mayor of the city as their president, even if the city is not the main funder or direct decision maker.[2]

## 5.5 Current trends in corporate fundraising

As the rate of change in society continues to accelerate, it is important that arts organizations evolve to address these changes. In this dynamic world, understanding trends is critical to the ongoing viability of cultural institutions in many respects, including corporate giving. These trends deal with industrial, cultural and social factors, and should always be

[2] Decreto Legislativo 29 giugno 1996, n. 367 / "Disposizioni per la trasformazione degli enti che operano nel settore musicale in fondazioni di diritto private"; Decreto Valore Cultura o Legge Bray (Legge n. 91, G.U. 08/10/2013).

carefully considered by development departments and senior managements in arts organizations, so their asking strategies are more effective. The common feature of these trends is that corporations – like any other entity – look more carefully at the complexity of the environment in which they are operating, and this complexity influences their decision-making. Financial crises (such as the 2008 downturn), big events (such as the COVID-19 pandemic) and the geopolitical changes of the last decade, with their long-term effects on populations, are something all decision makers must address. Furthermore, the impact of new technologies and the digital world will greatly influence future corporate decisions.

As already stated in this book, both arts organizations and businesses serve a community of people. The globalization of economies and culture, migrations and demographic shifts, and the recent COVID-19 pandemic have significantly impacted communities, resulting in great social displacement. Consequently, all entities including businesses and not-for-profits are having to grapple with issues regarding access to healthcare, access to education, inclusion and diversity, food security and so on. Arts organizations would be well advised to take this ever-changing environment into account when considering corporate giving strategies.

In addition, as previously mentioned, CEOs and top managers leading large corporations are no longer rooted in the local community, as was the case when the families that created the companies controlled them. These new corporate leaders are often not natives of the community in which their company is based, and may have no real allegiance to it. As a result, their philanthropic focus is usually global.

The changing demographics of many Western countries suggest that the traditional European art forms are no longer as dominant as they were in prior generations. Corporate leaders are aware of these shifts, and accordingly they are adjusting their philanthropic priorities.

To be successful in their corporate fundraising efforts, arts organizations must interpret these trends and the evolution in their communities, and adjust their approaches to potential business funders. At best, they can assist businesses as they look for opportunities to make deeper connections with communities. If this is done organically and authentically, those organizations that create programs to address these various social and economic challenges will be perceived to be good citizens. This will resonate with businesses and lead to deeper philanthropic connections.

One consequence of the increasing globalization of the world's economies has been the advent of mega-wealth industries. Technology, biotechnology, hedge funds, venture capitals and private equity are all sectors in which great wealth has been accumulated in a relatively short period of time. While these sectors have not traditionally had the arts as a philanthropic priority, some arts organizations have recently been able to secure support by aligning interests.[3]

Mega-wealth industries are more likely to have an international focus than family created companies of previous generations that were rooted in one community. Nowadays, international corporations donate to cultural institutions wherever they have a concentration of business interests and employees, no matter the continent or area. In general, companies that have a predominantly local impact report a lower percentage of international contributions (CECP, 2021).

Worthy of notice is the case of the so-called sin companies – those dealing in alcohol, tobacco, gaming and now legalized marijuana – that have occasionally sought legitimacy through giving to cultural institutions. These businesses tend to show their generosity even in difficult financial environments, but arts organizations would be well advised to consider ethical and reputational implications before accepting a gift from such companies (see Box 5.12).

Although this is not universally the case, modern corporate leaders in the United States tend not to be as culturally literate as prior generations. Moreover, the growing dominance of sports has captured the attention of corporate America, resulting in billions of dollars in sports sponsorships. Fortunately, there remains a certain status associated with involvement in the arts that some corporate executives have found enticing. That being said, the competition corporate sponsorship will be increasingly challenging for the not-for profit arts sector as sports and the for-profit culture sectors (e.g., the movie industry, commercial theatre such as Broadway and pop music) have become more dominant in the broadest sense of the American cultural landscape. In Europe, corporate leaders generally have a higher level of education, and when they decide to support the arts, it happens because there is either a business tradition or a personal connection with an art institution or art form.

---

[3] See also Chapter 4.

**Box 5.12 Japan Tobacco International and the British Museum**

A renowned business case related to these issues is that of Japan Tobacco and its funding of the British Museum. The British Museum still accepts this contribution twenty-eight years after it was rejected by the Tate. Japan Tobacco International, which operates under its more innocuous initials, JTI, provides funding to the museum's Asian department. Its brands include Benson and Hedges, Winston, Camel and Silk Cut. The JTI Japanese Acquisition Fund has enabled the British Museum to add 600 objects to its collection. JTI also finances a museum project curator for Japan. A museum spokeswoman says that "JTI have supported the museum since 2010 and we are grateful to JTI for their long-term partnership." Under the museum's 2016 Acceptance of Donations Principles, the trustees are required to consider "the economic benefits of accepting the money being weighed against the potential cost of reputational risks." This suggests that the museum does not consider that tobacco sponsorship has a negative impact on its reputation. However, although the museum accepts funding for acquisitions and curatorship, it would be unlikely to do so for more public activities, such as exhibition sponsorship. In general, sponsorship and donations for museums have recently come under increased scrutiny, as shown by protests over Sackler family grants – with London's National Portrait Gallery forgoing a donation recently and several prominent American institutions removing the Sackler name from various buildings, given controversies over the family's association with OxyContin.

*Source*: Author's elaboration from https://www.theartnewspaper.com/2019/04/02/why-is-the-british-museum-still-accepting-tobacco-sponsorship

As the central State usually provides general support to the arts in Europe, corporate support of the arts is mainly related to sponsorships and special-purpose initiatives with a quantifiable business return. This is also related to the local culture that gives governments of single member states the almost total responsibility of financing culture to enable wide accessibility to it. However, European corporations link arts funding with social recognition and managers' personal prestige. Actual trends in professional discussions show how the competitiveness for corporate funds is becoming more difficult in Europe too. As previously stated, sports and other not-for-profit sectors (such as healthcare or education) are powerful attractors of businesses' generosity, and arts organizations are required to develop more impactful proposals to make companies understand that giving to the arts is worthy.

One last important trend in corporate giving is that arts institutions need to consider that corporations require customization and/or exclusivity in their giving agreements. More and more frequently, businesses want to engage in a dialogue (negotiation) about specific benefits to be provided, about the price of those benefits and how a sponsorship or gift will benefit the business's employees as well as its customers. In respect to exclusivity, companies typically want to be the exclusive sponsor, at least in respect to category exclusivity. Common sense suggests that three banks sponsoring the same activity is not going to work. These matters have to be carefully negotiated, and the arts institution is well advised to keep track of the net level of funding before fully consummating a sponsorship or other contractual arrangement with a corporation.

## Keywords for arts fundraisers

Corporate philanthropy, corporate giving, corporate social responsibility, corporate foundation, the Gospel of Wealth, corporate citizenship, annual contribution, advertising, in-kind contribution, special fundraising events, cause-related marketing, licensing agreements, employee gift-matching, paid-release time programs, virtual volunteering, sin companies

## Suggested questions for meetings and discussion

- What are the key factors for successful corporate fundraising?
- What are the key motivators triggering corporations to donate to the arts?
- How can arts organizations approach corporations effectively to secure contributions/sponsorship? How does corporate philanthropy differ from corporate sponsorship?
- How dos an arts institution align its mission with a corporation or company? What the opportunities? What issues might surface?
- How would you develop your program to approach corporate funders?
- What are the various ways in which a corporation can supports arts organizations?
- What are the current trends in corporate fundraising?

- Among different corporate fundraising tools, can you give some examples of successful use of them in your institution or in arts organizations you know?
- In your experience, are there any case histories in corporate fundraising to set as a benchmark?

## References

ABA (Advisory Board for the Arts.) (2022). *Arts organization leader benchmarking*, March.

CECP (Chief Executives for Corporate Purpose) (2021). *Giving in Numbers: 2021 Edition.* Available at: https://cecp.co/home/resources/giving-in-numbers/.

Dang, A. and Nguyen, T. (2021). "Valuation effect of emotionality in corporate philanthropy," *Journal of Business Ethics*, 173 (1): 47–67.

FASB (Financial Accounting Standard Board). (1993). *SFAS 116, Accounting for contributions received and contributions made* (issued June).

Fry, L. W., Keim, G. D. and Meiners, R. E. (1982). Corporate contributions: Altruistic or for-profit?," *Academy of Management Journal*, 25 (1): 94–106.

Gautier, A. and Pache, A. (2015). "Research on corporate philanthropy: A review and assessment," *Journal of Business Ethics*, 126 (3): 343–369.

Gehringer, T. and von Schnurbein, G. (2017). *Corporate foundations in Europe*, European Research Network On Philanthropy 8th International Conference, Copenhagen.

Godfrey, P. C. (2005) "The relationship between corporate philanthropy and shareholder wealth: A risk management perspective," *Academy of Management Review*, 30 (4): 777–798.

Hopkins, K. B. and Friedman, C. S. (1997). *Successful fundraising for arts and cultural organizations.* Phoenix, AZ: Greenwood Publishing Group.

Schwartz, R. A. (1968). "Corporate philanthropic contributions," *The Journal of Finance*, 23 (3): 479–497.

Worth, M. J. (2016). *Fundraising: Principles and practice.* Los Angeles: SAGE Publications Inc.

# 6 Private and Public Grantmakers for the Arts

with *Agustí Filomeno*

## 6.1 Why governments support arts organizations

Governments regularly provide support to arts organizations, although approaches in Europe and the United States differ. In Europe, meaningful shares of public budgets are directly allocated to the arts, with governments owning the majority of cultural heritage institutions, including most of the buildings where arts events take place and the museums where artworks are exhibited. Tax exemptions favoring not-for-profit cultural institutions are another way in which European governments provide support. In the United States, champion of the so-called liberalist cultural policy model (Mulcahy, 2000), government supports the arts more indirectly, by granting tax deductions to private donors (who get tax benefits for their gifts) and exemptions (from local property taxes, for example) for not-for-profit arts organizations.

In the following paragraphs, we discuss the different mechanisms through which arts institutions are supported by public funders. We also explore in detail why governments support the arts and how the support is allocated. This review is not only theoretical, but also provides guidance for arts managers and policy makers who are advocating for a higher level of public funding for arts institutions (or at least no cuts).

### 6.1.1 *Why governments support the arts*

From an economic standpoint, scholars have agreed that public funding is necessary so that arts institutions can fulfil their mission. Artistic and cultural goods are public goods and cannot follow the rules of private goods markets. By definition, public goods consumption provides a healthy level of well-being in society when they are produced at an optimal level and the highest number of people have access to them. Conversely, the consumption of private goods provides the highest level of well-being in a society when competitiveness rules the markets, and companies and consumers share complete and perfect information (Towse, 2019).[1] Therefore, cultural economists have long demonstrated that if arts organizations operate as other businesses do, production and consumption of cultural goods is sub-optimal for society as a whole. This is because, if submitted to typical market rules, they would be forced for budgetary reasons to focus on demand preferences, thereby appealing to the widest range of consumers. This would consequently affect production choices, the variety of artworks available and the freedom of artistic expression. An example of this is provided by the opera industry. Opera houses all over the world regularly program their seasons with the same repertoire (for instance, *La Bohème*, *La Traviata* or *The Barber of Seville*) to fill the house and increase their earned income so they can cover costs. Without support from the public sector, alternative and less obviously appealing productions that would encourage the development of this art form and deliver variety would not find any space in their programming (Frey and Pommerehne, 1989; Turrini et al., 2008).

Another reason why arts markets "fail" is connected to the fact that the arts can be collectively consumed unlike private goods: the audience for a concert or visitors to a museum are not pure rivals in consumption, but share the same good. In addition, as the arts are collective goods, consumption cannot always be exclusive. For instance, freely accessible artworks (e.g., masterpieces placed in a public square such as Bernini's *Barcaccia* fountain or the Colosseum in Rome) are freely open for direct consumption. Because they are public, the arts can bring collective benefits (so-called positive externalities). These benefits are not exclusive to participants in the economic exchange (i.e., ticketholders and institutions), as they impact society at large. Typical examples are the indirect contribu-

---

[1] Private goods have two main features that cannot be shared with public goods: they are rivals in consumption (i.e., if someone consumes a specific private good, another individual cannot) and they are excludable (i.e., whoever buys a private good can exclude others from the same consumption, and enforcing exclusivity is easy).

tion of the arts to local tourism and development; the spin-off that affects other creative industries (i.e., fashion, design, advertising agencies); and the option that future generations have on the consumption of specific art forms, which reduces the risk of their disappearance (Hansmann, 1986; Scitovsky, 1989; Brosio and Santagata, 1992). In consequence, economic agents that are not directly involved in the ticketholder–institution exchange accrue benefits from arts consumption, with a consequent loss of market efficiency. Therefore, to re-establish equality between all actors who enjoy the positive externalities that emerge from the production and consumption of the arts, government regulation is required.

Finally, the conditions that allow perfect and complete information so the quality of products can be assessed are not guaranteed in the arts market. As cultural products are not commodities, there is no obligation to disclose all relevant information about the goods exchanged (as in the case, for instance, of shares traded in financial markets). The non-standardized nature of artworks and the aesthetic experience, added to the impossibility of assessing quality before purchasing arts products, generate information asymmetries between arts providers and consumers. In this context, government financial support or the use of not-for-profit status for arts institutions is a way to indirectly signal the quality of arts products before they are purchased, and to lower the perceived risk of disappointment (Hansmann, 1986). In this way, audiences can be assured that the money they pay (e.g., by purchasing a ticket for a concert in a public auditorium) is spent on the arts, and that there is no residual claimant lowering the quality of the cultural product to gain economic advantage. In sum, by funding the arts, governments avoid arts market failure by granting a better level of arts production and helping to fill the information gap regarding the quality of arts products, while also allowing arts organizations to set more affordable prices for their tickets to increase accessibility (Turrini, 2007).

The so-called Baumol cost disease (Baumol and Bowen, 1965, 1966; Blaug, 1976; Netzer, 1978; Felton, 1994) from which all cultural organizations suffer is another economic rationale for public intervention in the arts. According to this theory, arts organizations always experience an income gap, as they are labor-intensive organizations and belong to a stagnant industry. Stagnant industries do not benefit from technological innovations as progressive industries do. On the contrary, they experience little (or even negative) growth and an increase in their labor costs, because of the general increase in average wages that is linked to the higher productivity of progressive industries. This can be clarified with an example: the same number of musicians is needed to play a Mozart concerto today as was required in the 18th century: in other words, the productivity of classical music performances has not increased. However, real wages have increased substantially since the 18th century, affecting production costs significantly. Moreover, the income generated in the arts sector has not increased proportionally to production costs, as the selling price for artistic goods cannot increase as much as is necessary. This costs disease means that arts organizations (in particular in the performing arts) experience a growth in relative wages, an increase in labor costs per unit of output, an endemic increase in prices and a consequent contraction in demand (or even a deficit). This chain reaction necessitates government (or philanthropic) intervention and direct funding of the arts, thus eliminating the gap between costs and revenues and the risk of the sector becoming extinct.

The economic rationale is not the only one in support of public funding of the arts. Another set of arguments relates to the prestige and sense of identity and belonging that the arts can foster in a community. Cultural policies aiming to support national identity in a community can therefore be set in motion by the protection and restoration of heritage, by public works initiatives and by the launch of national awards. The arts also play a crucial role in fostering social cohesion. As discussed in Chapter 1, cultural institutions play a key role not only in their direct nurturing of the cultural capital of a community, but also by increasing its social capital, as they deliver relational goods that are experienced together (Putnam, 1993). Arts organizations strengthen social networks and mutual trust among citizens by entailing local development. The flourishing of industrial creative clusters in Italy, for example, derives from the presence of social and cultural capital that has accumulated over the years in a specific place.

As we describe in Chapter 8, cultural institutions also improve social inclusion and quality of life (Netzer, 1978). Regeneration projects with arts and cultural institutions as anchor organizations might help to revitalize socially or economically degraded neighborhoods (Cherbo et al., 2008). The Guggenheim Museum in Bilbao, Spain, is a prime example of this phenomenon (see Fig. 6.1).

The economic impact of arts festivals might also trigger increases in employment, spending and local wealth, and in a community's quality of life (Tyrrell and Johnson, 2006).

*Figure 6.1* The Guggenheim Museum in Bilbao

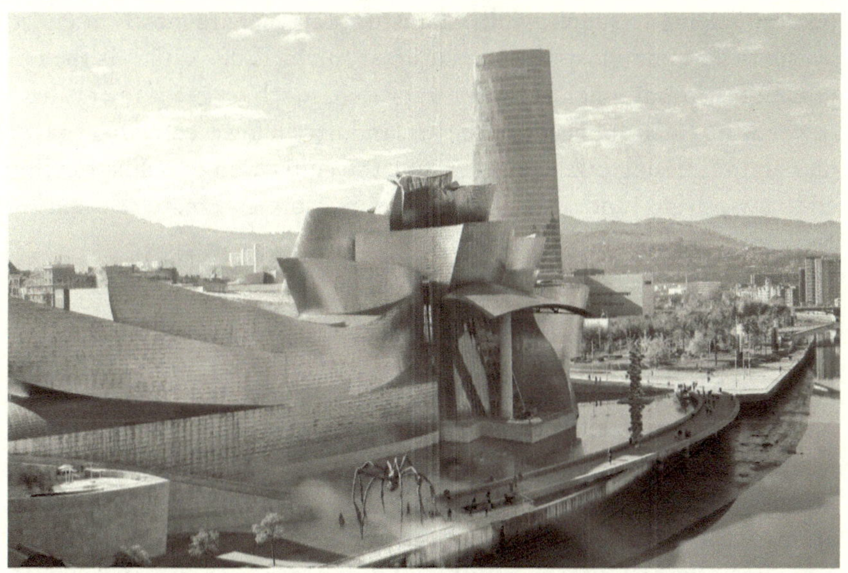

*Source*: Naotake Murayama, CC BY 2.0, via Wikimedia Commons

Individual and personal benefits brought by the direct exposure of people to the arts also motivate public support for culture. Such benefits include the cognitive improvements (e.g., for children and young people) that are accrued when individuals are frequently exposed to the arts. They can bring behavioral changes in terms of increased prosocial attitudes, stimulated by the opportunities to escape the daily routine that aesthetic experiences can offer, and increase openness to the diversity of opinions and ideas (McCarthy, 2004).[2]

Despite the long list of arguments that advocate public funding for the arts, criticism of it can be intense. The discussion is particularly animated in the United States, where liberal culture is stronger than in Europe. American scholars who criticize public funding for the cultural sector argue that this kind of financial intervention does not actually favor the maintenance of artistic freedom. Moreover, from an economic stand-

[2] See also Chapter 8.

point, public intervention in the sector has regressive effects: in a chain reaction, because of their funding through taxes, subsidies result in the poorest helping to support cultural institutions that are mostly attended by the richest and most highly educated (Turrini, 2007). This is the opposite of the traditional European approach, in which governments have covered the financial needs of the arts industry. However, owing to regular and increasing public budget cuts, the cultivation of public funding and new private fundraising are becoming more and more relevant for European cultural institutions.

### 6.1.2 *How governments organize public funding for arts institutions*

When we try to outline different cultural policies regarding arts funding (i.e., how governments organize their support for the arts), we should acknowledge how difficult it is to generalize and to find common threads among different countries. Figure 6.2 shows the share of national government spending in cultural services in different OECD countries as a measure of the relevance of cultural funding among other public policies.

*Figure 6.2* Cultural services as a share of total government spending, 2011 and 2019

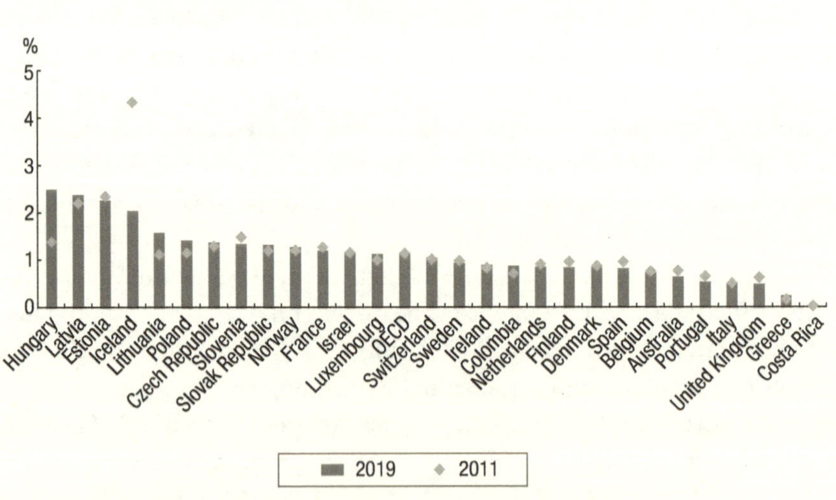


*Source*: OECD (2022)

The graph highlights the dissimilar contexts that arts managers experience in different countries: public financial support in 2019 for Hungarian arts organizations is, for example, about three times higher than that granted to Spanish or Italian cultural institutions.

The impact of different local cultural policies is also evident if we look at more detailed data. Let us consider, for example, the case of the opera industry. In the United States, about half of the total revenue of an opera house is covered by earned income (i.e., tickets, royalties, space rental), another 46 per cent is covered by philanthropy and only the remaining 4 per cent (as an average) is covered by public support. In Europe, the situation is the opposite. For example, the Italian Fondazioni Lirico-Sinfoniche receives 65–70 per cent of total revenue from public funding with notable exceptions like Teatro alla Scala in Milan.

Despite the differences in national cultural policies, it is possible to sketch some reference models (supported by published studies) to guide arts managers. By analyzing different approaches in national cultural policies, Lewis (2000) states that it is possible to cluster these policies into two main groups based on the breadth and extent of State intervention. To the first group belong countries where governments completely refrain from intervening in the arts sector, by letting private actors and market dynamics regulate national cultural development. This occurs, for example, in the United States.[3] In countries in the second cluster, public institutions intervene significantly, providing direct support to arts organizations' economic and financial needs, especially in the case of organizations that "deserve" protection and support (typically liberal or highbrow arts). This happens more frequently in Europe.

In his research, Lewis (2000) does not identify the reasons for these different approaches, so we must go back to previous studies to find possible explanations. Some scholars argue that the evolution of cultural policies in the United States can be traced back to some characteristics of American tradition and culture. Examples of these traits are a strong tendency to encourage individual initiative and action; respect for freedom of expression, belief, association and political opinion; the influence of a Puritan, utilitarian and pragmatic tradition regarding arts and cul-

---

[3] However, the United States indirectly provides support for much of the not-for-profit world, including the arts, by allowing private grants to not-for-profits registered with the Internal Revenue Service to be tax deductible.

ture; and even some concerns about possible failures of public programs (Cummings, 1982; Mankin, 1982; Wyszomirski and Mulcahy, 1995).

In respect of Europe, Cummings and Katz (1987) have studied the impact of the political and economic histories and cultural traditions of different European countries on the great variety of cultural policy approaches that we can still observe. Researchers argue that those countries (e.g., the Netherlands and the United Kingdom) that experienced an economic boom during the late 17th century – with the upsurge of a very powerful and influential class of merchants and the strengthening among the population of Protestant values – developed local cultural policies with weaker government intervention in the creation of public goods. Conversely, in countries (e.g., Austria and France) that experienced the authority of powerful and autarchic royal families (e.g., the d' Orléans in France and the Habsburgs in Austria), the long-lasting influence of the aristocracy and the relevance of values and beliefs related to Catholicism, have favored the development of local cultural policies that required a stronger intervention in public arts institutions. In these countries, State intervention has been consolidated through the creation of national institutions (an example being Vienna's Burgtheater opened in 1776 by Emperor Joseph II), aiming to glorify the founding royal dynasty with a clear symbol of their generosity (O'Hagan, 1998).

These models have remained substantially the same, even with the transition to democratic governments and the evolution of different political, social and economic systems. We can think, for example, about the relevance of private patronage in favor of artists and arts institutions (especially in the visual arts) as a sign of the new incumbent social classes' legitimacy. This is particularly strong in those countries where the austerity of Protestantism and the birth of the mercantile class have traditionally been relevant. However, after the Second World War, European cultural policies have gradually become more alike.

Examining the infrastructure and the organization of public funding of the arts, Cummings and Katz (1982) define two different organizational models. The French model of organization is based on the presence of a single strong public institution (e.g., a ministry) that is responsible for the development and implementation of most of the national cultural policies, while the Anglo-Saxon/American model is based on the establishment of quasi-public agencies or foundations that implement national or regional cultural policies. The latter represents an application of the so-called arm's length principle applied to the artistic and cultural sector (Hillman-Chartrand and McCaughey, 1989). This requires a clear administrative separation between political institutions and the agency that finances or manages cultural programs. In other words, the government decides the overall amount of cultural investment, but a separate and independent agency establishes which organizations or programs will receive it. Some examples of these agencies are the US National Endowment for the Arts (described in detail in Box 6.1) and the American State arts agencies, which arose from a Federal–State partnership program in 1967 to fund arts organizations and cultural districts.

The degree of decentralization/centralization of public funding decision-making is another feature that allows us to analyze types of government intervention in the arts. According to Mulcahy (2000), it is possible to classify countries into three groups. Statist countries present a strong centralization of responsibilities in decision-making related to the formulation, development, financing and implementation of national and local cultural policies. Localist countries have a higher decentralization of responsibilities in arts funding policy-making in favor of local governments. Pluralist countries, where local levels of government are decentralized and involve private actors in determining and deciding national cultural policies.

**Box 6.1 An application of the arms' length principle: the National Endowment for the Arts[4]**

In the United States, the National Endowment for the Arts (NEA) supports visual and performing arts organizations through the distribution of public funds and grants. The NEA receives an annual allocation from Congress, and decides au-

[4] The National Endowment of the Arts is one of the agencies of the National Foundation on the Arts and the Humanities which is an independent government agency created in the United States as a result of a legislative act (89-209) in September 1965. The other three agencies within the foundation are the National Endowment for the Humanities (supporting their protection, research, education and study), the Federal Council on the Arts and the Humanities (supporting and aligning the action of the other branches of the foundation) and the Institute of Museum and Library Services (managing federal programs that support museums and libraries of any kind, public and private).

tonomously how to distribute its funds. The link with political power is granted by the presidential appointment of the NEA chairman and the appointment of members of the National Council on the Arts, the advisory body of the chairman. Every year, the NEA launches general programs from which cultural institutions can apply for funding by proposing specific projects concerning dance, design, literature, multimedia arts (cinema, television, video art), music, musicals, opera, theatre and visual arts. Grants (typically matching grants) range from a minimum of $100,000 to a maximum of $500,000. The evaluation process has three stages. An initial examination is carried out by panels specialized in the art form most relevant to the project presented. The panels (there are about forty) are made up of artists, cultural managers, professionals, educators, representatives of other local agencies, private citizens, experts and connoisseurs. The selection of panelists is based on curricula and experience in the sector, and on criteria such as age, race, geographical origin and so on. Each panel is made up of five to twenty members, and possible conflicts of interest are avoided. Based on the opinion of these panelists, the National Council on the Arts makes its evaluations, and these are delivered to the President who has the final word.

The real selection is done by the panels, based on criteria that vary from program to program, but in general they are based on the quality and artistic merit of individual projects, their potential impact nationally and on local areas, and the ability of the proponent to carry out the project. The applicant organization must provide the NEA with all necessary information regarding the project, the proposing organization and other sources of funding at three points: when the application is submitted, when the grant is made and finally when the project is concluded. Selection through panels is important for non-profit institutions, not only for economic reasons, but also to obtain recognition of the quality of their cultural offering and their cost-effectiveness. As this is one of the few project evaluation processes in the cultural field, it represents an invaluable imprimatur and a seal of approval for a selected institution. The NEA also engages in other activities separate from funding: it plays the role of guide and catalyst for programs that have national importance, and collaborates with other public and private entities that operate in the cultural sector. The NEA plays a role on multiple levels. It supports State arts councils through unrestricted funds that State agencies can use to pursue the priorities they have assigned themselves. These grants are disbursed in the form of block grants (or basic State grants): one part is fixed (about $200,000), while the other varies on the basis of the sixty-two State arts councils' financial program and state populations. The NEA also supports regional arts organizations, both directly and indirectly, through initiatives such as the Regional Performing Arts Touring Initiative, which allows a better distribution of shows across different regions.

*Source*: Elaborated on Turrini (2007)

## 6.2 Public funding mechanisms to support arts organizations

Public funding of the arts can be addressed by referring to the traditional economic principles of supply or demand. Supply-oriented funding consists of direct subsidies provided to artists or cultural institutions. Demand-oriented funding provides incentives to the audience or private donors.

Public funding to arts institutions can take different forms according to constraints on the allocation of funds. Traditionally, especially in European countries, subsidies to cultural institutions have been provided as unrestricted funds. In other words, these funds are allocated for general operating support (i.e., to cover expenses that arts institutions sustain when carrying out their activities). As previously noted, the rationale of such subsidies is to discourage arts organizations from aggressively increasing their ticket prices and to make the arts accessible to the greatest number of people.

A large part of the relevant literature refutes arguments that are put forward in favor of public funding to arts institutions, giving several different reasons. First, as Seaman (2006) clearly demonstrates in his review of several arts demand studies, some features of audience buying behavior (i.e., taste cultivation, rational addiction, learning by consuming) weaken the assumption that higher ticket prices will automatically bring about a total collapse of paid attendance. Moreover, whether arts demand is price-inelastic (as the majority of the studies in cultural economics indicate) or there is a low elasticity to price (as seems to occur under certain circumstances) is still undetermined (Towse, 2010). Some studies even claim that demand for arts goods might be considered as similar to that for luxury goods because of its income elasticity rapport (i.e., the demand for arts goods increases more than proportionally as income increases) (Levy-Garboua and Montmarquette, 2003). In addition to all these considerations, the majority of studies evidence how education and cultural capital are the most powerful determinants of variations in arts attendance, favoring the provision of demand side subsidies rather than those oriented to supply (Peacock, 1993).

Another scholarly debate that criticizes public subsidies to arts institutions concerns the negative effect of direct public funding on the level of private philanthropy (so-called crowding out). According to this theory, if there is substantial public funding, private donors equate them with quasi-public agencies that are not in need of extra private funds (Friedman and Friedman, 1980). Furthermore, if an arts organization relies on extensive public funding, this could constitute a sign of its fragility, lack of autonomy or excessive reliance on public funds, which might dissuade private philanthropists from supporting it: they would be more likely to sponsor stronger and more independent organizations (Odendhal, 1990). Borgonovi (2006) replies to these concerns with evidence that the displacement of private donors only occurs when arts organizations receive a relatively high level of public support; a relatively low level of public funding can multiply and "crowd in" private donations. This effect depends on the potential increase in the reputation and credibility of institutions that obtain such public grants. In this regard, matching grants might be very helpful in avoiding the crowding out effect of private funding and in fixing a limit to government spending on a single project or organization (Schuster, 1988). Matching grants schemes follow two different logics: either they require that for every dollar/euro of public funding the arts organization must obtain a fixed percentage of funding from other public sources; or in the case of reverse grants, the government funds an arts institution only if an increase in private fundraising is achieved. An example of this approach is provided by the funding rules of the Italian Ministry of Culture in respect to the Fondo Unico per lo Spettacolo (FUS), which is the most relevant public funding source for Italian arts institutions.[5] For example, the Ministry of Culture assigns the Fondazioni Lirico-Sinfoniche 25 per cent of their FUS subsidy, matching the level of private funds that the organization raises over the fiscal year.

Recent debates about government support to the arts have highlighted the importance of some forms of demand-oriented funding such as voucher schemes (West, 1986; Turrini, 2005; Towse, 2010). With a voucher system, public or private grant-makers create a quasi-market system, facilitating access to the arts for specific (and typically underserved) categories of users. When an explicit or pure voucher mechanism is implemented (see Fig. 6.3), arts voucher users have a (fundamental!) duty to choose the event or the venue they want to attend. Once the voucher is used, the organization might be reimbursed (totally or partially) by the

[5] With a yearly amount of about €350 million in 2019.

*Figure 6.3* Pure or explicit voucher system scheme

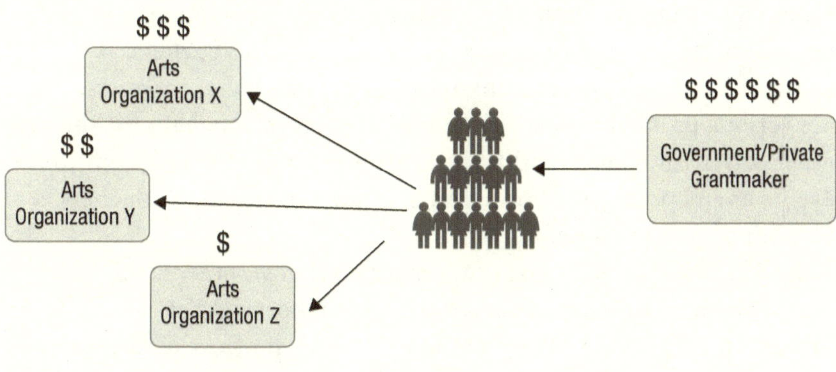


grant-maker. This means that users' choices drive the allocation of funding to a specific arts institution.

In order to make these mechanisms more effective, different ways of structuring voucher systems have been developed. For example, vouchers can be spent on the purchase of a fairly wide range of services to benefit a more or less large number of providers and users. The money transfer by the grant-maker (i.e., a public agency) can occur either in favor of the recipient organization (i.e., after the voucher has been spent) or in favor of the arts user (i.e., before a purchasing decision is made). Beltrametti (2004: 45) suggests that voucher systems should have some fundamental characteristics: (a) the face value of the voucher should be determined *ex ante*; (b) there should be an expiration date for the voucher; (d) issuers should determine *ex ante* the recipient of the voucher (especially in the case of a personal voucher); (e) the options available to the voucher holder should address the identification of the provider, the service to be benefited from and the time for which the voucher is valid.

By involving the final user (or the private donor), demand-oriented public support for arts organizations undoubtedly allows for more opinions and tastes in the decision-making process. However, such a decentralized and consumption-focused system tends simultaneously to disadvantage less renowned institutions or more innovative and experimental artistic projects. Accordingly, a public funding system based on direct subsidies might in principle give higher priority to the merit and the artistic quality of a cultural institution or an artistic project by involving critics or experts in the funding decision-making process. One major negative drawback of this demand-oriented system is connected to the emergence of secondary markets for vouchers. As Towse (2010: 150) recalls by referring to "classical liberal" economists, "there are serious problems with the administration of vouchers for the arts, especially with transferability: if consumers do not want to go to arts events at any price (even for nothing), they can sell their vouchers contravening their purpose."

Beside direct subsidies or voucher systems, governments might introduce tax incentives to encourage private support for the arts or to allow arts organizations tax exemptions. Not-for-profits can, for example, benefit from special reductions or exemptions from local property taxes. Private donors can receive tax benefits or deductions when they give. These are typical examples of indirect support (Throsby, 2010) (see also Box 6.2, which describes the Art Bonus benefit provided in Italy to all private arts donors).

In the United States, beyond very modest direct support, significant indirect support of the arts and all other non-profits with 501 (c) (3) status granted by the Internal Revenue Service is provided through the tax deductibility of gifts. In other words, with various limitations, individuals and companies contributing to arts organizations can deduct the amount of the gift from the gross income they report on their income tax returns, thus lowering their taxable income. Hypothetically, a person making $100,000 who makes a $5000 gift to an arts organization might only pay taxes on $95,000 of his or her income. The tax code is somewhat complicated and each situation is unique, but this results in billions of dollars of donations to the arts sector each year.

The rationale of these mechanisms is clear: with this kind of expansive fiscal policy, governments renounce some tax revenues that might have contributed to other public programs and give indirect support to the arts sector. However, it is useful to highlight some problems with these systems. First, as previously noted, the introduction of a system of tax expenditures is potentially inconsistent with tax rate reduction policies (Feld et al., 1983). On the one hand, the reduction of tax rates increases the disposable income of families and businesses (and potentially increases donations for cultural institutions); on the other hand, it reduces the benefits (and the incentives) to donating. In other words, the

**Box 6.2 A tax incentive for the arts: Art Bonus in Italy**

The Arts Bonus is a tax credit equal to 65 per cent of charitable contributions that individuals or companies can claim when they support arts organizations. Individuals or not-for-profit organizations can receive a maximum tax credit equal to 15 per cent of income, while for companies the tax credit cannot exceed 5 per cent of annual revenues. The tax credit is reserved for those donations aimed at restoring or maintaining the cultural heritage; supporting museums, libraries, archives, opera houses, theatres and archaeological parks; building new facilities for culture and entertainment or the restoration of existing ones related to all publicly owned cultural institutions. Donations addressed to private heritage or private cultural assets are excluded from the scheme. Donors can choose the organization or project to support by checking a website that lists all the fundable opportunities, and after having made a choice, they can contact the beneficiary to agree on the details of the donation. Introduced by decree in 2014, the Art Bonus generated €692.6 million in donations from over 28,000 patrons and benefited 2973 artistic and cultural assets throughout the country, with a greater concentration in central and northern Italy. The majority of gifts (17,864) came from private citizens, but companies (6651 in total) gave the greatest share of contributions, with €324.3 million given, followed by other non-commercial organizations. This initiative has been a success to various promotional actions, including the Art Bonus Project of the Year. This competition, which took place for the first time in 2016, invited citizens to vote for the best project that was undertaken as a result of the tax credit measure. In 2021, the competition recorded a surge in votes because of the extensive use of social media, resulting in 262,028 votes for 365 projects.

*Source*: elaboration on Mancini (2022)

introduction of tax exemptions for private donors together with a policy of cutting tax rates might lead to a reduction in donations, as it lowers the incentive to donate to cultural institutions. The second problem is connected to who is controlling the destination of taxpayers' money, as the system gives "high-income taxpayers excessive control over charitable tax expenditures" (Feld et al., 1983: 128). Finally, when governments rely on funding systems based on tax expenditures to support arts organizations, they might indirectly influence the fundraising strategy and internal decision-making of cultural institutions. Constrained by increasing competition in the arts philanthropy market, these organizations might, for example, lose their autonomy and independence, and favor the wealthiest donors at the expenses of minor or less influential supporters (Feld et al., 1983).

## 6.3 Foundations as private grant-makers for the arts

In the previous paragraphs, we have highlighted the importance of government and public agencies in funding arts organizations. However, at present, private foundations are becoming increasingly important as private grant-makers for the arts both in Europe and in the United States. Generally speaking, private foundations are legally independent entities funded by one or more sources of income created to grant funds to multiple recipients, typically through an application process. Box 6.3 outlines how European and American organizations differ and the role they play in arts fundraising.

### Box 6.3 Foundations in the United States and in Europe

In the United States, there are about 126,000 private and community foundations (Koob, 2021), covering about 19 per cent of total giving to not-for-profit organizations (CECP, 2021). They typically have one or few major sources of income (i.e.: individual, corporation, family) and they have a minimum payout requirement equal to 5 per cent of the average market value of the assets in their possession. In Europe, it is estimated that 147,000 foundations manage €511 billion in assets and endowments and give an estimated €60 billion annually (https://philea.eu/philanthropy-in-europe/about-philanthropy/). Of course, not having a minimum payout requirement makes the status and nature of private foundations in Europe different from the situation in the United States. Both in Europe and the United States, there are several types of private foundations. In the United States, family foundations (the largest category of independent foundations) have at least one family member serving as an officer or a board member, and that individual (or a relative) plays a significant role in governing and/or managing the foundation. Corporate foundations must avoid engaging in what are defined as self-dealing transactions, except where narrowly permitted by American or European regulations.[6] Finally, both in Europe and the United

[6] See also Chapter 5.

States, community foundations are public charities that support a geographical area by soliciting and catalysing donations used to fulfil community needs and local not-for-profits. They are funded by donations from individuals, families, businesses and sometimes government grants. There are approximately 900 community foundations in 23 countries in Europe and the same number operate in the United States.
Private foundation endowment can be made up of financial resources, tangible assets (e.g., jewellery, art, antiques, boats, cars and real estate, including residential, commercial and investment properties) and intangible properties (e.g., patents and intellectual property rights or publicly held, privately held or restrictively held stock). As private foundations are set up with the task of managing a fund that fulfils their mission, the issue of control is relevant. Each foundation should clearly and carefully determine: its mission; who the members of its governance bodies (i.e., the board) are; what are its investing policies and programs; and how and where funds are granted. In particular, the decision on whether the foundation has a limited life or exists in perpetuity is in the hands of the founder. This means that the control over the grant-maker and its assets can be passed to potentially countless generations of the founding family by perpetuating its values, continuing its charitable work and burnishing the name of the founder far beyond his or her lifetime (Reich, 2020).

In this paragraph, we highlight some risks of which arts managers should be aware when they approach private foundations in order to ask for funding (Turrini and Voss, 2021). The first risk is seeking grants from a foundation with funding priorities that are not in alignment with the arts institution's mission. Doing this may weaken the arts organization by encouraging short-term and mission misfocused thinking. The constant need for funds to cover increasing arts production costs might push organizations to apply for grants, even when the foundation grant-maker's areas of interest are not congruent with the arts institution's mission or strategies. Another risk involves cultural organizations writing and submitting proposals to grant-makers as a matter of routine, without considering whether receiving the grant is consistent with the broader strategy of the arts institution. To avoid this risk, which is common to many other fundraising strategies, arts organizations should instead focus on establishing a presence (Geever, 2012) and be consistent in their fundraising strategies, by establishing mission statements, programs and fundability criteria of each eligible project well in advance. Finally, setting funding priorities is particularly important, especially when the foundation that is approached might grant restricted as well as operational support.

A further potential challenge in approaching foundations is related to the level of funding request-tailoring. Arts organizations have the best chance of success when they address their funding requests to grant-makers who already have an interest in the arts, in what the arts institution does or in a specific project. However, even when the foundation has a pre-existing interest in the arts, the cultural institution seeking funding should customize the proposal in a way that is sensitive to the specific interests and objects of that foundation. The so-called donor–receiver fit is a rule that holds for foundations as well. The donor cultivation process is also relevant for foundation fundraising. In Chapters 3, 4 and 5, we emphasize the importance of building a relationship, gathering information about donors' interests and being transparent and accountable about the arts institution's programs when structuring a long-lasting relationship with individual donors and corporate givers. Arts fundraisers should be aware of these same issues when approaching foundations. In other words, arts organizations seeking support from private grant-makers should understand the grant-maker's point of view.

With this change in perspective, it becomes easy to understand that effective and focused proposal-writing is hard work. Arts fundraisers should collect all pertinent information about the fundable project (which also requires a full-immersion in what the core product of the arts institution is), conduct thoughtful research in the philanthropy market and identify, and select target foundations that might be the best fit with an organization's mission or projects. During this preliminary phase, arts fundraisers should also be aware of potential constraints (i.e., geographical, financial, political) that may prevent the organization from receiving a grant. As part of the arts institution's due diligence, the development department should explore whether there are any links with the foundation: as an example, these might include the arts institution's board members having a relationship with the family that funded the foundation. Of equal importance, the arts institution should have an understanding of the foundation's policies and grant cycle, and who is the most powerful decision-maker when making grants. This process should help inform the arts institution as it strategizes about the projects it should propose and the amount to request.

After this process is completed, the cultivation phase can start. At this point, personal contacts with the foundation are advisable (along with a letter of inquiry), especially when the request is unsolicited or does not refer to a formal request for proposal made by the grant-maker. Thanks to this initial contact with the foundation, arts fundraisers might receive feedback that will be helpful in defining and presenting the case for support.

After receiving a grant, the arts organization, should express gratitude and continue its stewardship of the foundation, as it is likely there will be other opportunities in the future to submit grant proposals. A successful grant proposal depends on the quality of its contents, particularly its case for support. Consequently, arts fundraisers should avoid writing weak proposals that do not convey the need that the organization aims to address through the proposed funding. A clear project description (avoiding wordiness and too formal writing), complete quantification of the estimated budget and a careful explanation of the reasons why the applicant deserves the grant are the contents of a successful grant proposal. Furthermore, in writing grant proposals, arts fundraisers should be able to share with a foundation clear evidence of the urgency and necessity of the foundation's intervention.

Broadly speaking, grant proposal writing should be simple, fluid and coherent. Customizing the proposal to the target foundation or the target funding program is also recommended. Finally, arts fundraisers should avoid sending more than one application at a time to an individual foundation or private grant-maker. Box 6.4 contains a template for structuring a winning grant proposal as suggested by the Foundation Center, which operates in the United States.

**Box 6.4 The structure of a winning proposal**

Executive summary (500 words)

The executive summary outlines why the project is necessary (i.e., the needs it will address), how the project will develop (i.e.: the activities and the expected result) the amount of money needed and why the organization deserves the grant.

**Statement of needs (1000–1500 words)**
The statement of needs expresses the issues that the project will address and in what way the proposed project will tackle these issues. Two main features of this section are important. First, the relevance and magnitude of the need should be evidenced with facts and statistics, anecdotes and quotes from target beneficiaries. Second, the proponents should outline why the project fits the need it is supposed to address. In describing the case for support, the organization outlines and documents its theory of change (the way in which the project produces its effects, change and impacts).

**Project description (2500–3000 words)**
This section should include the "how" of the project, and in particular:

- measurable objectives and target (coherent with the grant-maker's evaluation criteria);
- methods (detailed activities, timeline, staffing and administration);
- mechanism of evaluations (including a statement about when the project might be considered successful, consistent with the grant-maker's evaluation criteria);
- sustainability and future plans (what happen after the grant ends).

**Budget (one page)**
Depending on the grant maker's guidelines, this should include direct and indirect costs and a budget narrative if necessary).

**Organization expertise and basic information (500 words)**

**Conclusions (200 words, final appeal)**

**Appendices**

*Source*: adapted from Geever (2012).

## 6.4 What is the future of public support for the arts?

As emphasized in this chapter, public support for the arts is particularly relevant in Europe – where it covers about 65–75 per cent of arts institutions' budgets – but it also plays a role in the United States, where government indirectly supports private donations to arts institutions with tax benefits or grants tax exempt status to cultural organizations.

Despite the arguments for public support for the arts, there is also impassioned criticism on both sides of the Atlantic. This discussion is especially animated in the United States, where skepticism about government intervention in the arts is motivated by the fear that it could limit the best development of the arts market and reduce the true freedom of artistic expression. In Europe, the debate about government funding to the arts has become more vigorous, often highlighting some negative side effects of such public subsidies. One of them is reputational: the financial support provided by the government can create the impression within a portion of the broader population that the arts institution is a public bureaucracy, thereby losing support in the community. Other criticisms rely on the constraints that public funding imposes on arts organizations from a strategic point of view. For example, we can note the impact of public funding on the institutional decision-making process. The allocation criteria for public funds, for instance, are often historical, and consequently the assigned amount of public funding often depends on what an organization received in the past. This means that sizable changes in such amounts (when needed, for example, for a new venue, to celebrate an anniversary or to renovate facilities) are very difficult to obtain. At the same time, political cycles and changes can abruptly threaten the continuity of public support in favor of a specific arts institution, or they can affect its internal governance. When a newly elected public funder concludes that it has no obligations regarding past funding precedents, the relationship between the arts institution and the public funder needs to be totally rebuilt. This can generate additional advocacy and negotiation costs for the arts institution. Public sector financial support can also result in an arts institution being pressured when making programming decisions. For example, some public funders might attempt to influence an arts organization to engage more local artists or commission local composers. This might seem paradoxical given the mainstream advocacy for public funding, but it is something that many professionals face. A further drawback concerns the level of scrutiny – by the press or the broader public – that arts institutions are subject to, something that is very different when they appeal for a private donation. In recent years, social media channels have radically transformed how communication works, especially for public institutions. Consensus or criticism can be expressed more easily and with broader resonance than in the past. Citizens can give their opinion about public programs (or representatives) by endorsing or commenting on online posts and platforms. Common sense suggests that public funders will be very aware of arts institutions that receive positive as well as negative social media attention, which might impact their funding choices.

Finally, following a trend that began years ago but accelerated during the COVID-19 pandemic, European public funders tend to be more selective in their funding decision-making, and to look for evidence of positive economic and communication impacts of funded projects or institutions before assigning their grants.

For those institutions that are greatly dependent on public funding, being aware of these threats and trends is particularly relevant. To adapt to this ongoing change in the arts philanthropy market, arts organizations (especially in those countries where public intervention has been historically relevant) should first work to strategically diversify their funding sources, enlarging the private donor base at all levels (maybe investing more resources in major donors) and reducing the percentage of budget covered by public resources. Second, cultural institutions should change their approach in calling for public funds, developing expertise in designing more sophisticated and scope-oriented proposals, focusing on results and persuading public funders of the necessity of the required support. Internalizing these attitudes will enhance arts organizations' independence and help them to focus on their mission, increasing the consistency and breadth of their fundraising efforts.

### Keywords for arts fundraisers

Public goods, private goods, positive externalities, information asymmetries, market failure, Baumol cost disease, public funding, anchor-organizations, cultural policy, isomorphism, Ministry, quasi-public agencies, foundation, arm's length principle, National Endowment for the Arts (NEA), indistinct funds, subsidies, crowding in / out effect, matching grants, challenge grants, reverse grants, vouchers, cheques culture, quasi-market system, indirect support, tax expenditures, tax credit, grant-makers, proposal-writing, Request for Proposal (RFP)

**Suggested questions for meetings and discussion**

- What are the most relevant features of the cultural policies regarding funding for the arts in your country?
- What are the different ways the public sector supports the arts in your country? What are the main differences/similarities between American and European approaches for public sector investment in the arts?
- What cultural policies are adopted to encourage private funding of the arts sector (e.g., tax deductibility of contributions…) in your country?
- What are the arguments against public sector investment in the arts?
- What are the key drivers for public decision makers when allocating funds?
- How does the political environment influence the operations and strategies of arts organizations in your country?
- In your experience, when financed by public subsidies, are arts organizations able to define and develop their strategies? What are the strategic aspects that are most influenced by public decision-makers?
- How can arts organizations and leaders balance dependence on public financing with the need to maintain independence regarding artistic and operational decision making?
- Should arts managers receive incentives related to their ability to obtain public funding for their organization? Can you provide some examples? In your experience, what main differences/similarities can you see between American and European arts organizations in respect to this?
- What are the future trends in public financial support for the arts?
- In your opinion, what could be the future financial model for arts organizations regarding the balance between public and private support?
- In your opinion, is the rationale for public sector funding for the arts still legitimate? How are arts organizations looking at trends regarding the scaling back of public sector funding?
- How should arts organizations advocate for public funding?

- How can big crises – such as the pandemic and geopolitical unrest – affect the decision makers regarding public sector funding of the arts? In your experience, what main differences/similarities can you see between American and European arts organizations in respect to this?
- What is the role of private foundations in supporting the arts in your country?
- How can arts organizations successfully approach private and public grant-makers?
- What are the key features of a successful proposal?

## References


Baumol, W. and Bowen, W. G. (1965). "On the performing arts. The anatomy of Their Economic Problems," *American Economic Review*, 55 (2): 495–502.

Baumol, W. and Bowen, W. G. (1966). *Performing Arts – the Economic Dilemma*. Cambridge, MA: MIT Press.

Beltrametti, L. (2004). *Vouchers*. Bologna: Il Mulino.

Blaug, M. (1976). *The Economics of the Arts*. London: Martin Robertson.

Borgonovi, F. (2006). "Do public grants to American theatres crowd-out private donations?," *Public Choice*, 126: 429–451.

Brooks, A. (2000). *Who Opposes Government Arts Funding?*, eleventh ACEI Conference, Minneapolis.

Brosio, G. and Santagata, W.(1992). *Rapporto sull'economia delle arti e dello spettacolo in Italia*. Turin: Edizioni della Fondazione G. Agnelli.

CECP (Chief Executives for Corporate Purpose) (2021). *Giving in numbers: 2021 edition*. Available at: https://cecp.co/home/resources/giving-in-numbers/.

Cherbo, J. M., Stewart, R. A. and Wyszomirski, M. (eds) (2008). *Understanding the arts and creative sector in the United States*. New Brunswick, NJ: Rutgers University Press.

Cummings, M. C. and Katz, R. S. (1982). "To change a nation's cultural policy: The Kennedy administration and the arts in the United States, 1961–1963," in: Mulcahy, K. V. and Swaim, C. R. (eds), *Public Policy and the Arts*, 141–158. Boulder, CO: Westview Press.

Cummings, M. C. and Katz, R. S. (1987). *The patron state: government and the arts in Europe, North America, and Japan*. Oxford: Oxford University Press.

Feld, A., O'Hare, M. and Schuster, M. (1983). *Patrons despite themselves.* New York: New York University Press.

Felton, V. M. (1994). "Evidence in the existence of the cost disease in the performing arts," *Journal of Cultural Economics*, 18: 301–312.

Frey, B. S. and Pommerehne, W. W. (1989). *Muses and markets. Explorations in the economics of the arts.* Oxford: Basil Blackwell.

Friedman, M. and Friedman, R. D. (1980). *Free to choose.* New York: Harcourt Brace Jovanovich.

Geever, J. (2012). *The Foundation Center's guide to proposal writing*, sixth edition. New York: Foundation Center.

Hansmann, H. (1986). "Non profit enterprise in the performing arts," in DiMaggio, P. J. (ed.), *Nonprofit Enterprise in the Arts*, 17–40. New York: Oxford University Press.

Hillman-Chartrand, H. and Mccaughey, C. (1989). "The arms length principle and the arts: An international perspective – past, present and future," in Cummings, M. and Schuster, M. (eds), *Who's to pay for the arts? The international search for models of arts support*, 43–80. New York: ACA Books.

Koob, A. (2021). *Key facts on U.S. nonprofits and foundations, 2021*, Candid, Issue Lab. Available at https://search.issuelab.org/resource/key-facts-on-u-s-nonprofits-and-foundations-2021.html.

Lévy-Garboua, L. and Montmarquette, C. (2003). "Demand," in Towse, R. (ed.), *A Handbook of Cultural Economics*, 177–189. Cheltenham: Edward Elgar.

Lewis, J. (2000). "Designing a cultural policy," in Bradford, G., Gary, M. and Wallach, G. (eds), *The politics of culture: policy perspectives for individuals, institutions and communities*, 79-93 New York: The New Press.

Mancini, G. (2022). "L'Art bonus batte la crisi: in otto anni donazioni per oltre 690 milioni," *Il Sole 24 Ore*, 29 June.

Mankin, L. (1982). "Government patronage: An historical overview," in Mulcahy, K. V. and Swaim, C. R. (eds), *Public policy and the arts.* pp. 111-127 Boulder, CO: Westview Press.

McCarthy, K. C., Ondaatje, E. J., Zakaras, L. and Brooks, A. (2004). *Gifts of the muse,* Santa Monica, CA: RAND.

Mulcahy, K. V. (2000). "The government and cultural patronage. A comparative analysis of cultural patronage in the United States, France, Norway and Canada," in Cherbo, J. M. and Wyzsomirski, M. J. (eds), *The public life of the arts in America*, 138–169. New Brunswick, NJ: Rutgers University Press.

Netzer, D. (1978). *The subsidized muse. Public support for the arts in the United States.* Cambridge: Cambridge University Press.

O'Hagan, J. W. (1998). *The state and the arts: An analysis of key economic policy issues in Europe and the United States.* Cheltenham: Edward Elgar.

Odendahl, T. J. (1990). *Charity begins at home: Generosity and self-interest among the philanthropic elite.* New York: Basic Books.

OECD (2022). *The culture fix: Creative people, places and industries.* Paris: OECD Publishing.

Peacock, A. (1993). *Paying the piper: Culture, music, money.* Edinburgh: Edinburgh University Press.

Putnam, R. D., Leonardi, R. and Nanetti., R. Y. (1992). *Making democracy work: Civic traditions in modern Italy.* Princeton, NJ: Princeton University Press.

Reich, R. (2020). *Just giving: Why philanthropy is failing democracy and how it can do better.* Princeton, NJ: Princeton University Press.

Schuster, M. (1988). "Government leverage of private support: Matching grants and problem with "new" money," in Wyszomirski, M. (ed.), *The cost of culture: Patterns and prospects of private arts patronage*, 63–97. New York: ACA Books, American Council for the Arts.

Scitovsky, T. (1989). "Culture is a good thing: A welfare-economic judgement," *Journal of Cultural Economics*, 13 (1): 1–13.

Seaman, B. A. (2006). "Empirical studies of demand for the performing arts," in Ginsburgh, V. A. and Throsby, D. (eds), *Handbook of the Economics of Art and Culture* (Vol. 1), 415–472. Amsterdam: Elsevier.

Throsby, D. (2010). *The economics of cultural policy.* Cambridge: Cambridge University Press.

Towse, R. (2010). *A textbook of cultural economics.* Cambridge: Cambridge University Press.

Turrini, A. (2007). *Politiche management pubblico per l'arte e la cultura.* Milan: Egea.

Turrini, A., O'Hare, M. and Borgonovi, F., (2008) "The border conflict between the present and the past: Programming classical music and opera," *Journal of Arts Management, Law, and Society*, spring issue: 71–88.

Turrini, A. (2005). "Finanziamenti alternativi nei servizi pubblici: i voucher per le istituzioni culturali," *Economia & Management*, 3: 89–101.

Turrini, A. and Voss, Z. (2020). "Strategic fundraising in the arts: The mistake of selling," in: Addis, M. and Rurale A. (eds), *Managing Cultural Business*, 280–310. London: Routledge.

Tyrrell, T. J. and Johnston, R. J. (2001), "A framework for assessing direct economic impacts of tourist events: Distinguishing origins, destinations, and causes of expenditures," *Journal of Travel Research*, 40: 94–100.

West, E. G. (1986). "Arts vouchers to replace grants," *Economic Affairs*, 6 (3): 9–16.

Wyszomirski M. J. and Mulcahy, K. V. (1995). "The organization of public support for the arts," in: Mulcahy, K. V. and Wyszomirski, M. J., *America's commitment to culture. government and the arts*, 121-143. Boulder, CO: Westview Press.

# Part III
# Processes

# 7 Planning Fundraising for the Arts

by *Janet Clarkson Davis*

## 7.1 Purpose of a fundraising plan

> "Our goals can only be reached through a vehicle of a plan, in which we must fervently believe, and upon which we must vigorously act. There is no other route to success."
> – Pablo Picasso

Tied inexorably to an organization's strategic plan, the fundraising plan lays out the targets, strategies, estimated financial projections and resource requirements, and timeline that the fundraising team has designed in its pursuit of operating, capital and special project contributed income objectives set by the executive team and board of the organization. This chapter addresses the components that should be included in a fundraising plan and the people, process, and technology through which a plan is conceived, deployed and monitored. Emphasis is placed on ensuring that readers have the understanding and skills necessary to build a plan as well as strategies to secure organizational buy-in and endorsement by artistic and administrative leadership.

The conception and presentation of artistic and cultural programs is a process that begins years in advance of an audience's presence in a concert hall or gallery. Engaging artists, codifying the vision, funding design and creating the work are just a few of the activities that require in-depth planning and strategy for a successful opening. Arts administrators and boards recognize and invest in this process through the creation of multi-year strategic artistic and operational plans. However, securing the contributed income that will fund the presentation of these programs is frequently addressed far too late with little strategy and collaboration. Consequently, fundraising for arts and cultural organizations often does not produce financial results that transformational programming requires and deserves.

The purpose of a fundraising plan is to provide a three- to five-year road map for the staff and volunteers who have been tasked with securing contributed revenue in support of the mission of the organization. The plan is in close alignment with the artistic vision, strategic plan and business operating plan that have been created and adopted by artistic, administrative and governing leadership (i.e., the board). It captures the tactical aspects as well as the nuances of fundraising and, when thoughtful and comprehensive, serves as the framework upon which the long-term work of relationship development can thrive.

Practitioners may be tempted by "time-saving" products such as "An easy template for fundraising planning" or "Three simple steps to an effective fundraising plan." However, what may be gained by spending less time on the planning process or by involving fewer people is far outweighed by what is lost in short-cutting the planning process: understanding, inclusion, consensus, competitiveness, agility, innovation and ultimately financial sustainability. These elements are at the core of a comprehensive fundraising planning process.

Contributed income often comprises 40 per cent or more of an arts or cultural organization's income budget. Unfortunately, not-for-profit organizations (particularly arts and cultural ones) are often under-led, under-planned and under-resourced in the fundraising areas responsible for seeking that contributed income. Therefore, it comes as no surprise that in the United States, arts and cultural organizations historically receive only 5–7 per cent of total philanthropic giving in any given year (CECP, 2021).[1] Talented fundraising professionals and specialists are often lured away from positions in the arts to health, education and human services organizations – attracted not only by more competitive compensation packages, but also by these organizations' willingness and desire to invest in multi-year planning and growth. There are of course other market factors that impact these disappointing statistics about giving to the arts, but investing in leadership and planning is a primary means of igniting enduring change.

---

[1] As of 2020, this is at 4–5 per cent.

## 7.2 Components of a fundraising plan

A fundraising plan is a set of documents addressing five main components: some departmental goals and targets, a fundraising team, some articulated fundraising strategies, a pro-forma department budget and a suite of reports and dashboard. When complete, the fundraising plan is presented to the executive team and/or the board. The objective of this presentation is to secure clarity and agreement between the leadership of the arts organization and the fundraising team regarding the amount of contributed income to be raised and the related cash flow; the proposed fundraising strategies to achieve the objective; the structure of the fundraising team and skills necessary to do the job; the estimate of what it will cost to complete the approach and the corresponding ROI, and the recommended approach to measurement and reporting. In the following paragraphs, we describe the detailed content of each component.

### 7.2.1 *Department goals and targets*

Although the primary purpose of the fundraising department is financial – to secure contributed income – the achievement of this purpose is reliant upon reaching targets in other three functional areas: donors' relations, departmental operations and HR.

These targets are set in collaboration with the executive team and the board, and are driven by the overarching goals of the arts organization's strategic plan and the supporting business operating plan. As the fundraising department develops its targets, the team should consider that the targets will be monitored on a dashboard that is updated each week and presented to the executive team and the board on a regular basis. Targets should be inspirational, rational, achievable and measurable.

Financial targets are the first primary goal area of a fundraising plan. They are straightforward: income, expense and ROI. The contributed income target for the fundraising department is derived from the overall annual income budget for the organization in any given fiscal year (see Box 7.1.) There may be a secondary target in this area set for contributed capital or special project income that is required by the capital or special project budget for the organization in any given fiscal year. Contributed income targets should be expressed not only for a total annual number, but also for a monthly target that informs cash flow planning by the chief

**Box 7.1 How to set contributed income targets for an educational program**

The board and the executive team create an organizational strategic plan that demands growth in the educational program over a five-year period. The education department works with the executive team and the board to set specific, measurable outputs and outcomes related to this growth. (This could include output targets related to the number of students served, multi-year educational outcomes or evolving community impact.) The education department next determines the initiatives it recommends to reach these targets and estimates the direct and indirect costs of people, processes and technologies that will be required to implement its initiatives on an annual basis over the five-year period. A supporting five-year operating pro forma expense budget is developed that outlines the marginal expenses related to the acquisition/growth of these resources. Following the estimation of the expense budget, the education department works with the finance department and the marketing department to estimate the earned income that will be associated with the initiatives, such as tuition and fees. If the estimated earned income does not cover the estimated expenses, the department might request contributed income via restricted grants or via a share of contributed income as a supplement. Each department completes this planning exercise, and the resulting documents create the five-year business operating plan. In the event that the demands on contributed income are not within a reasonable range from year to year, it is likely that the department heads will need to revise expense budgets accordingly.

financial officer (CFO). Each department, including the artistic, curatorial or production departments, completes this exercise, and the total contributed income requirement is estimated as a sum. The total of the contributed income needs for all departments over this five-year period is the primary driver of contributed income targets for the fundraising department. It is the responsibility of the leader of the fundraising team to evaluate the feasibility of contributed income goals in the context of the plan, and to participate in the executive team's conversations regarding the overall business operating plan. Once agreement has been reached about the goals, they are submitted to the board for approval.

Financial contributed income targets are then subdivided into sources based on type of grouping and appeal. Allocations might vary between industry verticals based on best practices, market and history. For example, a theatre in a large metropolitan service area might allocate its contributed income targets between the following department divisions:

1. *Individual giving* (75 per cent of the overall goal – includes board giving)
   - General memberships
   - Major gifts/patron level memberships
   - Direct response appeals (direct mail, email, social media)
2. *Institutional giving* (15 per cent of the overall goal)
   - Corporate giving
   - Corporate memberships
   - Foundations
   - Government grants (local, regional, State, national)
3. *Events* (10 per cent of the overall goal)
   - Planned giving-realized gifts (usually not budgeted, but estimated)

The determined expense budget for the fundraising department in any given fiscal year is a goal that is set by the fundraising department. This includes personnel, costs of implementing fundraising appeals, administrative costs, technology, communications and events. Setting a target for cost per dollar raised (CPDR) is an industry best practice that refers to the concept that fundraising should be measured not only in total dollars raised, but also in ROI. To better understand their nature, these expenses can be divided into different categories, as highlighted in Table 7.1.

Donor relations targets are the second goal area of a fundraising plan. Donor relations is often equivalent to customer relations. This component of fundraising focuses on the investment of time and resources in activities that increase the level of loyalty between a donor and the organization, with the objective of longevity and increased giving over time. These objectives, together resulting in a concept referred to as "lifetime value of a donor," are discussed in depth in Chapter 3. As seen, this is an area that provides an opportunity for joint planning between the fundraising department and the marketing department, given that donors often begin their relationship with an arts organization as a ticket buyer, subscriber or member. The lifetime journey of such a customer must take into consideration the differences between the transactional nature of a ticket purchase versus the relationship development nature of philan-

*Table 7.1* Expenses plan to set financial targets

**General expenses**

a. HR – training and professional development for fundraising professionals, including memberships in industry-specific professional associations, attendance at conferences, executive coaching or further educational opportunities
b. HR – teambuilding for members of the development department, which can involve activities focused on developing trust, sharing knowledge, or industry-related social activities
c. HR – recruitment of new team members
d. IT – donor software/research specific to the development of leads for direct response appeals, screening lists for broad groups of prospects or the development of individual prospect profiles
e. IT – hardware, including laptops/pcs/and handheld devices that allow development officers secure and simple access to donor records, contact information, reporting, and data entry
f. IT – website, members of the fundraising team will have input into the development of website functionality, especially regarding messaging, links to giving mechanisms, and content related to case for support
g. office supplies
h. legal fees
i. credit card fees
j. stationery – including paper, card and envelopes
k. data hygiene – National Change of Address (annual)
l. communications
m. meals – for team meetings, committee meetings and staff meetings as appropriate
n. travel (including mileage) to non-donor related meetings and events
o. lodging and meals for conference attendance
p. printing of general collateral
q. postage related to general office mail and shipping
r. memberships and subscriptions to various professional associations and publications
s. gifts for volunteers and special project leaders
t. miscellaneous

**Individual giving expense**

a. stewardship/benefit fulfilment including premiums, concession tickets, complimentary tickets to organizational events and costs related to ticketing services
b. acquisition
   i. donor experience
   ii. outsource campaign
   iii. design and printing
   iv. postage
e. renewal
   i. renewal printing
   ii. renewal postage/mailshot services
   iii. business reply
d. upgrade
   i. research: prospect profiles
   ii. cultivation – 1:1 meals
   iii. total

| Major gifts expense: |
|---|
| a. stewardship/benefits fulfilment |
| b. printing |
| c. upgrade |
| d. cultivation |
| **Institutional giving** |
| a. corporate membership and sponsorship benefits fulfilment |
| b. foundation and government travel and cultivation |
| c. corporate foundation travel and cultivation |

thropic motivation. Donors' engagement is the first target in donor relations building. For purposes of the fundraising plan, donors should be considered customers of the fundraising department. Donors who consider themselves to be part of an organization (often taking an interest in the "behind the scenes" aspects of the work) are more likely to invest over and above the cost of admission or performance. Setting targets for levels of engagement (as perceived by both the staff and by the donors) ensures that staff are focused on working with colleagues throughout the organization to create opportunities for donors to feel as if they are an active and involved part of the organization's mission. Examples of this type of target could be "On the annual donor survey, 95 per cent of donors rate their level of engagement as "deeply engaged" or "80 per cent of donor participation rate in our volunteer workday." Measuring progress towards these targets should also delve into the relativity between higher levels of engagement with higher levels of household giving on an annual as well as a trending basis. Similar in nature to donor engagement, donors' satisfaction measures how donors feel about their relationship with the organization. Targets in this area could include statements such as "85 per cent of donors are highly satisfied with the level of communications they receive about the organization" or "Most donors feel satisfied with the number of events associated with their donation." Satisfaction is more likely to involve the service received through the box office, gift shop and restaurant/café or concessions operations.

The establishment of operational targets ultimately tied to team performance not only provides direction and focus for team members, but also justifies organizational leadership for investment in operational assets, including technology, HR, training and maintenance. This is the area of measurement most often *passé* in a fundraising department, frequently resulting in donor databases that are outdated and atrophying; team members whose skills are not competitive compared with their peers in health and human services or higher education organizations, poor relations with the finance department, and departmental policies and procedures that are irrelevant and out of date, exposing the department to risk. This can be clarified by sharing a simple example. Envision a direct-response fundraising appeal that is scheduled to be mailed to a large segment of the database of donors and prospects. For the appeal to reap results that meet expectations of gross as well as net income, the database must contain accurate contact information, be configured so that it can generate a list of the desired targets based on select attributes, be able to generate the list in a format that is efficiently used for mail merge and production either internally or by a third party and be configured so that gifts made in response to the appeal can be attributed to that appeal and reported appropriately. If these criteria are not met, the appeal will likely fail and cost the organization more than it earns. In a related example, even if the database meets the criteria listed earlier, the appeal will likely fail and cost the organization more than it earns if the team member responsible for managing the extraction of the list, the formatting of the appeal and the coding of the gifts is not properly trained. It may seem obvious that an organization would naturally focus on these operational areas. However, many arts and cultural organizations, especially those that are small to mid-sized, tend to set targets and objectives exclusive of operational performance and ignore the relationship between operational targets and financial targets. As a result, cuts to administrative operations budgets are made first if the need arises to cut expenses, often simultaneously with increases in financial income targets. In this case, the department has failed to make the case that the ability to succeed in reaching fundraising targets necessitates appropriate investment in fundraising operations. Marketing departments and fundraising departments often compete for resources. Just as a fundraising department requires investment to reach its targets, a marketing department requires parallel investment. The structure of access to operational resources and the deployment of those assets in any given sales and fundraising cycle is an opportunity to develop synergies between the departments by creating not a donor-centric or audience-centric culture, but rather by joining the two in a customer-centric culture. It can be beneficial to create a seamless and culture-based process for the weekly sharing of information, conflict resolution and creative problem-solving that involves all members of the marketing and fundraising departments. Targets for departmental operations are independent of the policies, procedures and structures of the department, which should be captured in annual work plans. Operational targets should be set in the following areas:

- donor information management (data cleanliness, clarity of policies and procedures, existence and consistency of communications);
- gift processing information management (in partnership with the finance department);
- communications technology (strategy, timing and quality of communications);
- reporting and dashboards (relevance, accuracy, consistency).

HR targets are set to ensure that the recruitment, hiring, training and retaining of professional fundraising staff is a priority for the organization. These targets should be developed in partnership with the HR office. In addition, the efficient and effective use of volunteers should be purposefully conceived and monitored. HR targets can include:

- employee satisfaction;
- professional development;
- achievement of skills and certifications;
- retention rate;
- interest in the organization by other professionals;
- quality of relationships with previous employees.

As members of the fundraising team work with their managers to set performance plans it is helpful to articulate whether the team members are novice, intermediate or masters of any given competency. This allows for conversation about growth and opportunity in employee satisfaction and professional development.

### 7.2.2 *Fundraising team*

Raising money for charitable causes is not a new endeavor. Charitable giving is referenced and encouraged in ancient religious texts for many faiths, and formally dates back to the 17th century. Leaping forward, fundraising in America began in the modern era in the early 20th century, furthered by the Revenue Act of 1913, which exempted organizations devoted to "religious, charitable, scientific or educational purposes" from paying federal income tax and prompted a distinct non-profit sector. As reported by the National Philanthropic Trust:[2]

> 1919: For the first time, Harvard University employs professional fundraisers to manage an endowment fund drive. Alumnus John Price Jones (1877–1964) leads the campaign, which raises USD 14.2 million in less than a year. Jones goes on to establish his own fundraising firm, among the first of its kind. More and more institutions follow Harvard's example, turning to professionals to wage effective campaigns and giving birth to a new line of work.

Since these early years, the profession of fundraising has grown significantly. In 1987, the Center on Philanthropy was founded at Indiana University,[3] with the mission,

> To increase the understanding of philanthropy and improve its practice through research, teaching, public service, and public affairs. The Center's goals include analyzing and interpreting the philanthropic process of associating, giving, and volunteering; teaching theory and best practices related to the philanthropic process and nonprofit structures; and providing public service and continuing education to volunteers and practitioners in the nonprofit sector.

With this step, the profession of fundraising moved from something fundraisers found themselves doing to a career choice.

Today, fundraising teams at major arts and cultural organizations are recognized as specialized professionals. That said, small- to mid-sized organizations often rely on the managing director (MD) or the marketing director to develop and operate a critical fundraising function. It is important for students and practitioners to understand and recognize the wide spectrum of types and members of fundraising teams.

The people who are responsible for researching, cultivating, soliciting and acknowledging donors who provide gifts and grants to arts and culture organizations are called a development or fundraising team or department.

---

[2] https://www.nptrust.org/.

[3] https://philanthropy.iupui.edu/.

Depending on the size of the organization, this group of people might be composed of a mix of professionals and volunteers. The leader of this department has the title of director of development, chief development officer, director of advancement or chief advancement officer. This person reports to the CEO, ED or MD of the organization. In some instances, a fundraising team is part of an external affairs team that might include marketing, public relations and fundraising. Figure 7.1 outlines three levels of organizational chart for various sized arts and culture organizations.

The fundraising plan should include not only current staff, but also outline, as contributed income targets increase, which team members will be added and at what cost, with associated expectations about income generation by each employee as appropriate. The department will be able to grow in size as annual contributions reach certain targets, and in association with growth in anticipation of a capital or capacity-guiding campaign. There will be cycles of years of investment when the CPDR is higher, and years of high return when the CPDR is lower, because the team is efficient and focused on higher level giving. Management should be oriented to these cycles as they will be included in the plan as part of the pro-forma budget is adjustments in compensation packages. In addition, the creators of the plan should reference industry and market research regarding salary or hourly compensation packages presented as part of the plan. Also included on the team are volunteers, and the fundraising plan should take into consideration the time and focus necessary

*Figure 7.1* Different sizes of a development/fundraising department

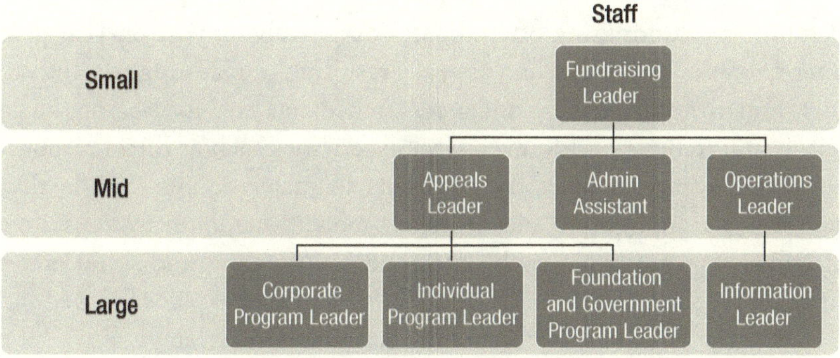

Staff

Small: Fundraising Leader

Mid: Appeals Leader; Admin Assistant; Operations Leader

Large: Corporate Program Leader; Individual Program Leader; Foundation and Government Program Leader; Information Leader to recruit, train and retain volunteers over time. Volunteers are often organized in a development committee staffed by the fundraising team, comprising leaders of the various strategies outlined in the fundraising strategies, who serve to provide community-based assistance. An example development committee structure is presented in Figure 7.2.

It is appropriate to ask both the paid staff and the volunteer members of the fundraising team to track how they spend their time – for example, how many hours a week a staff person spends writing grants, or how many hours a week a volunteer spends calling donors to thank them for their support. Tracking this time allows the measurement of ROI for HR.

*Figure 7.2* A development committee structure

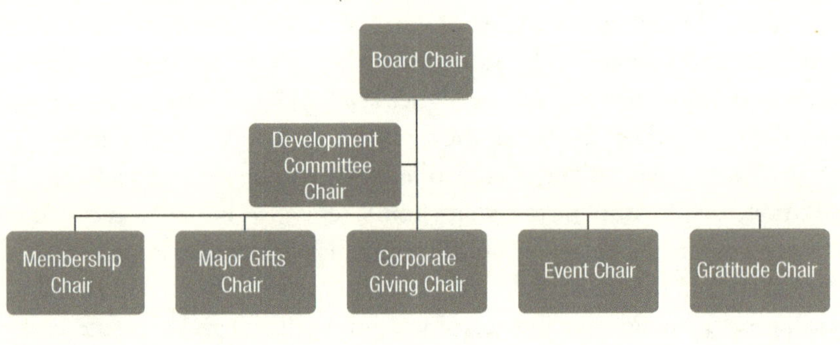


### 7.2.3 *Fundraising strategies*

Planning for fundraising often focuses exclusively on year-on-year planning for various divisions and appeals, resulting in plans for arts and cultural organizations that are under-researched and over-focused on the details of quarterly, monthly, even weekly activities such as direct response, openings, events, newsletters and visits to major donors. While these activities are appropriate and necessary tools to maintain in the suite of offerings that are deployed by the fundraising team, and some mix of these and other appeals should be included in the workplans for the fundraising office, none can be accurately described as a strategy. For a set of fundraising initiatives to work interactively toward a contributed income target, the initiatives and their corresponding appeals must be conceived as a result of the development of competitive fundraising strategy.

Michael E. Porter is widely recognized as a primary authority on strategy. His ground-breaking book entitled *Competitive strategy*, published in 1980, is recognized as having challenged industry to reframe corporate planning to focus not only on profit, but also on the "five forces" that should inform decision-making. In 1996, Porter re-evaluated and streamlined the topic of strategy in an article for the *Harvard Business Review* entitled "What is strategy?." In this article, Porter states that "Competitive strategy is about being different. It means deliberately choosing a different set of activities to deliver a unique mix of value" (Porter, 1996: 39).

Porter's theories from 1996 were evaluated and summarized in the subsequent article, "What is strategy, again" by Andrea Ovans. In it, she states:

> A tour de force by any measure "What Is Strategy?" is certainly required reading for all strategists. But it was far from the final word. One could perhaps usefully divide the vast universe of subsequent strategy ideas into those that focus on:
> - Doing something new.
> - Building on what you already do.
> - Reacting opportunistically to emerging possibilities. (Ovans, 2015: 4)

Extrapolated for purposes of fundraising strategy, the three ideas just noted argue that while standard categories of fundraising appeals are consistently and appropriately used by the majority of arts and culture organizations, the means by which these activities are deployed and the way that they are integrated should be unique to each organization and relatable to those strategic categories. Fundraising leaders should exercise discipline in preparing fundraising plans, and not vault from goals to initiatives and appeals without considering whether these initiatives and appeals are strategic in nature given market considerations and past performance. Fundraising strategies should be designed to support the pursuit of the departmental goals already described. If a strategy or an initiative does not advance the department toward the approved goals, then that strategy should be reconsidered for a different time or set aside.

Fundraising departments are supported by well-intentioned volunteers and donors who are often keen to suggest ideas such as events, appeals and communications ("Let's do a run/golf tournament/wine tasting!"). These ideas may or may not be rational, achievable, profitable or appropriate for a given community. More importantly, these ideas may not be relevant to the strategies that have been laid out by the professional staff. Explaining to a volunteer that his or her idea is not rational, achievable or profitable can be awkward. However, when the department has a comprehensive fundraising plan that is rooted in a well-thought-out strategy, that conversation becomes much simpler, giving the volunteer or donor the opportunity to understand how appeals are linked to strategy. Conversely, the staff could provide a framework in which to consider volunteers' ideas that could be innovative and effective in the right setting.

Figure 7.3 outlines examples of goals, strategies and initiatives. For each goal, there may be two or three strategies; for each strategy, there

*Figure 7.3* Examples of goals, strategies and initiatives in an arts organization's fundraising plan

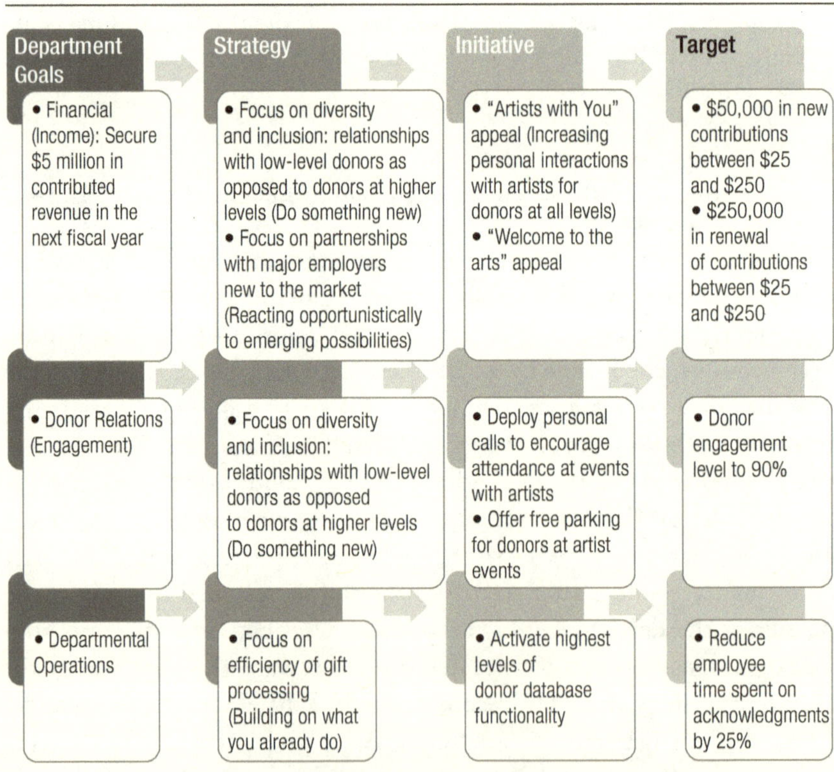

may be two or three initiatives. Strategies can be supported by initiatives, and ultimately appeals, in more than one goal area. For each initiative, there is a target. While appeals are not included in the fundraising plan, they should be included in the department work plans established once the fundraising plan is complete.

### 7.2.4 *Pro forma department budget*

A pro forma statement is a financial statement based on hypothetical scenarios. It is useful when planning, especially when testing assumptions about what a department can expect over time. It is a "what if" tool that allows a team to evaluate various options when considering the income and expense opportunities for the fundraising department. The pro forma budget should be fairly high level and does not require the amount of detail that will be necessary for department budgets. The template for the pro forma should be built at the beginning of the planning process so that it can be used throughout as a worksheet and checkpoint in terms of testing ideas. It should plan three to five years forward and include the following schedules:

- direct margin analysis (a summary of income, expense, and ROI);
- contributed income;
- fundraising staff compensation;
- fundraising initiative direct expenses;
- administrative expenses.

The pro forma should be used as a tool to evaluate the income and expenses related to various fundraising initiatives in pursuit of the total contributed income goals. An example of the pro forma direct margin analysis schedule is outlined in Figure 7.4.

As fundraising strategies and corresponding initiatives are envisaged during the planning process, estimates for resource requirements should be entered in the pro forma on the appropriate schedule. For example, the first initiative presented in Figure 7.3 ("Artists with You" appeal) has a total income target of $300,000 ($50,000 in new contributions plus $250,000 in renewals) and it might have an estimated cost of $10,000 (cost of the direct response campaign.) The income and expense estimates will be entered as line items of the contributed income and fundraising

*Figure 7.4* A pro forma direct margin analysis schedule

**Organization A**

*Proforma Financial Analysis - Cash Basis*

*Schedule 1 - Fundraising Direct Margin Analysis*

*Aug-20*

| | **Current Year** | **Plan Y1** | **Plan Y2** | **Plan Y3** | **Plan Y4** |
|---|---|---|---|---|---|
| **Contributed Income** | **$ 3,500,000** | **$ 3,900,000** | **$ 4,250,000** | **$ 4,500,000** | **$ 5,000,000** |
| **Expenses** | | | | | |
| Fundraising Staffing (excludes benefits) | $ (493,472) | $ (535,416) | $ (550,000) | $ (600,000) | $ (650,000) |
| Fundraising Initiatives (total) | $ (150,000) | $ (160,000) | $ (165,000) | $ (170,000) | $ (175,000) |
| Donor Relations | $ (10,000) | $ (12,500) | $ (14,000) | $ (16,000) | $ (17,000) |
| Administrative | $ (50,000) | $ (52,500) | $ (55,000) | $ (57,500) | $ (60,000) |
| *Total* | **$ (703,472)** | **$ (760,416)** | **$ (784,000)** | **$ (843,500)** | **$ (902,000)** |
| **Total Fundraising Expenses** | **$ (703,472)** | **$ (760,416)** | **$ (784,000)** | **$ (843,500)** | **$ (902,000)** |
| **Direct Margin from Fundraising Operations** | **$ 2,796,528** | **$ 3,139,584** | **$ 3,466,000** | **$ 3,656,500** | **$ 4,098,000** |
| **ROI** | **4.0** | **4.1** | **4.4** | **4.3** | **4.5** |
| **Cost to Raise $1** | **$ 0.20** | **$ 0.19** | **$ 0.18** | **$ 0.19** | **$ 0.18** |

initiative direct costs schedules. Once estimates for income, expenses, staffing, donor relations and administration have been completed, the direct margin schedule, which is linked to the income and expense schedules, will calculate direct margin and ROI.

As the group plans for year-on-year growth, it must maintain rational expectations. What might be considered reasonable growth for total contributed income financial goals over time? Usually, this is 5 per cent to 7 per cent per year: 10 per cent or more would be considered high in the non-profit sector. A three-year rolling average of ROI for a fundraising department should approach four to five times. That is, the total amount invested in fundraising should result in a four to five times return.

Another way to state this kind of measurement is the CPDR, which on a three-year rolling average should have a target of $18–20. The three-year rolling average is important because any given year might be a growth year, when a new position is added to the team or a significant investment is made in technology, for example. In those years, the return on that investment will not be high because the person or the technology requires time to generate results. In subsequent years, however (provided the investment is a good one), income will increase, and a significant improvement will be made to the ROI until it is time to grow again.

The pro forma tool is a critical planning tool that allows the fundraising team to make its case to the executive team for why spending money on the fundraising team and initiatives is a necessary investment as contributed income goals increase over time. Each year, the pro forma will be rolled into the departmental and organizational budgets in collaboration with the finance department.

### 7.2.5 *Suite of reports and dashboard*

Communicating the status of fundraising results is a primary responsibility of the fundraising team. This communication allows the executive team and the board to understand how to evaluate and respond to the success or failures of fundraising initiatives. The primary measure of overall performance is the department dashboard. This should be a one-page summary of the status of the major goals and objectives of the department. It should clearly and concisely communicate whether the fundraising department is on track to meet its goals, and should be prepared on a weekly basis for presentation to the executive team. Figures 7.5 and 7.6 show respectively a weekly dashboard and a sample suite of reports, including the primary audience(s) for each report and the timing of delivery of those reports.

*Figure 7.5* Weekly performance dashboard

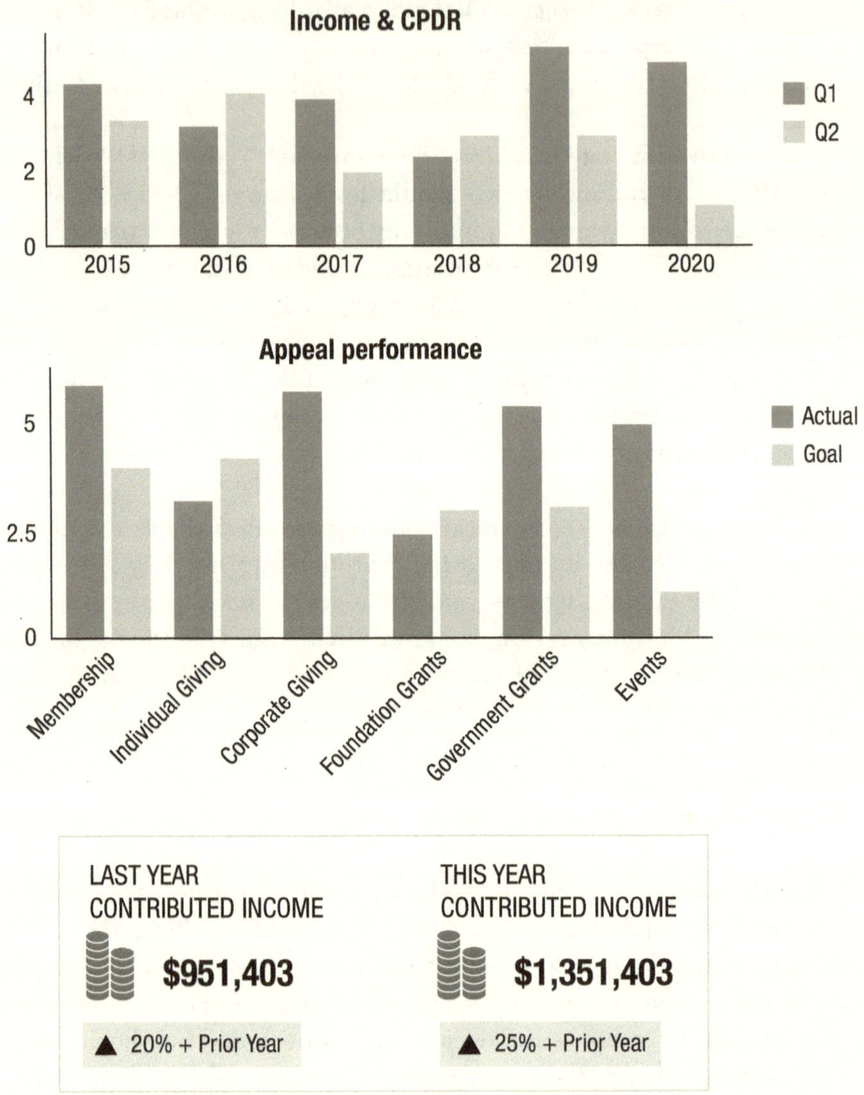

**Income & CPDR**

4
2
0
2015 2016 2017 2018 2019 2020
Q1
Q2

**Appeal performance**

5
2.5
0
Membership
Individual Giving
Corporate Giving
Foundation Grants
Government Grants
Events
Actual
Goal

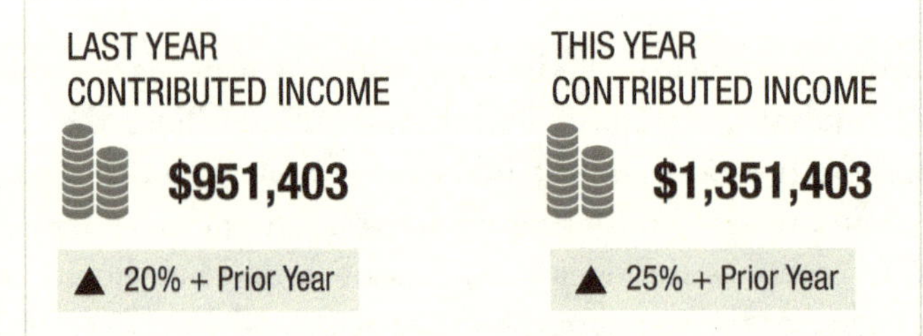

*Figure 7.6* Reporting

| Report Name | Frequency | Description | Primary User(s) | Generated By | Report Type |
|---|---|---|---|---|---|
| Fundraising Status Report | Weekly | YTD Goal v. actual of campaigns, funds appeals: Sums | Fundraising Leader | Fundraising Coordinator | Gift/Pledge |
| Individual Giving Status Report | Weekly | YTD Goal v. Actual | Individual Giving Leader | Membership Coordinator | Gift/Pledge |
| Corporate Giving Status Report | Weekly | YTD Goal v. Actual | Dir. Of Inst. Giving | Inst. Giving Coordinator | Gift/Pledge |
| Duplicate/ Incomplete Accounts Report | Weekly | Duplicate Incomplete accounts and fields requiring cleanup | Fundraising Coordinator | Fundraising Coordinator | Constituent Management |
| Monthly Reconciliation Report | Monthly | List of transactions for Previous Month | Fundraising Coordinator/ Finance | Fundraising Coordinator | Portfolio Management |
| Acknowledgement Report | Weekly | List of gifts requiring acknowledgement | Directors/ Managers/ Asst. to the Director | Fundraising Coordinator | Stewardship |
| Pledge Reminder Report | Monthly: Beginning of Month | List of pledges requiring reminders | Fundraising Coordinator | Fundraising Coordinator | Gift/Pledge |
| Prospect Interaction Report | Weekly | List of all interactions scheduled for current week & previous week | Fundraising Leader | Fundraising Coordinator | Portfolio Management |
| Weekly Transaction Detail | Weekly: Monday | List of all transactions for previous week | Fundraising Leader | Fundraising Coordinator | Gift/Pledge |
| Daily Transactions | Daily | List of all transactions for current day | Executive Team | Fundraising Coordinator | Gift/Pledge |

## 7.3 Building the plan: participants and process

> "A total work of art is only possible in the context of the whole of society. Everyone will be a necessary co-creator of a social architecture, and so long as anyone cannot participate, the ideal form of democracy has not been reached."
> – Joseph Beuys

Once the purpose and components of a fundraising plan are understood, a group should be assembled and a process defined through which the plan can be created. As in an artistic process, the planning process is enhanced by the participation of members of an organization whose work will involve or be impacted by activities and results of plan outcomes. Participants in the fundraising plan should include all members of the staff and volunteer teams who gain insight from previous years, to learn from experts in various areas and to activate participation and understanding about fundraising across the organization. When members of the team are engaged in building the plan, there is a greater commitment to and understanding of the concept of a culture of gratitude and philanthropy.[4]

Fundraising for the arts is always unique, given the varied nature of organizations and the environments in which products are presented. Arts and cultural organizations are mostly highly social and highly visible in a community. As a result, activities related to cultivating donors are social and visible. The fundraising team will be present at openings, dinners and events at private homes. Volunteer fundraising team meetings are often held at large corporation headquarters, in the office of a volunteer or in a private club. Members of other teams in the organization sometimes misinterpret this kind of activity. However, when other teams are represented in the fundraising planning process, these activities are explained as to their purpose and importance. The inclusion of teams across the board therefore helps to remove silos of work that can often arise in arts and cultural organizations – and the them and us atmosphere that often describes the relationship between artistic and administrative departments.

---

[4] See also Chapter 2.

Not all the participants will be active in all aspects of planning. Each will be involved as appropriate to their position and relevance. Specifically, participants in the planning process should include:

- *All members of the fundraising team.*
- *CEO/ED/MD.* The leader of the organization, usually the CEO or ED who reports directly to the board of directors or trustees, is the chief fundraising officer for the organization. Although the leader of the fundraising/development department has responsibility for designing and deploying the fundraising plan and is ultimately held accountable for the achievement of the goals of the plan, the CEO or ED should be actively involved in developing relationships and soliciting contributions for the organization.
- *Artistic director/chief curator/music director.* The leader of the organization's artistic vision and programs should actively participate in donor cultivation and solicitations. This person is the individual with whom major donors will want to interact. To that end, the artistic department should be involved in contributing ideas about how to facilitate this kind of interaction into strategies for the fundraising plan.
- *Production director/company manager/artist liaison.* Interaction with artists is a key element of fundraising success, both for major donor prospects as well as for members and event attendees. It is critical for members of staff who interact directly with artists and their representatives to participate in the planning conversation so that expectations and plans can be managed from the outset.
- *CFO/controller.* The fundraising plan includes monthly and annualized income and expense budgets for the fundraising department as well as goals, actuals and forecasts for contributed income. The CFO or controller will have information pertaining to the overall financial plans for the organization that is relevant to this information. Conversely, the CFO will require schedules and reports regarding the accounting and batching of gifts and pledges, collections and cash flow forecasts for each fundraising appeal.
- *Board/fundraising volunteers.* One of the most important responsibilities of board members is to assist the fundraising department with securing contributions. There should be a position on the board for a fundraising chair. This person reports to the chair of the board

and is responsible for making fundraising reports to the board on a regular basis. When the fundraising plan is nearing completion, this person should be briefed on the plan and invited to make final adjustments as necessary. Additionally, if there are fundraising events such as galas and auctions that raise financially significant amounts for the organization, the volunteer chairs of these events should also participate in discussions about the fundraising plan.

In order to achieve its primary purpose, success in securing contributed revenue, the fundraising team must build a plan that is inspiring, actionable, logical, rational, measurable and flexible. The process involved in creating such a plan is time consuming and requires clear-eyed and diplomatic leadership as well as excellent facilitation. The leader of the fundraising team should not build the plan (or even a draft of the plan) independently or in isolation. That said, planning is not, nor should it be, the forte of all team members; however, it should be a strength of the leader of the fundraising team. Just as the leader of the organization should have planning skills, so should the leaders of each department. If the fundraising leader does not have adequate time to steer the planning process, hiring a consultant or facilitator or assigning the leadership of the planning process to a team member with excellent organizational skills to organize the process are both excellent options. This can be a learning opportunity for a team member whose career trajectory is leaning towards becoming a director of fundraising or development. The planning process flow should develop as described in Figure 7.7.

The planning process also includes four main organizational steps or phases, will require approximately three months to complete and should be completed in time for the leader of the fundraising department to finalize and advocate for the resources (expense budget) required to achieve the goals as a part of the annual organizational budgeting process – approximately two months before the next fiscal year. Because the fundraising plan is a three- to five-year plan, once the initial planning process is complete, updating the plan for the next two to four years is not as time consuming. Each phase of the plan will:

- involve various members of the planning team as appropriate;
- produce specific deliverables;
- work within an expected elapsed timeframe.

*Figure 7.7* Planning process flow

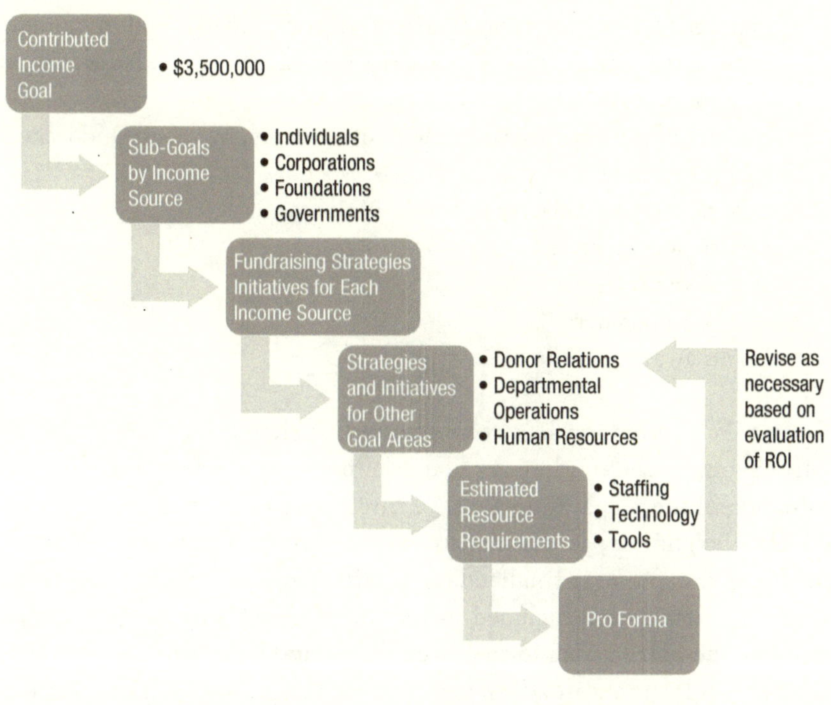


The objective of the first phase ("Prepare and Learn") is to ensure that the planning team is prepared with the information necessary to build a comprehensive plan. First and foremost, the team needs to understand what the executive team estimates for contributed income targets over time. Ideally, because the leader of the fundraising department is responsible for a significant amount of revenue for the organization, he or she has been an active participant in the development of the organization's three- to five-year strategic and operating plans and is therefore aware of and comfortable with the associated high-level contributed income targets. Second, the team will require contextual information that should include:

- an assessment of the organization's market placement as well as a competitive analysis for fundraising;

- historical financial performance of the fundraising department;
- an analysis of the lifetime value of the donor database;
- benchmarks for best practices locally, regionally and nationally within the organization's industry vertical (theatre, dance, visual art, opera, cultural center, etc.);
- surveys of fundraising team members, donors, members and ticket/admission buyers;
- experience and capacity of fundraising team;
- artistic footprint;
- size of house/facility;
- length in business;
- brand awareness and affinity.

Once this information has been amassed, it should be shared with all participants in the fundraising plan as a pre-read in advance of the culmination of the preparation phase: a three-hour kick-off meeting during which all planning participants are oriented to the planning process, the planning timeframe is finalized, and participants share their takeaways from the information included in the pre-read. This phase of planning requires the participants to step back from day-to-day work to gain perspective and context in advance of the planning process. This phase is also an opportunity for new team members to familiarize themselves with the department's structure and performance.

During the second phase ("Create"), participants are organized into groups that are assigned with creating the components of the plan as outlined in this chapter. Each group should be diverse in its composition, including relevant experts in each component area, representatives from the artistic department and key volunteers as appropriate. Each group will determine how many planning, design and review meetings it requires to prepare its deliverable component. The components of the plan that are driven by each meeting will address the question of the pro-forma and the annual contributed income goals for the entire team, and will be subdivided into targets for various sources. Figure 7.8 shows an example of how the high-level pro forma contributed income goal could be subdivided into these targets. Once these targets have been agreed upon, the plan components cascade from there into the discussion of fundraising strategies for each target. It is important to remember that this planning process is not intended to deliver details of work plans involved in implementing specific initiatives.

*Figure 7.8* High-level proforma contributed income budget

**Organization A**

*Proforma Financial Analysis - Cash Basis*

*Schedule 1 - Fundraising Direct Margin Analysis*

*Aug-20*

| | Current Year | Plan Y1 | Plan Y2 | Plan Y3 | Plan Y4 |
|---|---|---|---|---|---|
| **Contributed Income** | **$ 3,500,000** | **$ 3,900,000** | **$ 4,250,000** | **$ 4,500,000** | **$ 5,000,000** |
| **Expenses** | | | | | |
| Fundraising Staffing (excludes benefits) | $ (493,472) | $ (535,416) | $ (550,000) | $ (600,000) | $ (650,000) |
| Fundraising Initiatives (total) | $ (150,000) | $ (160,000) | $ (165,000) | $ (170,000) | $ (175,000) |
| Donor Relations | $ (10,000) | $ (12,500) | $ (14,000) | $ (16,000) | $ (17,000) |
| Administrative | $ (50,000) | $ (52,500) | $ (55,000) | $ (57,500) | $ (60,000) |
| *Total* | **$ (703,472)** | **$ (760,416)** | **$ (784,000)** | **$ (843,500)** | **$ (902,000)** |
| **Total Fundraising Expenses** | **$ (703,472)** | **$ (760,416)** | **$ (784,000)** | **$ (843,500)** | **$ (902,000)** |
| **Direct Margin from Fundraising Operations** | **$ 2,796,528** | **$ 3,139,584** | **$ 3,466,000** | **$ 3,656,500** | **$ 4,098,000** |
| **ROI** | **4.0** | **4.1** | **4.4** | **4.3** | **4.5** |
| **Cost to Raise $1** | **$ 0.20** | **$ 0.19** | **$ 0.18** | **$ 0.19** | **$ 0.18** |

| | Membership | Patron Membership | Corporate Membership | Artistic Projects | Education & Community Programming | Special Event | Small Events | General Operating | TOTAL |
|---|---|---|---|---|---|---|---|---|---|
| Individuals | $ 280,000 | $ 700,000 | | $ 600,000 | $ 25,000 | $ 800,000 | $ 60,000 | $ 140,000 | $ 2,605,000 |
| Corporations | | | $ 150,000 | $ 250,000 | $ 175,000 | $ 400,000 | $ 50,000 | $ 40,000 | $ 1,065,000 |
| Foundations | | | | $ 100,000 | $ 150,000 | $ 500,000 | $ 15,000 | $ 180,000 | $ 945,000 |
| Government | | | | $ 50,000 | $ 10,000 | $ – | $ – | $ 25,000 | $ 85,000 |
| | $ 280,000 | $ 700,000 | 150,000 | $ 1,000,000 | $ 360,000 | $ 1,700,000 | $ 125,000 | $ 385,000 | $ 3,500,000 |

The plan will require revision (Phase three: "Revise") to ensure that the target ROI is achieved. This process involves a negotiation between the managers responsible for each income area, source and the leader of the fundraising function, and should consider the concept of the three-year rolling CPDR discussed earlier in this chapter. Once compiled, the plan will be presented by the fundraising team to the executive team, and as a summary to the board (Phase four: "Present"). The team should plan to make minor revisions/improvements. Unless otherwise indicated in the organization's statutes, the fundraising plan does not require a vote of approval by the board.

*Figure 7.9* The 4 organizational phases in planning

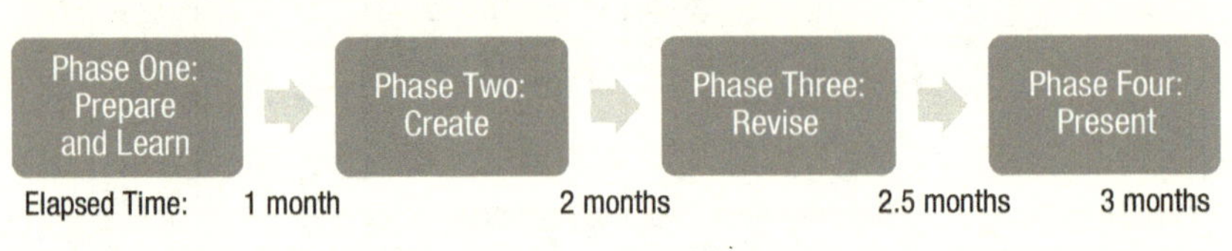


## 7.4 Using the plan and monitoring plan progress

The fundraising plan is a critical administrative project of an artistic or cultural organization, equal to the development of an artistic vision, strategic plan and business plan. The well-developed plan will be rooted in the contributed income targets prescribed by mission-related programming, and will include components related to goals, strategies, initiatives, targets and resource requirements. Success of the plan's implementation is driven by cross-departmental participation and consensus building. The executive team and the board should be made aware on a regular basis about the status of progress made toward plan objectives, and should be engaged in addressing any negative variances that may arise. Over time, a direct organizational investment in fundraising planning will increase the financial and therefore artistic sustainability of the organization. The planning process and its deliverables significantly advance arts and cultural organizations in terms of their ability to compete for contributed income, professional fundraising staff and, as a result, artistic outcomes.

Once complete, the targets of the fundraising plan are captured in the dashboard for the department. The dashboard is reviewed weekly by the leader of the fundraising team and the executive team. If the dashboard reflects performance outside a negative 2–3 per cent variance at any given time, the leader of the fundraising department will engage the fundraising team in a conversation about the performance deficit, whether the deficit can be reversed and the impact of the deficit on organizational finances. If the fundraising team cannot deploy measures to mitigate the negative variance, the board should be notified as a part of a monthly financial report. A secondary aspect of monitoring plan results

*Figure 7.10* The pipeline tool

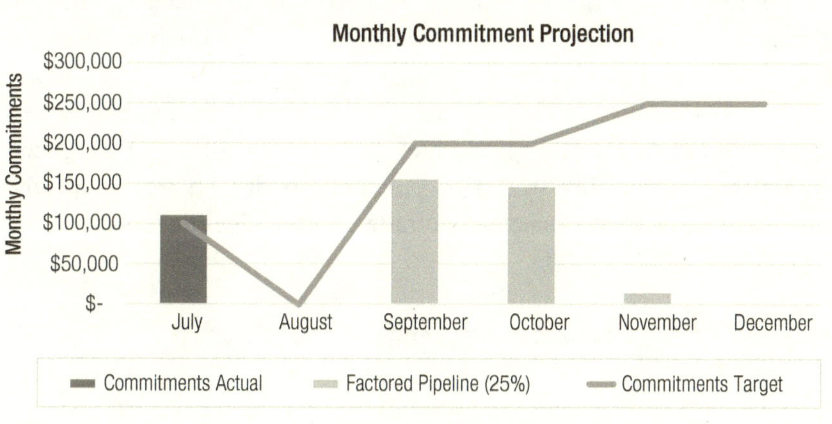


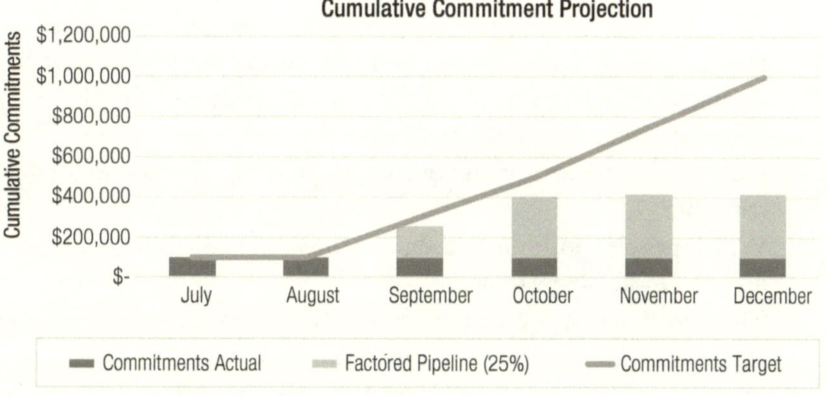

is accurate forecasting – reviewing the pipeline of active prospects and potential contributions. From a basic perspective, a pipeline measures target monthly and cumulative commitments versus actual commitments and commitments that are scheduled to be solicited. Figure 7.10 is an example of a pipeline tool.

The executive team and the board monitor the pipeline and the dashboard in collaboration with the CFO to ensure synergy between expectations and performance of the fundraising team in the context of its financial goals.

## Keywords for arts fundraisers

Fundraising plan, business operating plan, contributed income, cash flow; financial target, dashboard, chief financial officer (CFO), individual giving, institutional giving, expense budget, cost per dollar raised (CPDR), return on investment (ROI), donors' relations targets, operational targets, human resources (HR) targets, chief development officer, development committee, fundraising strategies, pro forma budget, direct cost, direct margin analysis, direct margin, planning process, pipeline tool

## Suggested questions for meetings and discussion

- What planning tools are useful in fundraising for the arts?
- What are the main components of a fundraising plan?
- What metrics should be used to monitor a fundraising process?
- How important is the learning process during the planning, monitoring and implementing of fundraising activities for the arts? What mistakes should be avoided?
- How would you design an effective fundraising plan for an arts institution?
- Which people (positions) need to be involved in planning and monitoring fundraising activities?
- Can you describe the various methods used to report fundraising results and the ways they are communicated?
- From your standpoint, what are the most important steps to be made for an effective fundraising planning?

## References

CECP (Chief Executives for Corporate Purpose) (2021). *Giving in numbers: 2021 edition*. Available at: https://cecp.co/home/resources/giving-in-numbers/.

Ovans, A. (2015). "What is strategy, again," Harvard Business Review Digital Articles, 12 May. Available at: https://hbr.org/2015/05/what-is-strategy-again.

Porter, M. E. (1996). "What Is Strategy?", *Harvard Business Review*, 74 (6): 61–78.

# 8 Measuring and Communicating Impacts to Attract Funding for the Arts

with *Pilar Cárdenas* and *Dan Wakin*

## 8.1 Why measuring and communicating impacts is important for arts institutions

Measuring and communicating the impact of the arts is a task that is becoming more and more relevant for arts organizations. There are several reasons motivating this trend. First, the increasing competitiveness in the philanthropy market to secure both private and public funds has forced these organizations to perfect their fundraising strategies. Consequently, arts philanthropy has become a true profession that has developed its own market, with its rules and logics, to which "competitors" must adapt. This includes providing funders with persuasive documentation (objective and subjective) about the impact of support from public and private sources. The value that donors expect to gain by funding an arts institution is related to the organization's capability to impact people's lives. This impact should be long-lasting and able to concretely improve people's well-being. Furthermore, it should be measurable and properly communicated.

Second, after the COVID-19 pandemic, cultural institutions are now required to rethink (and maybe re-legitimate) their role in the community. As discussed in Chapter 1, the interest in or the quality of an artwork cannot be considered enough to justify financial support. Today, arts institutions have to recover their original civic function: they have to become a resonant expression of the active citizenship that modern societies require. These trends are evident not only in the United States, but also in Europe. In the United States, social justice, diversity, equity, accessibility and inclusion are the new contexts in which arts organizations are going to be evaluated, as is detailed in Chapter 2. In Europe, while social justice matters are becoming more relevant, the focal point remains the organizations' relationship to their traditional funders: the state as well as regional and local governments. This means that even public arts organizations are increasingly required to provide reports and balance sheets that include not only their financial results, but also some key indicators of their impacts in external society (the so-called social balance sheet). Furthermore, in some European countries, access to funds is predicated on arts institutions addressing social development benchmarks. Overall, although the focus may differ, developing expertise in measuring, evaluating and communicating impacts is indispensable.

Third, as we live in a communication centered-society, arts organizations – even from their own standpoint – should be prepared to actively participate in conversations about issues that are relevant for the entire community. Moreover, when the discussed issue directly affects the arts, cultural institutions should be prepared to clearly advocate a position. Of course, an organization's advocacy is based on values and convictions that reinforce how its activities and specific programming impact the society. Following this path, funding an impactful arts institution becomes an endorsement and an indirect way to influence the development of a community: measuring and communicating the impacts of the arts is, then, a powerful task that can convert fundraising into institutional sustainability.

## 8.2 Impacts of the arts and ways to measure them

The arts matter. This clear declaration is the underlying rationale and inspiration for this book, dedicated to provide students and practitioners with the requisite tools and knowledge necessary for fundraising for the arts. Moreover, the increasing tendency to depreciate the value of the arts – occurring within some political circles and even broader segments of the population – suggests that measuring and communicating their impact is of the foremost importance.

Looking at the extant literature, the term "impact" often refers to "significant or lasting changes in people's lives, brought about by a given action or series of actions" (Roche, 1999: 21). Researchers also highlight the existence of connections between impact and social problems, arguing that the former is the root cause of the latter (Crutchfield and Grant, 2008).

As has been emphasized here, arts organizations are rooted in a community and they operate to improve the quality of life within it. Consequently, all arts projects frequently have a perceivable social outcome that is able to increase a community's social and cultural capital (Jeannotte, 2003; Leroux and Bernadska, 2014). This capability of the arts is particularly evident for so-called community arts projects. Leroux and Bernadska (2014), in particular, argue that community arts projects increase the development of social capital in a community because these collective initiatives create powerful, informal social structures among participants sharing a creative effort for a prolonged time. Moreover, Coleman (1988) and Putnam (2000) argue that the different dimensions of social capital (e.g., being trustworthy, informality in the exchange of information and the selfless and collectivity-oriented interests in actions) are drivers of behavioral changes both for individuals and the broader community. In these regards, audience-based arts participation projects (and also personal art creation) stand out as very effective in creating this type of community benefit, and arts organizations can focus on them when aiming to demonstrate their impacts (see Box 8.1 for an example).

**Box 8.1 Birmingham Opera Company and its community based artistic creations**

Founded in 1987 by Sir Graham Vick, the Birmingham Opera Company (BOC) has the ambition of "changing the face of opera." BOC has rooted its artistic programming in the belief that everybody can access opera. "We reflect the city we work in with our audiences, artists and stories that we tell" (from BOC website). BOC works all around the city of Birmingham (whose population is among the youngest and most diverse in the United Kingdom): although it hires renowned artists for its productions, it also trains hundreds of volunteers, citizens and emerging artists to create large-scale performances. Opera performances are staged in out-of-the-ordinary spaces: nightclubs, ex-industrial areas, hangars or power stations (and even in a burnt-out ice rink). The BOC projects have great artistic quality and have also occasionally competed for prizes with other more established opera production companies. This was the case for *Lady Macbeth of Mtsensk* and *Mittwoch Aus Licht*, which won the Royal Philharmonic Society Award for Opera and Music Theatre in 2019 and 2012 respectively.

*Source*: Author's adaptation from https://www.birminghamopera.org.uk/

While there are several ways to classify the various types of impact of the arts, the following sections present them in five categories: cultural, social, educational, economic and health. In the following paragraphs, we briefly review these different effects and outcomes and the ways in which arts organizations can measure them.

### 8.2.1 *Cultural impacts*

Almost as a truism, arts organizations have a cultural impact. Arts institutions play in fact a crucial role in defining, growing, and promoting the cultural identity of the community they serve by bringing people together around a collective experience. This experience has to do with common cultural roots and common referrals, shared communication codes and expression, but also with the creativity and the personal empowerment of the individuals within the community.

Arts organizations focused on increasing their cultural impacts normally pay special attention to the measurement of their cultural outputs. This means that they primarily focus on keeping the quality of their artistic offering high, but also pay attention to represent the different cultural identities of their community in their programming. In respect of the usable metrics, cultural impact is primarily evaluated in terms of productivity (i.e., the number for performances and productions per year) and in terms of artistic variety (i.e., artists involved and repertoire offered). In addition, audience development (i.e., size, demographics and geographic indicators; attendance rates, audience's average expense) and media reach (expressed, for example, by the amount of print and electronic press coverage as well as website metrics, such as website unique users and webpage viewers, and number of social media followers) also have a relevant role in measuring how culturally impactful an arts organization is. The higher these metrics, the greater an organization's impacts. Box 8.2 provides an example of how the Metropolitan Opera in New York City measures its cultural impact.

**Box 8.2 How the Metropolitan Opera measures its cultural impact**

At the Metropolitan Opera, the audience may be classified as local people, visiting the opera house physically; the audience around the country experiencing opera through live and encore high-definition transmissions in cinemas and live and recorded performances via radio broadcasts and satellites; and international audiences, who watch HD cinema performances, streamed performances or as tourists visiting New York. The value that the Met wishes to transmit is, first of all, the highest possible quality of artistic performance in terms of the creative teams: singers, directors, conductors and designers. The Met couples this goal with the provision of social value from involvement in social justice matters, such as supporting greater racial and ethnic diversity on stage and in the audience, and – at the moment – standing up for Ukraine in the face of the Russian invasion.

*Source*: Dan Wakin personal communication

### 8.2.2 *Social impacts*

Cultural and social impacts of the arts can often be coupled, as they both focus on collective experiences. By increasing the cultural capital of a community, the arts enhance the broader social capital. The arts are a repository for a society's collective memory, and can lead to the development of socially positive behaviors in the civic life of the community by helping build up its cultural infrastructure.

Research has highlighted the positive correlation existing between the level of their cultural consumption and people's social engagement. In particular, the higher the arts consumption, the more active people's participation in society, including voting in elections, supporting community causes, joining voluntary organizations (Leroux and Bernadska, 2014) and engaging with other players, such as local administrations, firms, community groups and funding agencies (Węziak-Białowolska et al., 2019).

Arts participation is also likely to promote empathy, kindness and positive feelings in individuals and they influence positive social behaviors, as well. As Matarasso puts it (1997: 79), "it is in the act of creativity that empowerment lies, and through sharing creativity that understanding and social inclusiveness are promoted."

The presence of arts organizations may also increase community cohesion and social well-being, especially in economically challenged neighborhoods. Indeed, according to the "Culture and Social Wellbeing in New York City" study, those neighborhoods with lower income but where cultural facilities are available record a drop of 14 per cent in child abuse cases and 18 per cent less serious crime than those without any (University of Pennsylvania and Reinvestment Fund, 2017). On-field research conducted in different contexts, an example being the immigrant communities of Philadelphia surveyed by Stern and Seifert (2002), have also highlighted how arts participation and projects – in particular those focusing on storytelling – are helpful in enhancing people's acceptance of a new culture, without losing connections with their own heritage (Leroux and Bernadska, 2014). Moreover, Stolle and Rochon (1998) state the existence of a positive correlation between the level of citizen participation in various cultural organizations and the degree of social tolerance.

The measurement of the social performance of the arts focuses on the impacts or results of an arts program (impact evaluation and outcome measurement), which are typically complex and interconnected. This assessment is often conducted after the implementation of an arts program and is primarily driven by funders (especially if they are foundations and governments). Typical questions that social outcomes analysis tries to answer are whether an arts program has improved cultural outcomes, increased people's quality of life and filled social gaps.

To answer these questions, the input–output–outcome model has been frequently used by public funding agencies interested in measuring the usefulness of public programs, including those relating to arts and culture (see Figure 8.1). This model evaluates the correlations existing among these elements:

- inputs given to the arts organizations to develop their programs;
- processes (or throughput) that arts organizations have developed to actuate these programs;
- outputs – the services provided or "products" supplied by arts programs;
- outcomes – the medium- and long-term results of arts programs, measured from an individual perspective;
- impacts – the significant and long-lasting changes in social life, measured from a community, population or ecosystem perspective.

*Figure 8.1* The input–output–outcome model

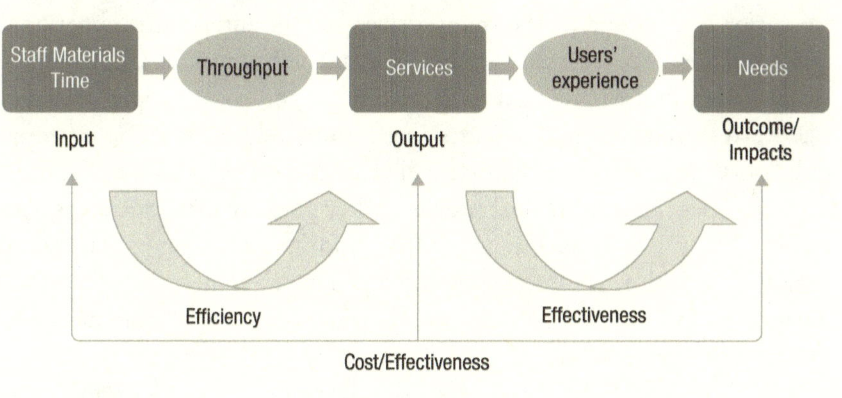


This model enables at least four reflections (Hatry, 2006; Poister, 2008). First, a public program or an artistic project is associated with a plurality of outcomes that can be expected and foreseen, but also unexpected and unforeseen (e.g., a festival or a big arts event might have unintended effects on traffic congestion and pollution) that can be measured and evaluated. Second, the action of an arts organization can produce a net of outcomes or impacts linked to each other by more or less strong causal links. To describe this causal chain of direct and indirect effects, Hatry (2006) refers to the health sector, specifying how the increase in the number of people who change their eating habits or lifestyles can represent an intermediate effect of a preventive health program, causally linked to the real final impact of the program, which is the improvement of health conditions. Similarly, an arts education initiative can directly influence the behavior of target students and have indirect/induced effects on their parents as well. Third, it should be emphasized that there is no certainty about the expected effectiveness of a cultural program, since its impact might not immediately correlate to the services provided. Outcomes and impacts can actually occur a long time after the program has been implemented, and can also depend on events or conditions that are not related to the original desires and scopes of the arts organization. To better understand this, we can think about the causal chain relating an education program to students' job placement. The likelihood of employment is linked to the classes and activities that a school provides and conceives to improve students' skills (i.e., the output of the program), but the latter is only one of the many drivers to the intended occupational outcome. The impact measurement of a cultural program (i.e., its effectiveness) is often carried out using methods and tools proper to social science research. Sometimes, arts institutions rely on specific outcome indicators to substantiate the external effectiveness or usefulness of their actions. These indicators (i.e., proxies or key performance indicators) can be very helpful in impact analyses based, for example, on experimental design or an ethnographic study. Table 8.1 gives some examples of indicators to use when implementing an input–output–outcome model in different arts organizations.

The table highlights how arts organizations can become more familiar with metrics and develop their own impact measurement systems, shifting to the (often public) funder the responsibility to measure the complex social impacts of arts programs. In order to create their own social impact measurement system, they should translate their institutional mission and aspirational vision into an operating set of strategies that focuses on the work to be accomplished. They should further articulate the scope and scale of their operations: the former identifies the activities for addressing the issue, while the project's scale refers to the size of the target. Arts institutions should perfect their

*Table 8.1* Proxies of input–output–outcome measures

| Kind of organization | Input | Output | Efficiency | Effectiveness |
|---|---|---|---|---|
| **Theatre** | production costs | # of performances<br>venue occupancy rate | $\frac{\text{Production costs}}{\text{\# of performances}}$ | $\frac{\text{\# of new subscribers}}{\text{\# of subscribers}}$ |
| **Library** | HR costs | # of library loans<br># of library visits | $\frac{\text{HR costs}}{\text{\# of library loans}}$ | $\frac{\text{\# of library users}}{\text{\# city residents}}$ |
| **Museum** | HR costs | # of visitors | $\frac{\text{HR costs}}{\text{\# of visitors}}$ | $\frac{\text{\# of visitors}}{\text{\# city residents}}$ |

ability to measure their outputs and eventually make claims around the outcomes, relying on the correct identification of the link existing between their outputs, the related outcomes and their final impacts through the creation of an appropriate measurement and control system (Ebrahim et al., 2014). The evaluation of the social impacts of the arts is also related to concerns about wealth distribution in our societies and about the relevance of arts philanthropy in this context. This discussion is particularly animated in the United States, but many European countries have begun to debate this as well. From the arts institutions' standpoint, the most relevant matter underlying the discussion is that socially conscious funders expect their grant recipients to be "good citizens" within the community, redistributing value in addition to creating and promoting great art. Consequently, when arts organizations are able to demonstrate the positive correlation that exists between arts production, participation and consumption, and social behaviors and attitudes that strengthen society, this can have positive influences on arts philanthropy.

### 8.2.3 *Educational impacts*

Cultural institutions throughout the world have long appreciated the educational impacts of the arts. They can motivate and inspire students, stimulating their desire to learn and their critical thinking, kindling skills that can make a difference in workforce requirements. Research highlights, for example, that exposure to arts activities increases the likelihood that individuals will undertake further education after eighteen years of age (Fujiwara et al., 2014); it also improves educational attainment, alongside literacy and cognitive abilities (Tripney et al., 2010). Moreover, the arts can impact in the long term the education-related social behaviors of the youngest members of the adult population. Catterall (2009), for instance, found a positive correlation between the participation of this segment of the population during middle and high school years in visual and performing arts programs and their higher propensity for activities such as volunteering and being engaged in school, neighborhood politics and community services.

Many practitioners assess that, given the significant reduction in funding for arts education in schools, cultural institutions are increasingly being expected to help fill educational gaps. In the United States, for instance, public funding cuts have disproportionately affected schools, especially those in areas populated by economically and socially disadvantaged people. While it is impossible for arts organizations to fully compensate for the dismantling of school arts programs, many cultural institutions have invested significant resources in educational programs that are now reaching millions of students. Carnegie Hall in New York, for example, has invested in a very large education department that has developed a national curriculum for teachers, provided lessons to students and additional educational support, suggesting that the music component of education has been outsourced by the schools accessing Carnegie Hall's educational resources. In Europe, the central State still covers most of the expenses of arts educational programs. Consequently, European arts organizations are not expected to provide core arts education in schools. However, European cultural institutions have been able to access special project funds controlled by the European Commission and to attract the attention of private sponsors who are interested in the institutional funding of targeted educational programs. With all that being said, American and European cultural institutions are investing more and more in education, and need to find authentic and meaningful ways to convey their impacts. Moreover, private funders (especially foundations and corporations) are increasingly responsive to contribution requests for educational activities promoted by arts institutions. This interest has become so intense that some funders have even restricted their philanthropy to educational programs that reach populations that are underserved by education.

Arts organizations can measure the impacts of their educational programs by referring to metrics such as the number, length and frequency of contacts, the earned revenue generated by ticket sales or fees for some programs, the contributed support for such programs and test scores. On the other hand, non-quantitative impacts may be recorded through expressions of appreciation for the program, including letters or personal messages received by the arts institution from students expressing appreciation and gratitude, and reports from teachers. Relying on experienced evaluators can also offer arts organizations a qualitative appraisal of a given educational program. However, funders often want to directly observe the impacts of the educational programs they are funding, and typically have reactions and thoughts about the programs that are unrelated to any other evaluation. Care and stewardship of these donors is critical if future funding is to be secured. Box 8.3 provides an example of how BSO measures its educational impact.

**Box 8.3 How the Boston Symphony Orchestra (BSO) measures its educational impact**

The BSO keeps records of all Tanglewood Fellows. These are emerging professional musicians who spend a summer or two in residence at Tanglewood, the summer home of the BSO. One way in which the BSO measures the success of the program is by the number of Fellows who advance into major positions throughout the music world. For example, Tanglewood Conducting Fellows include Leonard Bernstein, Zubin Mehta, Seiji Ozawa, Claudio Abbado, Lorin Maazel and Christoph von Dohnanyi. The success of the Tanglewood Fellows is a key marketing tool that is used by the BSO's development staff, and has resulted in millions of dollars of endowment for the program in addition to significant annual funding.

*Source*: Mark Volpe personal communication

### 8.2.4 *Economic impacts*

Economic impacts of the arts have been long documented. Several studies have demonstrated how the arts contribute to a country's economy at different territorial levels (i.e., national, regional and local). Not-for-profit arts organizations are active players in the business communities to which they belong. They are producers, consumers and employers, while their employees pay taxes and are often engaged in business organizations (e.g., a chamber of commerce or business circles). Moreover, as mentioned in Chapter 6, arts activities generate positive externalities for many different economic actors. Indeed, cultural institutions help promote the cities and regions where they are located and can enhance the touristic attractiveness of a territory. Conversely, arts consumers attending a theatre or a museum away from their hometown can benefit the local hospitality and tourist industry by buying air or railway tickets, booking hotels or eating at restaurants. Arts attendance helps revitalize whole quarters or districts, and enhances downtown sustainability. These are the typical arguments regularly used to persuade policymakers, corporations or other donors that funding the arts sector boosts the economy at large. Research undertaken by the National Endowment for The Arts and American for the Arts, for example, states that before the COVID-19 pandemic, in 2019, production of arts and cultural goods in the United States added 4.3 per cent to the gross domestic product, more than transportation and agriculture. Moreover, in the same fiscal year, the American cultural sector employed 5.2 million workers with a total compensation of $447 billion (AFTA, 2017; NEA, 2020). To compare these data with the European context, we can note that in 2018, in the United Kingdom, about 2.7 million people were employed in the arts (the majority in creative industries), with a total output of about £143.3 billion (Arts Council, UK, 2020).

In spite of all this evidence, criticism that there is a too narrow focus on the economic impacts of the arts is at the heart of the current debate. Among others, Sterngold (2004) argues, for instance, that an excessive concentration on the economic impacts of the arts, paying scant attention to other aspects, can even affect arts advocacy when legitimating financial support for the sector. Arts administrators, legislators and public funders may underestimate (or undervalue) the importance of non-economic benefits related to the arts and cut their contribution budgets.

In order to evaluate their economic impact properly, many arts institutions commission economists to produce ad hoc studies when they are making appeals to donors and governmental entities. These analyses aim to highlight the direct and indirect economic outcomes that arts organizations generate. Reports usually focus on data concerning employment (both direct and indirect), hospitality spending by visitors and direct spending (via suppliers, for instance). Moreover, they may consider financial injections into a region that are directly related to the presence of arts institutions, through from tourism, local spending flows and tourists' ancillary spending. Multipliers reflecting interdependencies between different economic and non-economic stakeholders should also be taken into account in these documents. Finally, it is noteworthy that, when limited to the analysis of ticket revenues and capital expenditures and the application of average multipliers, economic studies in the arts industry tend to be less impactful. Box 8.4 provides an example of such a study, which was commissioned by the BSO to evaluate its economic impacts.

Although indirect, cultural institutions also can enhance the property values in the neighborhoods in which they are situated. Moreover, companies and individuals are generally attracted to areas with abundant cultural activity, further stimulating economic energy and social dynamism. Cultural activities are especially attractive to highly skilled

**Box 8.4 The economic impact of the Boston Symphony Orchestra (BSO)**

In 2018, the BSO commissioned a study from the Center for Creative Community Development to evaluate the economic impact of its activities. With an operating budget of just under $100 million per year, the BSO produces about 327 concerts and 340 lectures, educational events and other activities annually. In total, the BSO reaches a total audience of more than 1.2 million every year. As such, it makes significant contributions to local and State economies as an employer and market for goods as well as being a critical component of the tourism product in Massachusetts. A 2008 study found that the BSO's total economic impact in Massachusetts was nearly $167 million. In Suffolk County, this includes the impacts of BSO, Pops, and Chamber Players events held at Symphony Hall and other local venues, as well as the free 3 and 4 July concerts on the Esplanade and additional non-ticketed events held at various outdoor locations. The analysis also includes the BSO's Education and Community Engagement programs, which serve tens of thousands of young people and families annually, and events held at Symphony Hall by outside presenters. This economic impact has been evaluated at a $148 million increase in economic activity for the City of Boston (Suffolk County). Tanglewood has served as the summer home of the BSO since 1937. One of the most significant generators of economic activity in the Berkshires, Tanglewood consistently draws thousands of visitors each summer to nearly 100 performances. Each season offers a vast quantity of music in a range of musical forms and styles, including performances by the BSO and TMC orchestras, recitals by the world's finest musicians, an internationally renowned Festival of Contemporary Music, family concerts and other educational events, and a popular artist series. Tanglewood performances and operations generate an estimated increase in economic activity for the Berkshire region of $103 million.

*Source*: The economic impacts of the BSO (Summary findings – April 2018), Center for Creative Community Development

and highly compensated individuals, who tend to have a larger economic impact on the region. When a new cultural venue opens in a specific area, the economic development of the region is stimulated: the building of arts venues and museums, for instance, can serve as a catalyst for other types of investment. Throughout the world, there is an extensive and ever-expanding range of building projects initiated by cultural institutions that stimulate further development. Some examples include the Lincoln Center in New York, Disney Hall in Los Angeles, Orchestra Hall in Detroit (which initiated the construction of restaurants, a performing arts high school, offices, a Black Box Theater and parking facilities adjacent to the hall), "The Egg" – the National Centre for the Performing Arts in Beijing, Guggenheim Bilbao, the Centre Pompidou in Paris and the Prada Foundation in Milan. Box 8.5 describes Tanglewood's building project in the Berkshire Region.

**Box 8.5 Tanglewood's building project in the Berkshire Region**

Tanglewood, the summer home of the Boston Symphony Orchestra since 1936, opened the newly built Linde Center for Music and Learning in 2019 (see Fig. 8.2). During construction, Tanglewood employment increased to 1400 jobs, resulting in a 1.5 per cent reduction in the unemployment rate in Berkshire County. Tanglewood generates more than $100 million worth of economic activity in the Berkshire area annually, making it the most important driver for tourism in the district. Tanglewood hosts 350,000 visitors each summer. The project served as an economic engine in Berkshire and received Mass Econ's 2019 Community Impact Award.

*Figure 8.2* Tanglewood's new Linde Center for Music and Learning

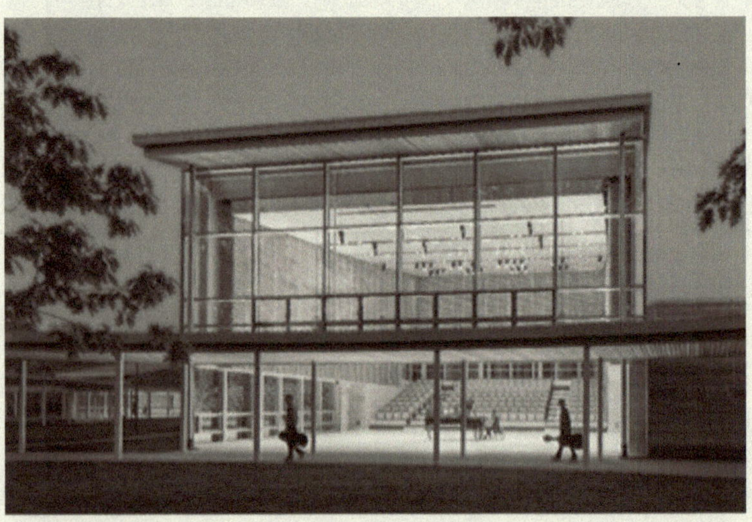

*Credit*: Robert Benson I Boston Symphony Orchestra

*Source*: Mark Volpe personal communication

### 8.2.5 *Health impacts*

The arts also have health impacts. In their research about the relationship between arts participation, personality and individual well-being, Lewandowska and Węziak-Białowolska (2022) review evidences from recent studies about the connections between mental and psychological health and the arts. Fraser and al Sayah (2011), for example, underline the power of the arts to express inner feelings and thoughts that can be difficult to formulate in words. By helping to develop people's self-reflection, exposure to and the practice of artistic and creative activities can be helpful in palliating anxiety, stress and depression (Stuckey and Nobel, 2010) and reinforcing the sense of belonging and socialization (Novak-Leonard et al., 2014).

The therapeutic power of the arts in symptom relief, in rehabilitation and in the improvement of patients' quality of life has been highlighted (Hamilton et al., 2003), since people engaged with artistic activities can benefit from the enhancement of their emotions, moods and psychological states (Lewandowska and Węziak-Białowolska, 2022). Moreover, the "Creative Health: The Arts for Health and Wellbeing study" (2017) states that music and art therapy are effective courses of action to reduce anxiety and deal with mental disease symptoms. The study also reveals that 45 per cent of medical institutions globally offer arts programs to their patients to accelerate their recovery (APPG, 2017). Furthermore, many practitioners indicate that different cultural institutions have developed specific projects or agreements with mental healthcare centers in order to exploit the healing power of the arts.

From personal experience, it is agreed that exposure to the arts can be effective in regulating or expressing human feelings and emotions. Moreover, researchers have highlighted the different health benefits that are available from different art forms. For example, making visual arts (e.g., coloring, painting or drawing) can reduce anger and anxiety (Drake et al., 2022). Listening to music can regulate emotions, increasing positive affect (Cook et al., 2019). Participating in acting classes helps to increase the use of adaptive techniques to handle emotions (Goldstein et al., 2013).

During times of particularly severe emotional stress, the arts have always played a healing role in terms of personal and collective well-being (Drake et al., 2022). After natural disasters, such as hurricanes or earthquakes, or during wars, children often rely on drawings to express their emotions.

Prison inmates can benefit from acting or from creative arts programs, which help to overcome sadness, anger and a sense of isolation. The World Health Organization even argues that the arts play a key role in promoting health and well-being, as they prevent psychophysical distress and help to alleviate both acute and chronic illnesses (Fancourt and Finn, 2019).

Researching the health and psychological benefits provided by the arts during the COVID-19 pandemic, Drake et al. (2022) highlight how – owing to the enforced pause of most social and leisure activities – many individuals turned to the arts for comfort and solace. Between May and June 2020, researchers surveyed a group of 486 individuals, and found that listening to music was the most comforting activity for them (19.6 per cent), while 14.2 per cent of those surveyed relied on reading novels, poetry or short stories to find relief during the lockdowns. Artmaking (e.g., painting, crafting, drawing) was chosen for the same purpose by 10.6 per cent. Less than 4 per cent stated that they relied on non-art activities for psychological help during the pandemic. Moreover, arts and crafts were parents' top choice to entertain their children during the long days of the lockdowns (Choi et al., 2020).

Measuring the impacts of the arts is becoming relevant for arts managers because it directly links to arts organizations' accountability. Impacts are a crucial indicator for both private and public arts funders, who want to know whether their contributions help to achieve a shared goal with the institution, or whether they should be given to other recipients or invested in different activities (Ebrahim et al., 2014). Currently, private and public funders require (and occasionally demand) that arts institutions provide more objective evidence of their supports' impact, relevance and effects. The number and variety of metrics and indicators that they use to quantify and describe their impacts (e.g., quantitative, qualitative, social, behavioral, economic) further indicates the complexity of this analysis.

## 8.3 Communicating impacts of the arts

An arts organization's ability to communicate its impact to stakeholders and other interested parties is critical to its ongoing viability. Communicating impact is a complex process, especially considering the multiple, sometimes overlapping, constituencies that cultural institutions must reach. Consequently, careful attention to the means, the frequency and the focus of each communication is imperative: a multilayered communication plan that can be customized for targeted audiences is indispensable to an arts institution that is making its case for relevance and, ultimately, support. Among the main targets of communication are:

- *External groups.* While an arts institution's websites and social media platforms can effectively be employed for external communications purposes, coverage in externally controlled print, electronic and new media remains very important in disseminating news about the impact of fundraising. Arts supporters tend to be literate and inclined to consume news, so positive stories in the press can be beneficial. Furthermore, given that virtually all press has been digitized, a story (positive or negative) in a local media outlet quickly becomes a national story or even an international one. This rarely happened before the digital age. Given this, the arts institution's development and public relations/communications/press departments should work together to formulate and coordinate stories on fundraising successes it believes are "press worthy." Matters such as type of media coverage desired (e.g., arts, society or business story), format of desired coverage (e.g., print, electronic or a combination – the press department should have current lists), content of a press release, timing of the release, possible visuals, specific journalists to approach (pre-existing relationships matter) and individuals offered to the journalists for interviews need to be carefully considered before a plan of action can be initiated.
- *Cultural community.* The local cultural community typically includes prominent, affluent individuals who tend to support various arts organizations and be involved in the governance of several institutions. The communication of impact to similar cultural institutions allows for the dissemination of information to an important group that tends to share intelligence through social networks. Occasionally, such news benefits other cultural institutions by inspiring their board members and supporters to make additional commitments.
- *Internal constituencies.* The three primary internal groups within an arts organization are the board members (and all other volunteers), artists and staff. Each has a unique part to play, but they all have communication responsibilities and thus need to be informed if the organization is to be consistent in its messaging; this starts with

board members. Among the main fiduciary duties of the board lies the understanding of the impact and mission of the organization, so it is necessary that they understand communication strategies and tactics concerning the institution's impact. With respect to staff, virtually all have some interaction with the public and the box office, and front of house personnel primarily deal with external constituencies. Therefore, it is important they are also equipped with sufficient knowledge about the institution's impact, as staff reach is broader than generally realized or appreciated. With respect to performers and curators, the artistic leadership is often the official and public face of the organization, so should be prepared to address matters concerning impact. Artists, musicians and other performers can also be considered public figures and therefore should be briefed by senior management on all relevant matters, especially those that help to make the case for supporting the artistic institution that employs them.

- *The opinion elite.* These are individuals who shape and ultimately influence perceptions of institutions, other noteworthy individuals, political movements and so on; they exist at every level of government and society. Occasionally, elites are grouped into governing elites and non-governing elites. Given the amount of public sector funding of the arts in Europe, the leaders of European arts organizations must develop a rapport with governing elites. In the United States, where the private sector is the primary financial supporter of the arts, non-governing elites play an outsized role, as such individuals serve in governance positions and provide significant financial support. While the governing elite remain relevant to artistic organizations in the United States especially in the context of tax policy, American cultural institutions are much more focused on the non-governing elite, especially those within the community in which the cultural institution is located. The non-governing elite come from leadership positions in many realms such as business, civic or social life, politics, religion and education. In some cases, they may be already involved in the governance of a cultural institution, so it is important for cultural organizations' staff to be aware of their presence. As an aside, within the context of social communications, influencers can be considered the modern equivalent of the opinion elite. Ideally, the board of an arts institution should be mostly populated by members of the opinion elite, and such members should be asked to invite other influential people to become involved with the arts organization. Although not directly involved in government, many members of the non-governing elite are politically engaged, and can be asked to advocate at various government levels.

Communication strategies should also be advocative. In other words, the role the arts institution plays in the broader community should be documented with metrics and anecdotal accounts, especially when the organization has (deservedly or not) an elitist image. This is especially true when addressing community and political leadership.

While traditional modes of communication such as letters or verbal conversations remain important for certain exchanges, the digital revolution has been transformational, as arts institutions can now extend their reach beyond what was once imaginable. This trend was accelerated during the COVID-19 pandemic when in-person encounters became impossible. One of the ironies of the pandemic was that while arts organizations were unable to generate much earned income, they greatly expanded their media audience by expanding their digital operations. Some performing arts companies even morphed into quasi-media companies as they could only disseminate their content through electronic means. The concurrent explosion in social media has also created many communication opportunities for cultural institutions. Such media can reduce the distance between an arts organization and their communities by stimulating and facilitating connections. However, some institutions have found their attention and focus on important matters diverted because they have to be reactive to social media posts. Given that social media is a growing force in the world that impacts consumer habits, arts organizations would be well advised to develop thoughtful, effective digital communications across all aspects of their operations, including fundraising.[1]

In communicating their impact to most groups, storytelling can be a very useful tool, as most individuals enjoy and are occasionally moved by heartfelt and authentic stories. The purpose of good storytelling is to emotionally connect donors to the recipients of their gifts, while highlighting the pressing needs that are addressed. Indeed, most pre-cam-

---

1 See also Chapter 10.

paign, in-campaign and post-campaign materials (either in printed or digital formats) are likely to include stories that document the impact of gifts. A story should be intentional, with a clear purpose, and it should activate empathy in the listener or reader, connect funders to a mission or cause and be supported when appropriate by visuals that help to make the case. They should therefore include data as well as a human-interest angle. Cause communicating through effective storytelling may change funders from passive to passionate, arousing their empathy or sympathy and inspiring action. At the same time, it may outline the challenges faced by the institution and encourage prospects or donors to help solve it.

The use of visuals alongside narratives can make for a more potent communication. Indeed, visually appealing documents keep readers engaged regardless of the content. Visuals may include infographics: timelines help readers to visualize the key milestones of a project, while bar and/or pie charts, tables and flow charts may also be used to illustrate a point. Poignant photos ingeniously incorporated can also make for effective messaging as can video messages if connecting through multimedia platforms. Communication materials prepared by the development team should use fonts, colors and other stylistic features that are part of the broader institutional palette to further reinforce the branding of the cultural institution. Visuals should reflect the quality and professionalism of the arts institution in ways that create a personal and trusting relationship with the designated audience.

Finally, as previously mentioned, there is a growing consensus that the success of not-for-profit philanthropy depends not only on economic and social factors, but also on the communication of transparency and accountability that enhances public trust of the institution (Rutherford et al. 2021). In Box 8.6, we provide an example of social reporting at Fondazione Orchestra Toscanini in Parma.

**Box 8.6 Introducing social reporting at Fondazione Orchestra Toscanini in Parma**

Fondazione Toscanini is among the most acclaimed and dynamic Italian musical institutions, producing symphony concerts and opera productions, and professionally training young musicians, honoring, not only in its name, the conductor Arturo Toscanini's artistic legacy and tradition of excellence.

Fondazione Toscanini includes two main artistic ensembles, which stage over a hundred symphony concerts and forty opera performances each year: the Filarmonica Arturo Toscanini, engaged in the great symphonic repertoire, and the Orchestra dell' Emilia-Romagna Arturo Toscanini, which provides regional educational concerts and opera productions. Fondazione Toscanini has recently founded a third ensemble, La Toscanini Next, which aims to promote and implement cultural initiatives that are accessible to all, through the enhancement, dissemination and safeguarding of artistic and musical heritage. Over the years, this institution has worked to pursue its mission of increasing accessibility to classical music, aiming to involve new generations and to enhance specific programs. Recently, Fondazione Toscanini has needed to emphasize its role in the community emphasizing how its value goes beyond economics, also having a social, spiritual, historical and symbolic impact. This significant attention to the community has prompted the foundation to equip itself with clear and effective reporting tools, useful for communicating the main economic and social results, both internally and externally, to its stakeholders. By publishing a social report, Fondazione Toscanini has been able to better communicate its value and the high potential of its cultural activities, together with the impact of the organization on communities. Measuring cultural impact remains challenging, because of the continuous evolution in cultural institutions' activities, but Fondazione Toscanini has been able to present itself through its social report, which has the following objectives:

- To create a valid reporting tool for the organization's activities, particularly the social ones;
- To deal with social needs and measure the impact of these actions, including the added value brought to the local area;
- To consolidate the involvement of all stakeholders, building privileged relationships and meeting opportunities for discussion, growth and exchange;
- To promote transparency inside the organization and build a useful internal communication tool.

The social report represented an opportunity for the foundation to give a voice to internal and external stakeholders, and to describe its identity, objectives and main results. It was an opportunity to outline a strategy, to reflect on the foundation's current and future activities, and to communicate its performance and objectives to a wider audience. The Fondazione Toscanini's social report, in line with the provisions of various theoretical studies, is divided into four distinct sections: the foundation's identity, activities, stakeholders and economics. The first section provides a general overview of the characteristics of Fondazione Toscanini, and presents its mission, principles, strategic policies, structure and governance model. The second section focuses on the foundation's social responsibility, as perceived by its institutional activity in terms of the plurality of stakeholders. In this phase, the activities and initiatives undertaken and its role with respect the reference community are analyzed in detail. The third section features a detailed mapping of the various stakeholders, through an analysis of their expectations and needs. The fourth section is characterized by an analysis and reclassification of the income statement in order to highlight the foundation's social externalities. The social report of Fondazione Toscanini contains much information, and is a communication tool that is capable of reaching a very large audience. The report is used to share all the foundation's activities, awards and positive results, and constructs aggregate measures that indicate the increasing numbers of, for example, personnel involved, artists, number of concerts and other activities that take place each year. It also contains aggregated measures and indexes that clarify the foundation's importance for the community. One of the main examples given is the "multiplier," which relates to public contributions received and how these are returned to the community: in 2021, wealth distributed throughout the region amounted to €6,989,534, which, compared with the public contribution disbursed by Emilia-Romagna (€3,500,000), indicates a multiplier effect of 2, meaning that for every euro invested by Emilia -Romagna, the foundation was able to produce and distribute two for the benefit of the region. The impact report is therefore an important tool for reporting on an institution's successes, ensuring an in-depth and reasoned summary of its real value, and a way of speaking to stakeholders and attracting potential donors, as it clearly indicates the value created by the institution and its primary role in the community.

*Source*: Alex Turrini personal communication

## 8.4 Community donors as a target for arts organizations

As previously discussed in this book, donors are motivated by a variety of factors, but virtually all of them want to understand the difference their philanthropy makes to a project or a cause. Most frequently, donors give because they share the institution's mission and values. Sharing particulars and metrics with them allows them to make informed philanthropic decisions. Researchers argue that arts organizations are shifting towards a community-centered fundraising strategy. These organizations now emphasize how their mission and programs provide shared benefits for the whole community they serve.

In their extensive arts donor survey,[2] the Advisory Board for the Arts highlighted the main drivers that motivate donors to support arts institutions (ABA, 2021). Among the most relevant findings, researchers note that for nearly two-thirds of donors (62 per cent), "love of the arts" is not the principal motivation for their contribution, and more American than European donors are motivated by transactional factors (such as tangible benefits received).

Particularly interesting in the ABA's research is the description of the segment of donors who are motivated by community factors. They represent about one-third of surveyed arts donors and are driven in their giving choices by a twofold motivation. Some of them want to impact the life of their community and support projects and community activities. Others are interested in being part of their community and in accessing the network of donors, in order to support friends and family. These community-focused donors represent about 31 per cent of donors overall and an even larger percentage of high-end donors to arts organizations (35 per cent). Beyond their financial contributions, community donors tend to be deeply engaged with the institutions they support in other ways, serving as board members or volunteers (50 per cent of community donors serve on arts boards). They are keen to participate in arts events and initiatives, and they aim to be more active in the greater community.

Their giving tendencies make community donors particularly interesting. They are the most generous of all donor types, giving about 25 per cent more than other donor categories: although they tend to give about the same amount as other donor types in their annual giving, they give about twice as much as other groups for special projects, galas and campaigns – being more likely to support this latter grouping at a level far greater than they support annual funds. Owing to its high potential, this category of supporters, if cultivated and advanced properly, can increase both the amount of granted funding and the number of donors to a cultural institution.

Community donors share the desire to contribute to the development of their community. This attitude goes beyond the concept of altruism, as it refers to a more rational and thoughtful investment in community social capital. Such donors position themselves as pillars of society, but

[2] A population of 5000 people based in the United States, Canada and United Kingdom.

they do not all behave in the same way. In particular, ABA refers to different segments within the category:

- donors motivated by community standing, wanting to raise the stature of their community in the eyes of others by ensuring that high-quality arts are thriving;
- donors motivated by belonging, wanting to be part of something bigger than themselves, a community that stands for ideals that they share;
- donors motivated by change, willing to catalyze change in society through the arts.

The study highlights that older donors tend to be motivated by community standing more than younger donors. Furthermore, younger donors are more driven by "belonging to something bigger" and "catalyzing change," so it is probable that over time we will see a shift toward the latter two categories.

Community-motivated donors and their powerful giving attitudes have been observed previously. A 2015 *Washington Post* article highlighted how community development was the giving priority of younger philanthropists. Moreover, if their interest in giving turns to the arts, they tend to support entities that offer impactful education and community development programs;[3] consequently, arts organizations attempting to resonate with younger donors should emphasize not only the quality of the arts, but also how the arts advance the overall interests of the community.

All this evidence tells us there is a large, generous population of givers who aim to be part of the "something else" that arts organizations can provide. Arts organizations can all bring to the community something unique and special: they just have to learn what community donors expect from them. The conclusion that ABA researchers draw from all this is twofold. First, an arts organization's purpose needs to be guidance for everything the institution does. The ideal that an organization stands for in the community matters at least as much as the quality of artistic expression it achieves. Organizations send messages with each communica-

---

3 https://www.washingtonpost.com/news/wonk/wp/2015/06/24/millennials-are-actually-more-generous-than-anybody-realizes/.

tion they share and activity they carry out, and those signals cumulatively present to donors and the broader community the institution's purpose. Second, if they aim to gain and retain the attention of audiences and philanthropic donors who are not avid arts consumers, arts organizations should rely on a purpose that is at a "higher level" than "just" making great art. This purpose must speak about the arts and something else; in other words, it should be related to what is accomplished for their donors and for the entire community. This "something else" can be referred to as shared values. As we detail in Chapter 3, a shared value is a belief that both an arts institution and its attendees or members have a higher purpose, impetus or vision of the world that brings meaning into their lives beyond an art form or the arts themselves. What a shared value does is to connect the organization's mission with the human values of the people in the community it serves. Consequently, arts organizations adopting and implementing a shared-values strategy in fundraising tend to be more attractive to donors, as they are perceived to consistently have more impact in the community they serve. In other words, if they succeed in positioning their brand by focusing on shared values, arts institutions are more attractive and have more meaning for all donors, whether large or small. To close, it can be argued that community donors are the segment that focuses on the full impact arts organizations have on people's lives. Their giving behavior is deeply influenced by the ability of these institutions to tell their story, reinforcing the impact that arts activities can have on the health of the community. To resonate with these donors, arts organizations should orient their fundraising strategies towards a community-centered approach. If they are perceived to be "good citizens" and socially active players, arts institutions tend to attract more support from a broader and more diverse group of donors. Elitist or privileged positioning is no longer the preferred messaging, as many donors want the arts to play an active civic role to foster community development.

## Keywords for arts fundraisers

Impact of the arts, social balance sheet, advocacy, cultural capital, social capital, productivity, artistic variety, audience development, media reach, social engagement, empathy, community cohesion, impact evaluation, outcome measurement, input–output–outcome model, public program, outcome, effectiveness, project scope, project scale, touristic attractiveness, multipliers, mental and psychological health, healing role, accountability, multilayered communication, opinion elite, influencer, storytelling, visuals, transparency, community donors

**Suggested questions for meetings and discussion**

- What is the impact that arts organizations have and how can it be measured?
- What metrics can be used to measure the impact of arts organizations?
- How can these metrics be a reflection on organizational strategies? What main differences/similarities can you see between American and European arts organizations in respect of this?
- How can arts organizations effectively measure and communicate their impact?
- On which qualitative and quantitative elements can arts organizations rely when developing their impacts communication strategy?
- How can arts organizations tell their story to "reputation givers" (critics, opinion leaders, politicians)?
- When arts organizations communicate their value, what types of impact should they emphasize?
- How do arts organizations make funders aware of the actual impact of their philanthropic contributions?
- When people contribute to arts organizations, what impacts do they indirectly have? Can you provide some examples? What are the differences/similarities between American and European arts organizations in respect to this?
- How can arts organizations influence opinion-elites?
- How are arts organizations using advocacy to advance their interests? In what contexts do such institutions use advocacy? What are the main differences/similarities between American and European arts organizations in respect of this?
- What is the role played by community donors in arts organizations you know?
- How would you develop your strategy to engage community donors in arts fundraising?

## References


ABA (Advisory Boards for the Arts) (2021). *Donors motivation and behavior research findings.* Available at: https://www.advisoryboardArts.com/webinar-recap-donor-research-findings.

AFTA (American for the Arts) (2017). Arts & economic prosperity 5. Available at: https://www.americansforthearts.org/by-program/reports-and-data/research-studies-publications/arts-economic-prosperity-6.

APPG (All-Party Parliamentary Group) (2017). *The Arts for Health and Wellbeing* Available at http://www.artshealthandwellbeing.org.uk/appg-inquiry/

Arts Council UK (2020). *The impact of arts & culture on the wider creative economy metro dynamics.* Available at: https://www.Artscouncil.org.uk/sites/default/files/download-file/Metro%20Dynamics%20-%20Arts%20and%20Culture%20Impact%20Report.pdf.

Catterall, J. S. (2009). *Doing well and doing good by doing art.* Los Angeles, CA: Imagination Group.

Choi, M., Tessler, H. and Kao, G. (2020). "Arts and crafts as an educational strategy and coping mechanism for Republic of Korea and United States parents during the COVID-19 pandemic," *International Review of Education*, 66 (5): 715–735.

Coleman, J. S. (1988). "Social capital in the creation of human capital," *American Journal of Sociology*, 94: S95–S120.

Cook, T., Roy, A. and Welker, K. M. (2019). "Music as an emotion regulation strategy: An examination of genres of music and their roles in emotion regulation," *Psychology of Music* 47 (1): 144–154.

Crutchfield, Leslie R. and McLeod Grant, Heather (2012). *Forces for good: The six practices of high-impact nonprofits.* John Wiley and Sons Inc., New York and London

Drake, J. E., Papazian, K. and Grossman, E. (2022). "Gravitating toward the arts during the COVID-19 pandemic," *Psychology of Aesthetics, Creativity, and the Arts.*

Ebrahim, A. and Rangan, V. K. (2014)." What impact? A framework for measuring the scale and scope of social performance," *California Management Review*, 56 (3): 118–141.

Fancourt, D. and Finn, S. (2019). "What is the evidence on the role of the arts in improving health and well-being?," *Health Evidence Network Synthesis Report nr. 67,* World Health Organization.

Fraser, K. D. and Al Sayah, F. (2011). "Arts-based methods in health research: A systematic review of the literature," *Arts & Health*, 3: 110–145.

Fujiwara, D., Kudrna, L. and Dolan, P. (2014). *Quantifying and valuing the wellbeing impacts of culture and sport.* Research paper. London: Department for Culture Media and Sport.

Goldstein, K. (2013). *Human nature in the light of psychopathology.* Cambridge, MA: Harvard University Press.

Hamilton, C., Hinks, S. and Petticrew, M. (2003). "Arts for health: still searching for the Holy Grail.," *Journal of Epidemiology & Community Health*, 57 (6): 401–402.

Hatry, H. P. (2006). *Performance measurement: Getting results.* Washington, DC: The Urban Institute Press.

Jeannotte, M. S. (2003). "Singing alone? The contribution of cultural capital to social cohesion and sustainable communities," *The International Journal of Cultural Policy*, 9 (1): 35–49.

Leroux, K. and Bernadska, A. (2014). "Impact of the arts on individual contributions to US civil society," *Journal of Civil Society*, 10 (2): 144–164.

Lewandowska, K. and Węziak-Białowolska, D. (2022). "The impact of theatre on social psychology outcomes: systematic review and meta-analyses," *Arts & Health.*

Matarasso, F. (1997). *Use or ornament: The social impact of participation in the arts.* Stroud: Comedia.

NEA – National Endowment for the Arts (2022). *The US Arts Economy in 2020: A National Summary Report.* Available at: https://www.arts.gov// sites/default/files/NationalReportCompliantMarch11.pdf.

Novak-Leonard, J., Baach P., Schultz, A., Farrell, B., Anderson, W. and Rabkin, N. (2014). *The changing landscape of arts participation: A synthesis of literature and expert interviews.* Chicago: NORC and the Cultural Policy Center at University of Chicago.

Poister, T. H. (2008). *Measuring performance in public and nonprofit organizations.* Hoboken, NJ: John Wiley and Sons.

Putnam, R. D. (2000). *Bowling alone: The collapse and revival of American community.* New York, NJ, Simon and Schuster.

Roche, C. Jr (1999). *Impact assessment for development agencies: Learning to value change.* London: Oxfam.

Rutherford, A. C., Hogg, E. and McDonnell, D. (2021). "Incentivizing regulatory participation: Effectiveness of a fundraising levy," *Public Administration Review*, 81 (3): 532–542.

Stern, M. J. and Seifert, S. C. (2002). *Culture builds community evaluation summary report.* Philadelphia University of Pennsylvania School of Social Work.

Sterngold, Arthur. (2004). "Do economic impact studies misrepresent the benefits of arts and cultural organizations?. *Journal of Arts Management Law and Society*. 34: 166–187.

Stolle, D. and Rochon, T. (1998). "Are all associations alike? Member diversity, associational type, and the creation of social capital," *American Behavioral Scientist*, 42 (1): 47–65.

Stuckey, H. L. and Nobel, J. (2010). "The connection between art, healing, and public health: A review of current literature," *American Journal of Public Health*, 100 (2): 254–263.

Tripney, J., Newman, M., Bird, K., Vigurs, C., Kalra, N., Kwan, I. and Bangpan, M. (2010). *Understanding the impact of engagement in culture and sport: A systematic review of the research on the learning outcomes for young people participating in the arts.* London: Institute of Education, University of London.

UPSIAP-RF – University of Pennsylvania Social Impact of theArts Project and Reinvestment Fund (2017). *Culture and social wellbeing in New York City: Highlights of a two-year research project.* Available at: https://repository.upenn.edu/siap_culture_nyc/2.

Węziak-Białowolska, D., Białowolski, P. and Sacco, P. L. (2019). "Involvement with the arts and participation in cultural events – does personality moderate impact on well-being? Evidence from the U.K. Household Panel Survey," *Psychology of Aesthetics, Creativity, and the Arts,* 13 (3): 348–358.

# 9 Capital Campaigns for the Arts

with *Edilia Gänz*

## 9.1 Campaigning for the arts: basic definitions

While annual fundraising remains essential to the ongoing daily viability of most arts organizations, there are times when an institution has an opportunity for transformation, either by creating or renovating physical spaces or by endowing programs that are central to the institution's identity and mission. When not-for-profit organizations have these opportunities, they often engage in a capital campaign.

Broadly speaking, capital campaigns are intense, concerted fundraising efforts implemented to raise a large amount of money (often millions of dollars/euros) in a designated period of time (typically between three and five years) in order to achieve a specific purpose or set of purposes (Tempel et al., 2016). The typical aim of a capital campaign is to raise money to cover capital costs, such as building renovation or expansion, or even the acquisition of facilities (e.g., land on which cultural institutions can build). In the United States, capital campaigns are also initiated to augment or begin an endowment. More frequently than not, capital campaigns for new construction and/or renovations to existing physical plant also include an endowment element.

Capital campaigns are intended to have significant, long-term institutional impact and they require very sizable gifts from the institution's wealthiest donors. In quantitative terms, capital commitments are usually a healthy multiple of annual fund gifts, with campaign pledges typically fulfilled over a period of several years. Given the magnitude of most campaign "asks," gifts can be made in the form of cash, appreciated securities, real estate and, in the United States, often planned gifts.[1]

Capital campaigns are different from special project campaigns or purpose initiatives (Kihlstedt, 2005; Worth, 2016). Special project campaigns usually have smaller goals than capital campaigns, they tend to be shorter (one to three years) and they have a "cross-funding" logic. An example can help clarify this. If an opera house is organizing a special project campaign for the restoration of a ballet rehearsal room, it might decide to solicit only regular supporters of the ballet company instead of its whole donor base. By tailoring special project campaigns in this way, arts organizations can avoid positioning the initiative as the top giving goal to the entire supporter constituency and can match donors with their specific interests. In other words, these campaigns allow arts organizations to focus their solicitations on prospect donors who have a more specific connection with the initiative. Consequently, by embracing these campaigns, institutions can raise considerable additional money beyond annual fundraising.

Beyond achieving its principal goals, a successful capital campaign has some less obvious ancillary benefits. The expression "success begets success" can certainly apply to initiatives of this kind. Indeed, it is not unusual for arts organizations to experience a noticeable increase in annual giving after a successful campaign. In addition, investment in communications while the institution is in "campaign mode" can result in increased ticket sales as well as press attention, and may even have long-lasting benefits for its reputation and image. Thanks to the strength of their purpose, campaigns can often offer arts organizations new opportunities to improve or change their approach to and conversation with donors. Lastly, a successful capital campaign can even positively influence the entire fundraising ecosystem of a community (Worth, 2016; Woronkowicz and Nicholson-Crotty, 2017).

While capital campaigns have been prevalent in the United States for decades, European cultural institutions have not, until fairly recently, included them in their strategic planning. This relates to the structure for funding European arts organizations that has existed for many generations. As previously noted, European arts organizations have historically benefited from generous public support (e.g., local, regional and

---

[1] See Chapter 4.

national, and even from the European Commission), which has covered most of the costs that are usually the focal point of capital campaigns. However, owing to the recent social and geopolitical changes throughout Europe, further accelerated by the COVID-19 pandemic, reductions in public support for European cultural institutions is no longer a remote risk. Consequently, over the last two decades, arts institutions in Europe have been showing an increasing interest in finding alternative resources to finance their capital costs. As is the case in most of the world, earned income covers just a part of arts organizations' operational costs and is only very rarely available to fund capital needs. Consequently, European cultural institutions have worked not only to develop systematic philanthropic programs (i.e., memberships or annual programs) that can provide unrestricted gifts to fund operations, but also to explore new opportunities for raising greater amounts of money for capital needs. Some European arts organizations are now initiating campaigns that attempt to match potential donors with capital or special purpose projects, especially those that have a specific impact on the life of the wider community. An example of this new trend is provided in Box 9.1.

**Box 9.1 FEDORA: innovative philanthropy at European level**

FEDORA – the European Circle of Philanthropists of Opera and Ballet – is a not-for-profit organization that was created in Paris in 2013 under the presidency of Jérôme-François Zieseniss and the directorship of Edilia Gänz. Paying tribute to Rolf Liebermann, the well-known composer and former opera house director, FEDORA is committed to supporting and contributing to the renewal of opera and dance, supporting the artists of today and reaching out to younger and more diverse audiences.

FEDORA experiments with and builds new complementary funding models that support innovative and artistic opera and dance co-creations led by emerging artists and staged by opera houses, dance companies and festivals internationally. As a unique European ecosystem enabler in the opera and dance sector, FEDORA brings together the key actors of the industry: emerging artists and their new works, cultural institutions, international philanthropists and audiences.

In 2014, FEDORA launched a privately funded international competition, FEDORA Prizes, rewarding cutting-edge international projects in the areas of opera, dance, education and digital innovation; it is recognized as the "world's largest opera and dance competition" (*Das Erste – Europamagazin*).

In 2021, FEDORA and Opera Europa launched the Next Stage Initiative to trigger change and recovery in the opera and dance sector behind and beyond the stage. This initiative provides financial support and skills development to boost innovation through sustainability, inclusivity and digital transformation. The Next Stage Grants financially support the projects that help to create new industry standards and opportunities for change.

Over the past decade, FEDORA has invested over €2 million of private funding in seventeen new opera and dance projects, involving sixty-seven co-producing cultural institutions, with performances attended by over half a million people and hosted by twenty countries. The FEDORA platform is a beneficiary of the European Commission's Creative Europe Program, benefiting from an accumulated co-funding of over €4 million to scale its impact – together with its members across Europe.

*Source*: Edilia Gänz personal communication

When cultural institutions commit to a campaign, they must be prepared to commit a large portion of their fundraising resources to the campaign for its duration, as the process for asking higher-level donors for so-called stretch gifts (seemingly out of proportion to a donor's giving capacity) can involve multiple conversations. Furthermore, arts institutions should be aware of the risk that the capital campaign will undermine the annual fund, with donors choosing to partially fund their capital pledge with money that would otherwise have been contributed to the annual fund. Given that annual funds are usually the lifeblood of cultural institutions, effective communication about the value of both the annual fund and the capital campaign can mitigate this risk.

To reduce the risk of cannibalization, campaigns in the arts sector often go beyond the capital needs of an organization and are comprehensive in focus. These comprehensive campaigns require the arts institution to make a substantial effort in involving its entire donor base (Weinstein and Barden, 2017). Rather than appealing to donors to support a capital project, comprehensive campaigns raise funds that cover the whole spectrum of a cultural organization's financial necessities. In a campaign of this kind, donors, both large and small, can feel as if they are actively contributing to "the campaign" and making a difference. What is more, arts organizations can offer donors with different interests alternative giving choices, with all gifts counting towards the campaign goal. This means that – unlike in traditional capital campaigns – a donor's contribution to the annual fund, to a capital project or to the endowment counts as a gift to the comprehensive campaign. Of course, it is imperative that the institution continues to emphasize the importance of the annual fund when marketing a comprehensive campaign.

As contrasted with comprehensive campaigns, arts institutions periodically initiate targeting campaign fundraising (primarily addressed to the board and other major donors already close to the institution) when confronting the effect of an externally precipitated financial crisis. This has recently happened during periods of financial upheaval such as the great recession of 2008 or the COVID-19 pandemic in 2020–2022 (see Box 9.2). During the pandemic, with the reduced ability to generate earned income, arts organizations turned to their boards and other loyal long-term major donors for gifts to offset the precipitous drop in ticket sales. These campaigns have been reactive, rather than proactive or strategic, and their focus has been quite narrow. Even concerning the urgency of their financial necessities, organizations should note that when campaigning is conducted this way, it tends not to have clearly predictable and consistent results. Moving on in our discussion, we will explore how capital campaigns are planned and executed, and how it is possible to measure their impacts.

**Box 9.2 Special project fundraising in times of economic uncertainty**

In its more recent history, the Boston Symphony Orchestra (BSO) has been forced to rely on special fundraising appeals to address some crucial moments of special need during periods of economic uncertainty. The first was in 2004, when the BSO raised $3 million during a mini-special campaign in order to completely restore and endow for the future maintenance of the Aeolian-Skinner 5,000+ pipe organ in the Symphony Hall, which was close to being irreparable. Then, in 2008, the BSO raised $12 million to offset losses in endowment incomes, precipitated by a market collapse. More recently, in 2020, BSO succeeded in raising $21 million in addition to its annual fundraising, which along with over $16 million from the federal government resulted in the Orchestra being financially well positioned after the COVID-19 pandemic, with an operating cash balance approaching $50 million.

*Source*: Mark Volpe personal communication

## 9.2 Capital campaigns: features and key successful factors

Broadly speaking, fundraising campaigns should be aligned with the cultural institution's vision and mission. 2 However, capital campaigns have a specific purpose, a defined goal and are accomplished in a defined period. According to this strict logic, arts organizations should detail the purpose of their campaigns into specific objectives that are related to the strategic priorities of the institution. Any fundraising effort without a clear and differentiated goal, that is intended as to "raise as much money as possible" or continues until a certain total has been achieved will not be successful. Establishing clear deadlines is necessary to ensure a campaign's effectiveness and momentum. Deadlines and objectives must be widely communicated so that all individuals involved know what is expected. In addition, beyond serving as an impetus for insiders to focus on in a disciplined way, communications regarding timelines and deadlines to the broader donor community can instill a sense of urgency. (Worth, 2016; Weinstein and Barden, 2017).

All these elements can be important motivators for those invested in a campaign's positive completion. The commitment of board leadership and CEO is therefore essential if it is to be successful. When the arts organization's leadership commits itself to a campaign, the consistency and credibility of the effort increase significantly in the public eye. In Chapter 2, we discuss the relevance of developing a culture of philanthropy that encourages the involvement of the entire organization (not just the fundraising department) in its development efforts. This concept becomes even more pertinent when an art organization is in campaign mode (see Fig. 9.1.)

Hopkins and Friedman (1997: 12) use the word "impetus" to describe the powerful internal engine of a successful campaign. This expresses the shared desire of all elements of an arts organization to achieve a major goal that usually has to do with a change: a building renovation, a change

[2] Vision is a clear declaration of what the cultural institution hopes to be in the future. Mission includes the institutional priorities and strategies that the cultural institution employs to make the vision become reality. In other words, mission is the pursuit of a goal that can differentiate an arts organization from its competitors, emphasizing its core values. Mission statements should be a well-balanced mix of general purposes and specific focuses, involving people in terms of broad themes and also prioritizing activities and resources.

*Figure 9.1* The nine key factors for a successful capital campaign

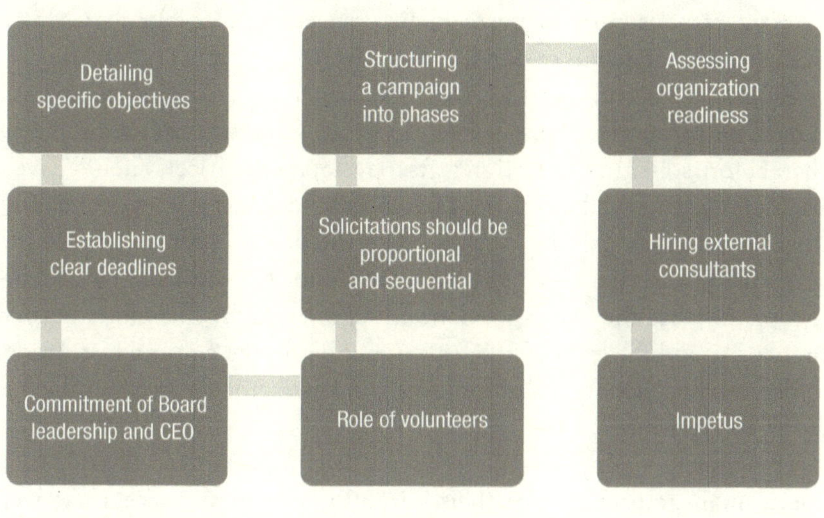


in general programming, institutional stabilization. Consequently, it is very important that everybody in the cultural institution feels the same acute need on which the campaign aims to focus. To create this emotional (almost intimate) connection with the campaign's purpose and share it with the community that the organization serves, the role of volunteers is of the utmost importance. As people tend to follow the example of those whom they admire or with whom they wish to be associated, arts institutions can engage prestigious volunteer leaders (who are typically already involved with the institution) to authenticate the case for support. Arts institutions should have their volunteer leaders serving in visible roles (e.g., as chairs or co-chairs or as members of the campaign leadership committee). To inspire further donations effectively, leading volunteers should be willing to contribute directly to the campaign, and to cultivate and solicit other prospects (Kihlstedt, 2010; Worth, 2016). Committed volunteers can serve on the organization's board or board committee, be a member of the organization's constituent groups (e.g., friends, members) or be philanthropically minded members of the community. These people can become potential major benefactors of a successful capital campaign. Because of this, fundraisers should have at their disposal a list of potential leading volunteers who have the ability to "make a difference" in a campaign. In this search for leading volunteers, development officers have the responsibility to create an effective engagement strategy, which will inspire individuals to participate actively in the arts organization.

Rosso (1991) and Worth (2016) recommend that capital campaigns should be designed so that solicitations are proportionate. This means that, before soliciting campaign gifts, development officers should have a sense of the financial capacity of prospective donors. All too frequently, institutions under-ask (i.e., for less than the donor might be inclined to give) or over-ask (i.e., for more than the donor has available for philanthropy) because they have not done enough research. Therefore, beyond propensity and the level of interest a donor has in the cultural institution, understanding donors' ability to give is a key factor for successful campaign fundraising.

Structuring a campaign into phases is also important: an organization has to manage each one of them carefully to achieve success. As well as being proportional, campaign solicitations should be sequential. As previously noted, when embracing a campaign, arts institutions should address their board, their most engaged donors and their major prospects first, as they have the higher giving capacity and represent the heart of the institution's donor base. Only later should the campaign reach out to the broader campaign prospect pool. (Tempel et al., 2016). Even if this process can be complex and difficult to sustain, case histories confirm this approach is essential if campaign results are to be maximized. Setting the correct timing is very important, so that the campaign's results are not affected by premature or late actions.

In our discussion, we have noted that a campaign can consume considerable resources. When a campaign is under way, numerous commitments have to be secured in a relatively short period from contributors who have to be specifically cultivated and solicited. Consequently, assessing an organization's readiness for a capital campaign before launching it is fundamental. This is not only a matter of calculating the costs of running a campaign, but also takes into consideration time and commitment. During a campaign, the CEO, development director and development staff will be fully engaged, and it is very important that they have time and energy to sustain their efforts. Considering the burden and the complexity of well-designed campaigns, hiring external consultants can be appropriate, even if it brings extra costs (Kihlstedt, 2005). Consultants can give helpful professional advice and provide additional human resources, while also offering a less self-referential perspective in the development and implementation of a campaign's feasibility study and its planning documents.

## 9.3 Carrying forward a capital campaign for the arts: key stages

All arts organizations are unique. They have their own history, fundraising practices and, of course, culture. Therefore, even if there are some commonalities in the ways they develop a campaign, no general prescription is possible. At this point of our discussion, however, we have to state again that capital campaigns are intended to provide the necessary resources to fulfil an organization's long-term mission and, consequently, actuate its vision. This is why an arts organization should focus on and understand the "why" that moves it before a campaign is launched. This understanding goes beyond financial targets, since the impact of the campaign affects the organization at all levels: it involves artists, community and project legacy. Only when the purpose is clear can the message be formulated and the target identified.

As previously mentioned, campaigns are usually conducted in phases. Some of these phases regard the actual development of the campaign; some others start well before the campaign itself is planned. Lindhal (2008) suggests that core planning should be divided into three sub-phases: leadership, growth and goal-line. The leadership phase is the period during which the organization should focus on securing commitments from the institution's board leaders and other historically generous donors. The institution should start with donors who are most ready to commit and then leverage those commitments to stimulate and/or inspire their peers to join the campaign. This phase can be determinant to the success of the campaign, and fundraisers should wait to move to the next phase (i.e., growth) until a high percentage of the overall goal (between 40 and 60 per cent) is committed. During the growth phase, the prospect list of donors is expanded as contributors to the leadership phase motivate the next circle of donors through cultivation events and solicitations. In the final goal-line phase, organizations focus on committed donors whose assets are more modest and major donors who want their gifts to bring the campaign to a victorious conclusion. Another more popular way to analyze the macro-phases of a capital campaign is by distinguishing a quiet (private) phase from a public (community) phase (Tempel et al., 2016; Worth, 2016). The rationale behind this is that, for an initial limited period, a campaign's planning and preparation are circulated only among the organization's internal constituencies, with the launch to a wider public only taking place when at least two-thirds of the campaign goal is achieved.

On this basis, what we will try to do here is provide a possible approach to structuring a campaign that is derived from observing case histories in the arts sector and the literature. The campaign structure that we propose here for arts organizations is that suggested by Tempel et al. (2016), and comprises six main steps:

- feasibility study;
- planning;
- kick-off and public announcements;
- campaign closing and celebration;
- stewardship;
- impact evaluation.

Figure 9.2 outlines the relationships among the different phases of a campaign. We discuss each of them in detail in the following paragraphs.

*Figure 9.2* The phases of a capital campaign

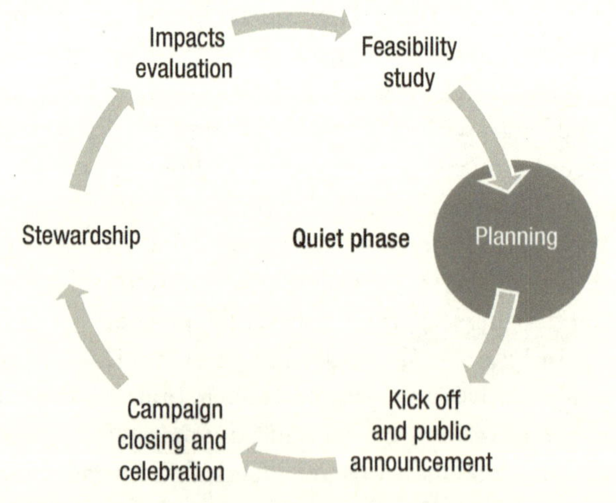


*Source*: Author's elaboration from Tempel et al. (2016)

### 9.3.1 *Pre-campaign steps: the feasibility study*

A feasibility study is the first step in planning a campaign. The results of this, which should be conducted with the professional support of external consultants, give arts organizations an overview of what they should know before starting. The study can even help the institution to evaluate whether there is an enough interest to start a campaign at all. In addition, a feasibility study helps them determine if they are prepared for the rigor of an ambitious, multi-year campaign (Tempel et al., 2016). This pre-campaign phase is also relevant in that it allows those involved in the campaign (i.e., executives, board members, development staff and leading volunteers) to start thinking about how the campaign should develop, not only from the organization's perspective, but also from that of the prospects.

The feasibility study is the result of two different but complementary analyzes: an external study of the philanthropy market and an internal audit.

The external study, through a PEST(EL) analysis, which focuses on political, economic, socio-cultural and technological (environmental and legal) factors, helps the institution understand the external conditions that inevitably impact the proposed campaign. This, and a SWOT analysis (strength, weakness, opportunity and threat[3]) in which the institution's relationship with the external world is examined, are important steps in the preparation of a campaign.

The internal audit can provide arts organizations with an overview of their current institutional and fundraising situation. In particular, this assessment should clarify what resources – human (e.g., staff, board, volunteers) and business (e.g., technology, systems, financial means) – are internally available before the campaign starts. The core deliverable of virtually all feasibility studies, which relates to propensity (i.e., interest in making a major gift) and capacity (i.e., the amount that the organization can reasonably solicit), relies on this internal assessment of the arts institution's current donor base.

The process begins with the campaign volunteer leaders, the professional leadership and the consultant agreeing on the donors who should be interviewed. After this, consultants confidentially interview these

[3] See the glossary for further definitions.

donors to gather information and collect some of the data that will be used to draft the feasibility study. Beyond non-board member donors, the consultants will want to interview key members of the board, senior staff and leaders in the community including corporate and foundation leaders. These conversations are typically the most delicate moments in the pre-campaign phase. However, the information gathered can be reliable and, on many occasions, invaluable. Effectively conducted, these interviews inform the arts institution of the amount that may be raised in a campaign and the key drivers that will motivate current and prospective donors. This analysis should be conducted from both the organization's and the donors' perspective.

The presence of external consultants aims to provide the arts institution with a more objective and neutral perspective in gathering this qualitative information. This process is delicate and, of course, demands considerable resources. It is very important that leaders are ready and willing to accept the findings. A summary of collected responses (without identifying individual respondents) is usually shared with the campaign planners. Findings of these preliminary studies can help campaign planners adjust or change campaign goals or planned actions, saving resources and improving effectiveness. Therefore, it is very important to avoid short cuts or poor communication.

During the pre-phase of a campaign, arts organizations are required to develop a compelling case for support that will drive all subsequent campaigning actions. Drafting a case for support is complex, so campaign planners should conduct conversations with people at different levels of the organization, in order to fashion a statement that will represent the whole institution's perspective. Through this process, all involved people are required to think carefully about the organization's mission, structure and current effectiveness in delivering its services or activities, to fully understand and express why a campaign is necessary. This process is usually supported by personal interviews with the key players in the campaign. Once the case for support is generated, it should be tested with current and potential major gift donors (Worth, 2016).

Current major donors can be the most important allies of an arts institution during the campaign pre-phase. As these donors already embrace the cultural institution's purpose, involving them in pilot projects or smaller initiatives that might lead to a more wide-ranging campaign will allow the development staff to understand the pitfalls and risks (and also the opportunities) that should be considered. For this testing to have effective results, arts organizations should be able to count on well-structured lists of donors so they can select the profiles that are most suitable for their purpose. Moreover, as previously noted, knowing donors personally is important so it is possible to rate them before a campaign is launched. If a realistic assessment of the organization's fundraising potential is not made, the risk that the campaign will fail is very high (Tempel et al., 2016). After all pertinent information has been gathered, the consultants, in conjunction with the organization's development department, should be able to draft the feasibility study document. Some consultants refer to this as a campaign planning study, since the recommendations may go beyond the feasibility of the specific campaign goal (Worth, 2010, 2016; Tempel et al., 2016). In any case, the final document typically leads to a campaign plan that encompasses the final goal and the changes that the organization should adopt before launching the campaign (see the next phase).

The feasibility study may also include a recommendation that the arts institution should invest in additional staff and the professional support of a consulting firm.[4] A campaign budget and a description of the scope of the consulting services for the next phase complete the document. When the feasibility study is encouraging, the arts organization gains confidence that the campaign can proceed to the next step. Of course, good governance requires that the board should arrange a formal presentation of the feasibility study, as it is imperative that the leadership understand the magnitude of the opportunity and have a sense of the role that they will be expected to play.

The organization's communication skills play a key role during all phases of a campaign, including its preliminary steps. Communication must be focused on the campaign goals and be clear and impactful not only for the external, but also for the internal groups that are involved in the fundraising effort. While donors are the primary addressees, there should be a consistency of style, tone and visuals across the entire spectrum of campaign communications.

---

[4] The campaign consulting firm is frequently not the same firm as the one that conducts the feasibility study.

### 9.3.2 *The quiet phase or campaign planning*

Between the feasibility study and the public announcement of most campaigns, board leadership, executive leadership and development staff conduct the so-called quiet phase, which consists of campaign planning and the solicitation of board members and other donors closest to the institution.

Campaigns are adopted to raise money to cover capital costs and last for a period that often overlaps with that of a general strategic plan (i.e., three to five years). Consequently, arts organizations are better able to plan their campaign after the board has adopted the strategic plan. A campaign plan should always begin with a "statement of strategic direction" (Tempel et al. 2016, 245) that reflects the organization's identity and its vision of the impact the campaign will have (O'Brien, 2005).

During this phase, several activities typically occur (see Fig. 9.3).

*Recruitment and appointment of the campaign committee*: As in most endeavors, leadership is critical to success. It is essential that the board chair and CEO recruit a campaign chair (or chairs) who can make leadership gifts and are willing to inspire and solicit peers to join them in support-

*Figure 9.3* Activities that take place during the quiet phase of a capital campaign

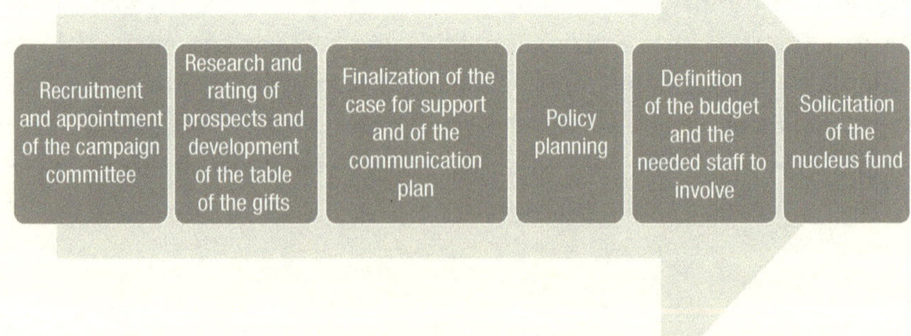

ing the campaign. Once the campaign chairs are appointed, they must assemble a capital campaign committee (sometimes known as the campaign steering committee) that will oversee the entire campaign. Broadly speaking, such a committee can include the CEO, the chief development officer, a campaign chair and a board chair together with influential board members who may also be major donors or have the potential to be so. Typically, a campaign committee reports to either the full board of directors (which in the United States is ultimately responsible and must exercise the highest standard of care) or to the executive committee of the board, which acts on behalf of the entire board with powers and responsibilities delegated by law. Best practices suggest that the campaign committee should make periodic reports to the executive committee of the board or to the entire board of directors. In order to encourage ownership of the campaign throughout the organization, the campaign should be a standing topic on every board meeting agenda. This may also be true for reports to the creative teams, staff and volunteers – the internal constituents. The appointment of a campaign committee can occur at different stages of a campaign. Occasionally, the committee is appointed before the feasibility study is conducted; while other institutions wait to appoint a campaign committee until after the board votes to initiate a campaign after reviewing the feasibility report. For the purposes of this section, we will assume that the campaign committee is organized after the board has voted to launch a campaign. In this sequence, the campaign begins the process of reviewing objectives and goals, and fine tunes the case. Perhaps the most important step in the campaign committee's work involves campaign members working together to solicit each other's gifts. Board leadership, development staff and campaign counsel should carefully coordinate this activity. Securing commitments at the highest possible level is critical, as these individuals will be able to leverage their "stretch gifts" to secure commitments from their assigned prospects. Of course, in appointing the campaign committee, the predisposition they might have to make a meaningful donation might be the most important criterion. After the campaign committee members have all made commitments, other board members and major donors should be approached during this quiet phase. The aggregate of all of these early gifts will constitute the first nucleus fund of the campaign (Kihlstedt, 2010; Worth, 2016). These individuals are the prospects closest to the institution and should be making the most generous contributions to the campaign.

*Research and rating of prospects and development of the gift range chart*: Before asking for their commitment to a specific campaign timeline, prospects should be screened through research, analysis and assessment of their propensity and capacity to give. In particular, this analysis should include an understanding of prospects' past giving, giving to other institutions, real estate ownership, stock holdings and club memberships. In the silent phase, arts organizations can also select the date at which gifts can begin counting towards the campaign goal. This deadline is typically shared only among a restricted group of stakeholders at this point: the administrative leadership, the governing board, key volunteers and major donors, fundraising staff and other related audiences. Even if both the money goal (or range) and this first deadline are clear, a final target does not yet have to be established (Tempel et al., 2016). In this phase, it could also be useful to refer to a table/pyramid of gifts (Hopkins and Friedman, 1997; Worth, 2016), which identifies the different levels of gifts needed to achieve the campaign goal (see Fig. 9.4).

The campaign committee should then create an inventory of donor recognition opportunities; this is a very useful tool in campaign marketing. The inventory should be carefully crafted to encourage prospects to stretch their thinking in respect to gift size. While such donor recognition vehicles are too numerous to list, a few examples include the naming

*Figure 9.4* Template of gift range chart

| Goal: $/€1.3 million | | | | | | |
|---|---|---|---|---|---|---|
| Number of gifts | $/Euro amount of each gift | $/Euro amount from level | Cumulative amount | % of total | Multiplier | Prospects needed |
| 1 | 250,000 | 250,000 | 250,000 | 19% | X2 | 2 |
| 2 | 125,000 | 250,000 | 500,000 | 38% | X2 | 4 |
| 4 | 50,000 | 200,000 | 700,000 | 54% | X3 | 12 |
| 8 | 25,000 | 200,000 | 900,000 | 69% | X3 | 24 |
| 10 | 10,000 | 100,000 | 1,000,000 | 77% | X3 | 30 |
| 20 | 5,000 | 100,000 | 1,100,000 | 85% | X3 | 60 |
| 30 | 2,500 | 75,000 | 1,175,000 | 90% | X4 | 120 |
| Many (50) | < 2,500 | 125,000 | 1,300,000 | 100% | Many (X5) | Many (250) |

of a curator's chair at a museum; the naming of a space (e.g., lobby, stage) within a building or, for a mega-gift, the building itself; an opera production; a chair or position in an orchestra. Aside from naming, there are other donor privileges that can be offered, special tours, events, dinners and conferences, for example, which can take place in special locations on notable occasions. Publicizing major gifts via the arts organization's communication channels is also an effective way of celebrating a donor's generosity. When establishing the table of gifts and the recognition they might receive, organizations should always remember that the very top of the pyramid can produce upwards of 50 per cent of the goal – and the inventory of gift recognition vehicles should be managed very carefully.

*Finalization of the case for support and of the communication plan*: Before moving to the public phase of the campaign, the campaign planning committee must undertake a concluding review of the case for support and agree to a final version. Moreover, a communications plan through which the case for support is shared with multiple constituencies must be outlined. During this process, it is possible to involve the closest, long-time supporters by asking not just for a gift commitment, but also for a sincere reaction to the case for support. When undertaking this test, arts organizations should be prepared to welcome both constructive suggestions and possible criticism, and ultimately be willing to incorporate such feedback in a refined case statement. The final output of this process is a document whose focus should be a clear and effective explanation of the need that is being addressed in the campaign and how the successful completion of the process will be transformative for the arts institution, its projects and, consequently, the community it serves. The case of support will be the content basis for all the campaign material (i.e., printed material, press statements, online posts, other communication materials, and also internal document and reporting). Of course, the campaign staff will produce diverse materials for the various groups impacted by the campaign throughout its sequential phases. The communication plan of the entire campaign should be outlined during the quiet phase, in order to prepare for the presentation of the campaign to the wider public.

*Policy planning*: Throughout the campaign, various policy issues will arise. While some matters will require the attention of the full board, most will be addressed by the campaign planning committee. The implementation of campaign policies is a very delicate process, since these are the behavioral path that the arts institution will follow throughout the campaign. Policies that the campaign planning committee will need to address include some key issues. For instance, the pay-out time for pledges is worthy of note as the cultural institution must balance its immediate cash needs and the financial flexibility that it is willing to allow. Another policy matter concerns the staging of the various phases of the campaign, including the duration of the quiet phase, which, as noted, is contingent on the percentage of campaign goal achieved. The campaign planning committee should also organize the various ways in which gifts will be acknowledged (e.g., personal letters, calls, possible press dissemination) and create a list (occasionally described as "menu") that is organized by giving level, showing all the ways in which donors can contribute to the campaign. Finally, the committee should be prepared to periodically report the progress of the campaign to the full board and other pertinent groups, using relevant data.

*Definition of the budget and the staff to be involved*: When considering the duration of a campaign and its potential financial goals, case histories suggest that arts organizations should foresee a campaign budget that does not exceed 5 per cent of the funds to be raised. Such a budget should include all costs associated with the campaign (e.g., consulting expenses, staffing, materials, events, etc.). This should be defined separately, in order not to lose overall focus on the campaign goal. An organization can decide either to add the budget to the campaign goal, or to cover the expense of the campaign with different resources. In respect to staffing, the campaign manager is a key role, in addition to a dedicated team of fundraisers. This position is responsible for all operating aspects of the campaign and the careful coordination of all groups involved, including board leadership, other volunteers, staff, donors and prospects.

*Solicitation of the nucleus fund*: During the quiet phase, insiders will develop a deep knowledge of the anticipated campaign goal and all other aspects of the campaign. Solicitations follow a very carefully planned top-down/inside-out process and solicited gifts will be included in the campaign's nucleus fund. The nucleus of very close prospects that is drawn upon is the key pool of donors. Scholars recommend that the objective should be achieving commitments that will cover between 40 and 60 per cent of the ultimate campaign goal (Lindahl, 2008).

There is no golden rule about the exact duration of a well-balanced quiet phase. As a general rule, it should last long enough to determine whether the campaign goal presented in the feasibility analysis is realistically achievable (Tempel et al., 2016). For example, a disappointing amount committed by the nucleus fund might lead the arts institution to reassess the campaign goals or consider lengthening the quiet campaign period before launching it to the public. The quiet phase ends with the public announcement of the campaign's goal and timeline. Box 9.3 describes an example of capital campaign conducted by Boston Symphony Orchestra at Tanglewood.

**Box 9.3 Tanglewood Learning: when campaign planning wins**

Tanglewood is the summer home of the Boston Symphony (BSO), situated on 500 acres of land and including over 100 buildings. Historically, it had two primary activities: a summer music festival that is regarded as the most important in the United States and a music center in which the next generation of professional musicians receive instruction from members of the BSO and some of the world's greatest artists. However, in spite of Tanglewood's success, there were several significant concerns that needed addressing. Consequently, a strategic planning committee proposed a building project that would address three main concerns and opportunities:

- Tanglewood Music Center: the summer program attracting 150 of the most talented young professionals in the world, needed more rehearsal and performance space.
- Baby Boomer generation: the largest generation in history, which accumulated significant wealth, began retiring at the end of the last century. Its members had disposable income, and were looking for opportunities to learn more about music.
- Tanglewood's buildings: there are 100 buildings on campus, none of which were winterized with the consequence being that the towns in which Tanglewood is situated could not use Tanglewood facilities during the offseason for civic, community and educational purposes.

The campaign steps outlined in this chapter were all followed in the project: there was a pre-campaign audit and strategic plan drafted, the campaign committee began to meet monthly and a budget was developed. This budget included an estimated $32 million in building costs, a projection of the Tanglewood Learning

Institute's (adult education program) operating costs, the forecast of the building operating costs, and expenses related to off-season use resulting in a campaign goal of $70 million including a significant addition to the endowment intended to cover all operating costs. A gift table was built, with naming rights priced.
A lead gift was secured for $35 million, and the campaign exceeded its goal with $72 million raised. As a result, a four-building complex was completed (winning top US architectural awards) that addressed the programming needs identified at the advent of the initiative.

*Source*: Mark Volpe personal communication

### 9.3.3 *Campaign kick-off and public phase*

When a campaign goes public, the excitement generated when the arts institution's initiative becomes more visible can inspire and stimulate the campaign team while also adding stress and time pressure.

The public phase usually begins with a large-scale official event. At this point, the campaign manager and the development staff should have compiled a list of all the commitments made and a list of remaining prospects who need to be solicited before the campaign concludes. Prior to the official launch, development staff should confidentially and privately inform some of these prospects about the upcoming announcement, so they are not surprised. If this is done effectively, these prospects feel that they must be important as they are receiving special treatment. Managing these communications and expectations requires sensitivity and nuance.

Scholars usually adopt the metaphor of a football game when describing the official presentation of a capital campaign (Kihlstedt, 2010; Tempel et al., 2016; Worth, 2016). The public phase starts with a kick-off and ends with a victory celebration, during which donors should appreciate that their generosity has made the campaign's success possible, despite challenges and obstacles.

The kick-off is the official event that opens the public phase. This event should include background about the arts institution, the challenges and opportunities to be addressed by the campaign, a recognition of the donors who have contributed to the nucleus fund and the campaign timeline. The campaign team should plan the kick-off event carefully and consistently with the campaign's primary focus: the campaign for the building of a new auditorium will require a different kick-off event than one that aims to create or further build an endowment.

In addition to the wide public of potential stakeholders, all key people involved in the campaign project should be involved in the kick-off, with the aim of generating excitement, visibility and optimism that will inspire the campaign's leaders as well as those potential donors who are yet to be solicited. Fundraising practitioners recommend that arts organizations time the public announcement of their campaign to coincide with at least 40 to 60 per cent of the goal committed. Publicly announcing a campaign when only 25 or 30 per cent of the goal has been achieved will create the impression that the campaign has little momentum, while announcing it when 65 or 75 per cent is committed will create the impression among remaining prospects that their generosity may not be needed (Tempel et al., 2016: 250). Campaign case histories also document that a certain number of donors like to make gifts late in the campaign, so that it appears their gift helped to successfully close the campaign. However, campaign statistics tend to highlight a significant drop in interest among a broader donor pool when the campaign is at between 95 and 110 per cent of completion level and a drastic fall in donors' attention as soon the goal has been achieved. These findings reinforce the importance for an organization to be focused on goal setting throughout the entire campaign effort. In order to manage this risk, using a variable goal throughout the campaign's different phases may be advisable – setting one goal during the quiet phase with the possibility of revising it during the public one. For example, when a campaign is going well, announcing a higher goal with the message that the institution will be able to provide extra value to a community beyond the original promises in the case can be quite effective.

Communication is important throughout the various phases of the campaign, with its significance increasing once the campaign has been publicly announced. By definition, when a campaign becomes public, additional scrutiny can be expected. Managing the messaging is critical when addressing questions from the press or disseminating information through the institution's analogue and digital channels. Such communications need to go beyond the immediate stakeholders and should be addressed to the broader community, even those who have little interest in the organization. Creating a buzz across the whole community can only have a positive impact on prospective donors.

When the campaign goal has been shared with the larger community, arts organizations should pay attention to donors' reactions. Duncan

(2004) suggests that campaign donors want to make a real difference, so they may be motivated either to be the first or the last donor (this is the impact philanthropy theory). Taking a contrary perspective, Andreoni (1990) states that donors are motivated by good feelings regardless of other donors' intentions, thus being equally likely to give at various points during the campaign's life cycle. Business research argues that the more demanding the goal, the higher the performance improvement because of the challenge that donors perceive (Locke, 2001). While they are not consistent, these assertions about donor intent confirm one truism: it is very important for an arts institution to have a sense of the motivation of each donor. With respect to the broader pool of donors, sharing campaign progress on a regular basis is a good way to keep donors interested and invested. Peer-to-peer solicitations and communications are still the recommended approach.

### 9.3.4 *Campaign closing and celebration*

The approaching of a campaign's official deadline gives arts organizations the opportunity to further perfect their fundraising efforts. Tempel et al. (2016: 251) argue that an impending deadline can give new donors an opportunity to be part of a successful effort: as the cliché goes, everybody supports a winner. Moreover, when the deadline is approaching, the organization can solicit the last "not-yet-committed" donors. These are usually individuals who might have been expected to commit at the very beginning of the campaign, but for whatever reason did not. With a compelling result and deadline on the horizon, a new ask for funding could be effective. Finally, campaign closing is the moment to resolicit donors who made commitments that were significantly below expectations. This must, of course, be done with finesse and respect in order not to discount the importance of major gifts secured at the beginning of the campaign.

Typically, the end of a campaign is marked by an official closure event during which the campaign leadership announces results, in particular the amount of money raised and the top objectives achieved. Such celebrations should involve lead donors, other contributors, staff, the artistic team, community leaders, politicians, possibly press and sometimes beneficiaries of the campaign (for example, if the campaign had a educational element, including impacted students can be meaningful). While the accomplishment of a monetary goal should be acknowledged, more emphasis should be placed on the donors themselves, and the difference their generosity will make for the arts institution and the broader community.

A campaign closure event presents a valuable opportunity to demonstrate that a theatre, museum, symphony or other arts organization does not undertake a campaign simply to raise money. A campaign's greater accomplishment is found in the connections that are made between donors' passions and an organization's need. Furthermore, a successful campaign can provide encouragement to the arts institution to undertake a future campaign with a degree of confidence. But nothing is possible without the effective and thoughtful stewardship of donors.

### 9.3.5 *Campaign stewardship*

After a campaign has been successfully concluded, the greatest risk for an arts organization is complacency and a lack of sensitivity towards those who have worked hard to make the campaign successful. Good stewardship at this stage should involve everyone who has been involved in the campaign, recognizing their efforts and expressing acknowledgement and appreciation. During this phase, it should be reinforced to each campaign donor that their gift was invaluable and that a specific institutional need was addressed. The institution's leadership should be personally engaged in these stewardship efforts.

Personal stewardship should be preferred wherever it is possible. The leaders of a campaign should always find the time to meet donors in person and thank them for joining and supporting the project. This includes not only major donors, but also those new ones who show promise for long-term engagement and continued future support. Other useful stewardship strategies can be pursued, including permanent signage that acknowledges the campaign's efforts, the amount raised and the impact, thereby creating a long-lasting memory of the campaign period. Post campaign stewardship might also include events that involve the campaign's volunteer leadership and donors who have contributed with particular generosity, as well as reports and summaries (e.g., impact reports and figures) about the usefulness of a campaign, which may also include a list of the donors involved. Digital communications (to be shared, for example via email or official website) also work very well in expressing gratitude and acknowledgement. Highlighting the names of volunteer leaders and major donors (or other key figures) in a variety of settings can also enhance stewardship efforts.

### 9.3.6 *Evaluating the campaign impacts*

The concluding phase of a campaign is the perfect moment for the campaign team to look back at the entire process to evaluate all aspects of the campaign so as to inform future campaigns or other fundraising efforts. It is very important to dedicate a separate phase to this work, as the campaign staff will be fully occupied with the campaign while it is in progress.

While many institutions choose to evaluate a recently completed campaign internally, post-campaign assessment that is supported by an external consultant can provide more objective and reliable information. This review and evaluation will also be fundamental to the planning of future campaigns. Analyzing processes and results (in terms of internal policies and organizational behavior) is very useful in helping an arts organization focus on the most effective way of functioning as a development office even when no campaign is under way. In addition, the expertise gained during a campaign can shape future fundraising efforts by developing internal leadership and raising the sights of donors, thereby leading to a greater level of support (Hopkins and Friedman, 1997). By focusing the attention of the overall community on the organization and its needs, cultural institutions can unite potential prospects around a common cause. This is a powerful precondition for developing future campaigning initiatives.

The evaluation of a campaign's impacts has to include both quantitative and qualitative factors. Quantitative factors can be, for example, the aggregate money raised, the number of donors, the number of contacts reached or the economic impact on the area where the organization operates. Qualitative indicators measure the impact that a campaign has on the entire community, especially in social and cultural terms. Measuring the impact before planning for further campaigns is very important in terms of the organization's external validation, as successful campaigning has so many positive dimensions beyond what an arts institution can imagine when it begins. A campaign is very helpful in strengthening relationships between an arts organization and its city or community, as it can highlight which its value to the broader through the generosity of the donor community (see Box 9.4).

With respect to future campaigning trends, issues such as social equity and justice will gain most attention, both in the United States and in Europe.

**Box 9.4 Detroit Symphony: matching community needs to start the rebirth**

In 1990, the Detroit Symphony Orchestra (DSO) was a very good orchestra that played conventional concerts in a fine hall – surrounded by a crack cocaine corridor that required the presence of eighteen fully armed security guards at every concert or event. At the time, the DSO had a budget of roughly $17 million but had accumulated $18 million in bank debt and had not paid creditors: this meant it was insolvent and was contemplating filing for bankruptcy. The board asked the musicians and staff to accept massive pay cuts while plans for the future were made. The process began with an assessment of the market which led to the conclusion that the orchestra did not have artistic challenges, but rather an urban challenge. The riots of the late 1960s had decimated whole neighborhoods in Detroit, so the city was much more concerned about urban renewal than it was about artistic accomplishment. Therefore, the DSO was not relevant and had become disconnected from the community in which it operated: indeed, in an informal poll that was conducted by the orchestra's CEO it was ranked thirty-second out of thirty-three cultural and educational institutions in terms of importance. The institution learnt a valuable lesson: that it should be aware of the market and the community around it. Although the artistic teams can be more internally focused, the leadership of cultural institutions should be both internally and externally aware. The orchestra therefore engaged in an ambitious project and avoided insolvency; this ultimately led to $250 million in investment in a project that helped to initiate Detroit's rebirth. The approach included strategic observations of the neighborhood in which the orchestra's hall was situated. As a consequence, during the first years of the 1990s, the institution bought 18 acres of land surrounding the hall, secured a federal grant to demolish vacant buildings and engaged architects to create various plans for the surrounding the hall including an office building for Detroit Medical Center's administrative staff, a related parking garage for the medical center's staff that also would be available for the Symphony's attendees at night, a restaurant an expansion of the hall, with the addition of a black box theatre that was mostly dedicated to community programming, to ensure that the hall would be a destination for the all. Concurrently, the leadership of the DSO attended many school board meetings and helped to create messaging and support for a $110 million bond issue for the construction of a Performing Arts High School next to the DSO's hall. The funding for the project came from both public and private sources, with many generous donors committing gifts to the largest campaign in the history of the orchestra. These were augmented by grants from the State of Michigan and the City of Detroit. The project generated enormous good will from virtually the entire city, and was frequently front-page news in both of the major daily papers while it was under way.

*Source*: Mark Volpe personal communication

Consequently, the ability of an organization to show itself to be a credible community player in respect to these themes will make a difference to prospective donors. Being able to describe in a campaign report that the initiative has constructively impacted diversity, equity and inclusion can positively influence not only the public debate in respect to what the organization has been able to do, but also the preparation for future initiatives' accountability. This sensitivity towards community issues is compelling in the multiracial (and less Eurocentric) societies of Western countries: cultural institutions seeking funding from private and/or public sources are having to rethink their positioning in society, and must find contemporary ways to describe and evaluate the impact of their activities. As addressed in Chapter 8, accurate metrics are needed to measure social impact, and much of the donor community, especially younger entrepreneurs, will expect arts institutions to provide these.

### Keywords for arts fundraisers

Capital campaign, capital costs, endowment, special project campaign, planned gift, campaign pledge, stretched gifts, comprehensive campaign, cross-funding logic, campaign fundraising, major gift, proportional and sequential solicitations, campaign phases, vision and mission, leadership phase, growth phase and goal line phase, quiet phase, public phase, feasibility study, internal audit, external study, case for support, PEST(EL) analysis, SWOT analysis, campaign plan, campaign chair, capital campaign committee, nucleus fund, top-down/inside-out process, kick-off, victory celebration, impact philanthropy theory, post-campaign assessment

### Suggested questions for meetings and discussion

- What roles do capital campaigns play in shaping fundraising strategies in the arts?
- What are the differences between capital, comprehensive and special projects campaigns?
- What kind of arts organization can initiate such campaigns? Can you give some examples/cases from your experience? What are the

main differences/similarities between American and European arts organizations in respect of this?

- What are the key steps to make and the right people to involve in order to effectively plan and execute capital campaigns?
- How would you plan a successful capital campaign for the arts? What are the stages of a capital campaign?
- What is the role of campaign committees? Who may/should be included? What knowledge/information is necessary?
- How can arts organizations evaluate and communicate impacts of their capital campaigns? What are the metrics to be used?
- What information do PEST and SWOT assessments provide a cultural institution as it considers beginning a capital campaign? How should arts organizations consider the external environment during the various stages of a capital campaign??
- What is the purpose of a feasibility study in the context of campaign planning?
- What will be the future trends of capital campaigns in arts fundraising?
- Have the effects of the COVID-19 pandemic altered the thinking regarding capital campaigns in the arts? How do arts organizations analyze these trends? What are the main differences/similarities between American and European arts organizations in respect to this?
- Are there case histories of successful campaign that you can recall?

## References

Andreoni, J. (1990). “Impure altruism and donations to public goods: A theory of warm-glow giving.” *The Economic Journal*, 100 (401): 464-477.

Duncan, B. (2004). “A Theory of Impact Philanthropy,” *Journal of Public Economics*, 88 (9-10): 2159–2180.

Hopkins, K. B. and Friedman, C. S. (1997). *Successful fundraising for arts and cultural organizations*. Phoenix, AZ: Greenwood Publishing Group.

Kihlstedt, A. (2005). *Capital campaigns: Strategies that work*. Sudbury, MA: Jones and Bartlett Learning, Inc.

Lindahl, W. E. (2008). “Three-phase capital campaigns,” *Nonprofit Management & Leadership*, 18 (3): 261–273.

O'Brien, C. L. (1998). "Thinking beyond the dollar goal: A campaign as organizational transformation," *New directions for philanthropic fundraising*, 1998 (21), 9–22.

Tempel, E. R., Seiler, T. L. and Burlingam, D. F. (2016). *Achieving excellence in fundraising*, fourth edition. Hoboken, NJ: Jossey-Bass.

Weinstein, S. and Barden, P. (2017). *The complete guide to fundraising management.* Hoboken, NJ: John Wiley and Sons.

Woronkowicz, J. and Nicholson-Crotty, J. (2017). "The effects of capital campaigns on other nonprofits' fundraising," *Nonprofit Management and Leadership*, 27 (3): 371–387.

Worth M. J. (2016). *Fundraising: Principles and practice.* Los Angeles: SAGE Publications, Inc.

# 10 Digital Fundraising in the Arts

with *Stefano Prestini* and *Michele Mario Stanta*

## 10.1 Digital revolution in the arts industry

During the last couple of decades, the digital revolution has deeply influenced how people and organizations function in their everyday lives, especially in the context of communication and relationship-building.

In business terms, digitalization has become so important that, for most organizations, being online (for communications and/or service delivery) has often become synonymous with being alive, and because of this trend, the "digital affair" has deeply affected the life of arts organizations. Can you, for instance, remember when you last went to a ticket office in person to buy a ticket for a performance or an exhibition? Similarly, when did you last look in a newspaper instead of on an official website or social media platform for information about a theatre or an opera house programming? Maybe several years ago (or never!).

For the arts industry, going digital has resulted in a completely new approach to communications and service delivery. As a result, arts institutions have attained a much better balance between benefits and costs, with this change in approach meaning that organizations can generate value from each web contact by being able to sell tickets and provide information at any time. The reach and richness of digital systems has provided arts organizations with the opportunity to get closer to their audience and other constituencies, thereby furthering the relationship-building essential to their viability. Finally, tools such as databases and customer relationship management (CRM) software, especially when connected to the booming social media platforms, have helped arts institutions to customize their messaging and services. These efficiencies have given rise to significant improvements in the ROI of their marketing expenditures.

Of course, this digital affair is clearly not just a service-related matter. In these times, both business and personal relations flow more and more frequently through digital channels: The internet has become a new meeting space, where people can be in touch, share contents and experiences, and communicate, despite distance and boundaries. This was never more evident than when the COVID-19 pandemic restrictions were implemented.

As already noted, many times, effective fundraising strategies are based on the ability of arts organizations to build a long-term relationship with their donors. With respect to audience engagement, arts organizations can rely on greater expertise in managing relations with their attendees. Accordingly, when soliciting donations, arts fundraisers should pay more attention to their relationships with donors and to their continued evolution: these changes can affect the development of effective relation-based digital fundraising strategies.

## 10.2 Digital can help to develop relationship-based fundraising

Relationship-based fundraising is not a sequence of one-shot solicitations of donors. Rather, it is based on a long-term dialogue with donors and supporters. When they build relationships with their donors, arts organizations should look at them not simply as funders, but also as ambassadors, spokesmen and volunteers (Burnett, 1992). This implies that they should look for connections with their donors, taking into serious consideration their needs and points of view. Digital technology is making this dialogue change rapidly, especially in terms of personalization and customization of adopted approaches. Furthermore, digital tools can enhance organizations' ability to embrace successful techniques to widen their donor base and tighten the legacy pipeline.

Ken Burnett for the Charities Aid Foundation,[1] and Burnett and Fowler (1997), highlight six key steps that bring about successful relationship-based fundraising.

First, an organization should start by telling a story that will be interesting for potential supporters, explaining why giving makes sense. Sec-

[1] Burnett, K., "Learn to Build Long Term Relationships with Your Donors," CAF (Charities Aid Foundation). https://www.cafonline.org/charities/webinars/learn-to-build-long-term-relationships-with-your-donors.

ond, it should work to build a relationship with prospective donors, making them feel they are part of a community of people that is involved in sharing something valuable. Third, the organization can ask for support for a project or its institutional activity. Fourth, to keep potential donors engaged while pursuing common goals, a consistent dialogue should be developed with them. Fifth, the organization should collect data on anyone it connects to in order to keep tabs on how fundraising is progressing, so that ineffective approaches can be modified. Sixth, with the help of data monitoring, an organization can learn how to develop its storytelling, so the process of relationship-based fundraising can begin again. In summary, digital technologies can offer immediate and innovative ways in which all these steps can be supported.

As the desire to share values, experiences, emotions and creativity among people who feel part of the same community is a core component of arts organizations, the evolving digital environment is a natural context in which these attitudes can be perpetuated. Moreover, thanks to digital advances, organizations have a concrete opportunity to convert web followers into donors, exploiting the viral power of web reactions by connecting with volumes of contacts, to raise a little money from many individuals. In some cases, the value of the donations collected by numerous small donors might occasionally exceed the total amount of money given by the big donors, thanks to digital technology. Web platforms (provided with a simple donation button) can be an always open window: anyone who is interested can look in, gather information, follow and share what an organization posts, and can then join, give and encourage other people to do the same.

Furthermore, engaged followers can share their experiences spontaneously with other online users and underline what is relevant for them, both positively and negatively. As a consequence of this transparency, other users who read their comments, watch stories or receive suggestions related to the organization will perceive them as more authentic. If the wave of sentiment that is generated by this transparency is positive, this can influence other people in their perception of an arts organization and in their potential willingness to give. This contact chain, which adopts an earned media approach,[2] is as important as direct giving because it

---

[2] Earned media is publicity or exposure gained from methods other than paid advertising. Typical examples are social media and word of mouth. Earned media

can trigger a multitude of potential supporters and help organizations to reach their fundraising goals. Digital technologies have also led to a strong democratization of public relationships, particularly between arts institutions and their stakeholders. As a consequence, these organizations can, for the first time, communicate even more directly with their audience (and, more widely, with all their stakeholders) and receive feedback in almost real time. Finally, in spite of the criticism that digital solutions are impersonal, digital marketing tools and social media offer arts institutions significant opportunities to personalize their fundraising strategies. By reducing response time and by reworking the old-fashioned "word of mouth" into the viral output of social media communication, digital advances offer the arts sector new opportunities and challenges when building up and managing their communities, with clear implications for their fundraising strategies. Therefore, the digitalization of fundraising techniques helps organizations to reduce obstacles and develop their relationship-based fundraising effectively. Immersive storytelling on social media, for example, is incredibly powerful in enhancing the success of fundraising activities, and also provides interesting insights about donors' behavior.

Immediate and bidirectional communication between organizations and consumers enhances community engagement in a way that standard web pages cannot do. Arts organizations are now able to develop their storytelling for a wider audience, which can be converted into an endorsed team of supporters. These supporters can then help them to further build their networks of volunteers, donors or spokespersons with a long-term perspective, but only if the organization's reputation and authenticity are well established and its actions are consistent. Digital channels are effective in ensuring higher donor engagement, involving supporters of different ages and backgrounds who can make a contribution regardless of a lower financial capacity. For example, experiences of volunteering shared online can help to build the donor–organization relationship and a call to action.

When developing their digital strategies, arts organizations also have to consider that opening their doors to a wider universe of connections brings new challenges, most of all in terms of community and reputation

---

operate primarily through enhancing enjoyment, and are at the heart of the newest digital marketing strategies (Lovett and Staelin, 2016).

management. Giving and receiving feedback in front of an always active group of people has made arts organizations more transparent as they attempt to build their reputation and increase their influence with the endorsement of web communities. Once donors have made a commitment, organizations should share with their web communities how that money is spent. Moreover, they should ask donors for feedback to share with all trustees in order to reinforce donors' trust. This process works not only on content related to what the organization stages or shows (e.g., videos or pictures of performances, backstage, events, exhibitions), but also on how it can directly influence people's lives.

## 10.3 Threats and opportunities in the digital environment

The digital wave has precipitated the extreme evolution of the concept of corporate social responsibility in brand activism (Sarkar and Kotler, 2018), manifested mainly, but not only, through social media.[3] Organizations, including arts institutions, speak to people online, via their social media accounts, and can declare their position for socially relevant causes (e.g., community diversity, gender equality, climate change). This approach (identified, as noted, as brand activism) can significantly impact an arts organization's activities. Online buzz can influence decision-making at several levels and impact an arts organization's reputation. Ultimately, such a buzz can affect the artistic choices that an organization makes, such as the kind of plays theatres produce or which artists' works are exhibited in a museum or gallery. Additionally, this process can influence how arts organizations define their human resources hiring procedures, the energy policy they adopt for stage lighting and decisions about the use of paper for theatre booklet programs.

During the COVID-19 pandemic and the forced shutdown of theatres, music halls and museums, arts institutions used digital media to stay connected with their stakeholders. The internet was almost the only means of communication with donors and all other interested individuals.

---

[3] Brand activism consists of business efforts cantered on a brand that aims to "promote, impede, or direct social, political, economic, and/or environmental reform or stasis with the desire to make improvements in society" (Sarkar and Kotler, 2018: 554).

In order to stay connected, past and new performances were streamed, meetings and events were organized online, and virtual tours and exhibitions that reached millions of people were created, thus keeping the conversations with audiences and stakeholders alive. For the most part, this necessary transition has been beneficial to arts organizations. However, the rush to digital was in some cases undertaken without a clear strategy or long-term goal. In other words, some organizations moved online more as an immediate reaction to the emergency than as a mindful choice. Thanks to the easy accessibility of some digital tools, many of them have assumed that moving online means simply doing online what they usually do offline, but that is of course a misunderstanding. It is not enough to stream a good opera production via YouTube or to ask people for a donation online, without considering that posting a video that is longer than sixty minutes or making donation requests on an online platform without clever community management activities or a good digital visibility strategy are simply ineffective. Digital will never be able to replace the live experience, and arts organizations should understand that their digital strategy will complement their various activities, not replicate them in the digital realm.

Arts organizations should also be aware of the risks related to online development. On the one hand, reach and richness in communication, ease in reaching wide groups of people, the receipt of immediate feedback (that can become direct giving) are clearly positive. On the other hand, owing to the unbounded universe of the internet, arts organizations must be aware of the potential for opacity in relations with web users that can affect the possibility of converting clicks into something valuable. Moreover, risks related to intellectual property, privacy violation or to fraud (e.g., personal data theft, credit card cloning, fake payment buttons) can be an enormous threat to an organization's accountability, as arts institutions frequently request personal information, especially when selling tickets or securing donations online. In sum, we can assume that the internet makes things simpler but not always easier. Arts institutions must think about their digital strategies with the same care they exercise for all other strategies, developing an approach that addresses efficiency, security, consistency, vision and shared values.

In order to cope with these changes, web strategies and the related community management activities have become so crucial that many arts institutions have created new units (usually related to marketing and development offices) focused on the management of these issues and their various implications, including the possibility to monetize digital efforts. According to ABA (2019), by November 2019, 69 per cent of internationally surveyed arts organizations from Europe, Canada and the United States disclosed that they generated revenue from digital (ABA, 2019). Of these, 43 per cent did it by asking for voluntary donations in exchange for some digital content, while 26 per cent generated revenue by selling digital tickets or subscriptions. Of the same institutions, 31 per cent divulged that they were active in digital without generating any income. Of this group, 53 per cent stated that they were intentionally *not* attempting to generate revenues from digital, but using it as a tool to stay in touch with their audiences. The remaining 47 per cent hoped to generate revenue from digital in the future but had not developed or implemented approaches to do that. One can surmise that the percentages of arts institutions generating revenue through digital channels will continue to increase over time (ABA, 2019).

Arts organizations that have invested in their digital activities for the past couple of decades are surely better positioned to think strategically about the digital revolution, as they realize that digital is a tool and not an aim. Perhaps the single greatest focus regarding their digital investments is related to how they can monetize their digital efforts, not only by selling digital tickets, but also by raising money through what we will label digital fundraising.

## 10.4 A definition of digital fundraising

Digital fundraising describes the ways in which arts organizations can raise money online using a variety of tools and techniques. This definition applies not only to methods of payment (e.g., credit cards, PayPal accounts, Facebook stars), but also to applications utilized to connect with donors (e.g., platforms, sites, apps, crowdfunding platforms, social media accounts). Digital fundraising refers also to the different actions and tactics (e.g., online donation buttons, contribution forms or digital fundraising events) that develop online fundraising activities.

The main feature of digital fundraising is that it is community-based. In other words, with the flat philosophy of the internet, digital fundraising works with the aim of involving and embracing small donors and spokespersons in a huge community of web followers. For this reason, it requires arts organizations to develop not only strong technological skills, but also compelling content and community management. The use of digital technologies allows arts institutions to engage their web audience in real-time conversations, which, if done effectively, enhance knowledge of the broad digital audience. Indeed, according to the results of research by Liu et al. (2021), a potential funder accepts the institution's social network profile attributes as an evaluation of the institution's digital reputation, as he or she makes funding decisions (the study analyzed the crowdfunding setting). Accordingly, organizations should continually improve their digital communications, by addressing web user issues or concerns and by sharing valuable digital assets (e.g., pictures, videos, texts, and also experiences and stories) to stimulate and animate potential supporters to become engaged.

During the first months of the COVID-19 pandemic, the majority of arts organizations focused their resources on free digital initiatives because staying connected with all interested individuals was the primary objective. However, as the crisis was revealed not to be temporary, arts organizations focused on digital in order to reduce the heavy impact of the sanitary restrictions that were imposed by governments. This change of approach led them to develop a more stable model to monetize digital. In the digital marketplace, online revenue typically derives from a large number of individuals spending or contributing small or modest amounts of money. While this approach works for disaster relief efforts, digitally earned revenue efforts are unlikely to generate significant income in the arts sector in the near term. They currently provide some income and valuable marketing intelligence about audience preferences, but arts institutions should continue to invest in digital fundraising competences if they want digital revenues to grow.

### 10.4.1 *Different approaches in digital fundraising*

During the COVID-19 pandemic, donations have proven to be the biggest digital monetization success for arts organizations: many have been pleasantly surprised by the number of donors reached through digital channels. In this context, to benefit from the indirect path to revenues provided by digital fundraising, organizations have framed different approaches when asking for funds. We can cluster these in two groups:

*Content accessibility-based approach.* To raise funds online, arts institutions continue to ask people for money in exchange for access to digital content, such as artistic productions (e.g., performances, exhibitions) or bonus materials (e.g., backstage, dress rehearsal, special events) that have been captured and made available via live streaming or on demand. Content accessibility-based digital fundraising helps arts organizations to attract potential new donors online, as digital fundraising often appeals to crowds of not-yet-engaged small supporters. With this approach, donors receive a direct benefit in return for their gift. Content accessibility-based digital fundraising works better for campaigns developed for general institutional support, rather than for project-related initiatives, as it requires a lower level of involvement for donors and refers to them almost as paying audiences. When using this approach, organizations should pay attention in particular to costs related to digital content production, as direct donations usually only partially cover them.

To benefit from the bilateral interaction between the arts institution and its supporters, which is made possible by the internet, some arts organizations have built a content-based pricing that mixes pricing and fundraising techniques. Some have, for example, adopted a pay what you want (PWYW) approach, allowing backers to "pay what they can" instead of "nothing" to access organization's digital offerings. Others have added to the PWYW a suggested price, with a higher impact on revenues, even if this is not stable over time. A final group of organizations has applied the PWYW + Donation scheme, which seems to work best: in many settings, yielding higher revenue than either "fixed price" or standard PWYW. Even if it looks like a transaction, this online pricing makes the relationship between the potential supporter and the organization stronger, as "buyers" are mindfully involved in the value definition process. To convert pricing into actual fundraising, the next step for an institution will be to engage givers in the arts organizations' activity as more stable donors. Box 10.1 provides an example of content-based digital fundraising.

*Community interaction-based approach.* When following this approach in digital fundraising, arts developers work on the interaction between the arts organization and its potential supporters with the aim of achieving a shared goal. In this context, organizations usually make an appeal for

**Box 10.1 The National Theatre digital model**

The National Theatre (NT), London, has developed a mixed model in order to maximize revenues from its digital efforts. At the basis of the digital donor pyramid, from April to July 2020, the NT has boosted a crowd of "unknown donors" reaching them via YouTube by the weekly posting of free content and a request for a donation. With 15 million viewers in sixteen weeks, the NT received more than 25,000 donations. In addition, the NT has launched the National Theatre @home platform (supported by Bloomberg Philanthropies) with a regular ticketing plan (£9.99 for a single play, £12.99 per month, £129.99 per year, with unlimited access) mixed with fundraising tools. At the beginning and at the end of each production, users are required to make a donation, as a "form of applause" reacting to what they have seen. High spending subscribers also benefit from bonus content, which increases the value of their subscription.

*Source*: Author's elaboration from nationaltheatre.org.uk

individual donations – often during a live digital event or the launch of a project-based campaign – with the specific aim of stimulating and encouraging people to give, so they feel part of the same community. These techniques exploit the interactive power of the internet by soliciting people to give in reaction to an appeal for a specific cause or to support a project or a defined situation. As members of a community focused on a project, online donors can also become digital ambassadors for the organization and ask their network (more or less directly) to join and give as well. Emotional impact and involvement are crucial to developing these fundraising techniques successfully. The *leitmotiv* connecting all the campaign steps and orienting community management actions should be the clear perception that, by a little giving people get a lot, and can create something valuable for the community to which they belong. The Royal Opera House in London has been especially effective using YouTube to create a community of donors (see Box 10.2).

**Box 10.2 Royal Opera House for the World Ballet Day**

In its dialogue with potential supporters, the Royal Opera House (ROH), London, has always stated that the main purpose of its activity is to ensure the future of opera and ballet. This is the reason why the ROH refers to its donors as a community, linked to those artists who are on stage and the artisans who work behind the scenes. The ROH uses this tone even more in its digital communication. In October 2020, the ROH solicited YouTube donations for the World Ballet Day, involving the dancers of the Royal Ballet. The message was clear: to support with a donation the recovery of their community of artists, freelancers, craftspeople and theatre workers after eighteen months of closure. In its message, the ROH stressed its gratefulness to potential supporters in a special moment of the house's life and shared the full morning class of the Royal Ballet, broadcasted live from the main stage. The declared aim was involving donors in something "greater," relying on their emotional connection with all the employees who were working hard to overcome the ravages of the COVID-19 pandemic. In under an hour and a half, this fundraiser attracted 660,000 viewers and donations of $100,580.

*Source*: Author's elaboration from Royal Opera House official social media accounts

## 10.5 The main digital fundraising techniques

Even if many of the "traditional" offline fundraising techniques have their digital equivalent, it is important to underline that developing digital fundraising strategies means not only moving online what has been usually conducted offline, but also to focus on opportunities and advantages (and on the risks and threats) that digital brings.

When arts organizations design their digital fundraising model, they should have some milestones clearly in their mind:

- *Focusing on fundraising goals*: to choose the most appropriate digital technique, arts organizations should clearly define their fundraising objectives. For instance, crowdfunding sites or online fundraising events are more effective for single project campaigns.
- *Content sharing*: disseminating information through digital newsletters or other digital means can keep significant donors close to the arts institution.

- *Analyzing and monitoring the results of their activities*: arts organizations must analyze the pros and cons of each digital fundraising technique before adopting one or more of them. The approach and the language to use, the rules, the contents and the targeted audience can all influence the effectiveness of a strategy. Furthermore, there are digital tools such as Google Analytics that make the monitoring of results from digital activity much easier to access. If used correctly, these tools should make arts institutions' fundraising more efficient.
- *Being consistent*: digital fundraising must be coherent and complementary to what the arts organization offers offline and should always be supportive of the arts institution's mission, vision and value proposition. Online donors should feel the same consistency and authenticity experienced by those who join, for instance, a more traditional fundraising meeting.
- *Being technically skilled*: there are no effective digital fundraising strategies if the arts organization does not possess the knowledge and experience required to manage digital and analytical platforms. This necessitates adopting the most appropriate – and recent – tools and channels to interact effectively with the "donor journey."

### 10.5.1 *Crowdfunding*

Crowdfunding is one of the most popular bottom-up digital fundraising techniques that exploits the community-based profile of the internet, by using the viral effect of digital and social media communication. The working principle of crowdfunding is raising money from the crowd – in other words, reaching fundraising objectives by relying on a huge volume of small contributors. The majority of crowdfunding campaigns are "U-shaped" (Mitchell et al., 2017). This means that donations are concentrated at the beginning and the end of each campaign. Consequently, in order to avoid the risk of affecting the overall success of the campaign, some arts organizations can decide to rely on matched crowdfunding.[4]

Transparency is very important in crowdfunding campaigns, so that supporters are well informed about the development of the project. In

---

[4] See Section 10.5.3.

addition to content production, this fundraising technique also requires emotionally persuasive storytelling related to the project, which will attract potential donors and generate interest from "the crowd," with the aim of converting it into an engaged community of supporters. It is possible to differentiate two major clusters of crowdfunding techniques, analyzing them from the perspective of the donors or the project's success. In the first case, we define the different kinds of crowdfunding techniques by considering what donors expect in return for their donation. In the second case, we can differentiate crowdfunding techniques according to the degree to which fundraising goals are achieved.

When speaking about crowdfunding techniques from the donors' perspective, we note:

- *Donation-based crowdfunding* is the most popular digital crowdfunding model. In this technique, donors are asked to contribute small amounts towards a much larger target while receiving no benefits. In other words, donors do not receive any material benefit in exchange for their donation, but just the "feel-good factor" and improved self-perception, derived from supporting a cause in which they believe. As emotional involvement and being part of a community of supporters make this technique work, donation-based crowdfunding is particularly effective when arts organizations want to raise funds for a specific project. Examples include a theatre raising funds to restore part of a venue, an orchestra needing to replace a piano that was destroyed in a basement flood or a museum seeking funds to purchase new changing tables for mothers visiting exhibitions with their babies. For donation-based crowdfunding, storytelling and follow-up actions with digital content about the initiative are very important, as well as intensive communication that reaches a high number of potential supporters.
- *Reward-based crowdfunding* works by following an "exchange for" logic, as donors are motivated to support a specific cause in return for receiving a direct reward for their contribution. With this approach, donors receive rewards proportionately to the amount they are willing to give. While this technique allows it to control inventory, using reward-based crowdfunding risks under- or overestimating the willingness of each donor to give. As the motivation to give connects to donors' personal feelings and depends on the value that

they give to their own experiences, organizations can fail to correctly estimate the value people give to a donation if they link it to modulated but standardized rewards. On the other hand, rewarding donors' engagement with specific endorsement actions observed by a wider community (more than with a reward), can be even more effective in making donors feel part of the journey.

When focusing on crowdfunding techniques in terms of a project's success, we can note:

- *All or nothing*: in order to enhance organizations' commitment to boosting their crowdfunding activities, some platforms require the arts organization to reach or exceed its goal before releasing the money raised. In other words, the organizations get money only if they fully reach the targeted fundraising objectives, otherwise the campaign fails and donors get their money back. In this situation, the moderation and intermediation of platforms are crucial, as they collect and keep money until the campaign is completed. As crowdfunding is a project-related fundraising technique, many sites tend to use this "all or nothing" rule as a condition to launch projects. This feature can help organizations to focus more carefully on their communication initiatives, which are intended to create a sense of urgency as well as "we are all in this together" mindset among their donors.
- *'Keep it all'*: This is the opposite of 'all or nothing' crowdfunding, as arts organizations have the right to funds that are raised even if the crowdfunding campaign does not reach its targeted goal. The biggest risk in this case is that organizations can finish the campaign with a very small amount of money for a project, as the incentive to achieve the goal is not as pronounced (or obvious) as in the 'all or nothing' approach.

Crowdfunding is so popular that smaller arts organizations are able to choose from many web tools to develop a campaign even if their communication budget is modest. They can launch crowdfunding campaigns via donation platforms, where donors can gather detailed information about the project, the goal to reach, the conditions for giving, the time in which money has to be raised and the number of supporters already involved. Among the most popular platforms are Kickstarter, Indiegogo, Artist-

Share and Change.org, which provide both standardized and customizable tools that each organization can use according to its communication needs and fundraising objectives. These platforms usually ask fundraisers for a subscription or keep a percentage of raised funds. The main advantage in choosing one of these platforms is that arts organizations can benefit from tools that have already been developed and that users are familiar with. Furthermore, as these platforms usually organize and host projects and campaigns in specific categories, they can benefit from an established targeting process of potential donors that is guaranteed by the site. However, because every institution is sharing potential prospects, organizations run the risk of not being competitive if they cannot distinguish their project as outstanding and worthy of support within the platform. Of course, it is critical that the institution does its "due diligence" to assure the accountability of the selected platform and its adherence to the highest ethical standards. Box 10.3 provides an example of a crowdfunding project developed by the Louvre Museum in Paris.

**Box 10.3 *Become a patron!* The Louvre Museum's crowdfunding project**

Launched in 2010, the Become a Patron! crowdfunding project has become one of the biggest fundraising developments for the Louvre. Each year, thousands of people support the acquisition or restoration of important art works such as the Winged Victory of Samothrace (2013), the mastaba of Akhethetep (2017), the Book of Hours of Francis I (2018), the Arc du Carrousel (2019), the Grande Allée des Tuileries (2021) and the Miseroni Cammeo (2022). This crowdfunding initiative has helped the Louvre collect several thousand modest donations. For instance, in 2022, with a four-month campaign focused on Miseroni Cammeo, the Louvre raised €1 million, thanks to the mobilization of more than 5,600 donors with an average donation of €178. Using a crowdfunding platform called iRaiser and a specific communication campaign, the Louvre truly engaged a massive number of people who wanted to become patrons for a single day (#tousmecenes). A good communication campaign combined with the institutional reputation have been key elements in reaching campaign goals. In this sense, clear objectives and processes for the crowdfunding project together with an emotional reward for the potential donor – recognition as a donor in a public list on the Louvre's website – inspired many to become involved in this noble cause.

*Source*: https://www.louvre.fr/en/support-the-louvre

### 10.5.2 *Social media crowdfunding*

As a direct consequence of its high dependence on crowds of donors to be successful, crowdfunding needs a good digital communication strategy if organizations are going to achieve their fundraising objectives. For this reason, arts organizations with stronger and more effective web communication are typically more successful when adopting crowdfunding campaigns to support their projects. The boom in social media communication and marketing offers a further booster to crowdfunding techniques, as the buzz generated on social media channels about a fundraising project can take it viral. By matching these increasing needs expressed by different kinds of organizations all over the world, there are now social media tools for crowdfunding that rely on these platforms' huge communication potential. The most popular web spaces where people meet are indeed social media platforms. In particular, social media crowdfunding helps to amplify a solicitation message, without compromising an organization's relationship with the other side of the digital divide. Social media crowdfunding can be very useful, especially for small arts bodies, which through these media have access to funding possibilities that bely their modest budgets.

Facebook is the most popular generalist social media in terms of number of subscribers.[5] Beyond the reach of an arts institution's database, Facebook adds the richness of its communication potential, with arts institutions gaining the potential to address any communication to a large yet targeted segment of users. Facebook works well when arts organizations need to build awareness and interest around a crowdfunding campaign. Through targeted ads on Facebook posts, cultural institutions can describe their project, tell their story, promote their campaign and – thanks to the donation buttons available – even raise money directly. According to Facebook policies, this tool is at the disposal of any organization that can certify (via a simple online process) that it is entitled to raise funds for its project as a not-for-profit organization (Liu et al., 2021).

Facebook has also developed so-called Facebook stars, a sort of virtual coin that allows organizations to receive donations from fans on their Facebook pages or during paid online live streaming events, in addition to the digital ticket that is purchased to access the content. Each star is

---

[5] The younger generation – GenZ – is more active on Instagram, though.

worth $0.01 and each user is free to send the institution the desired number of stars, which are monetized as voluntary donations.

As it is a social media form specifically for images and storytelling, Instagram is very effective in presenting a crowdfunding campaign from a more intimate and human point of view. This is particularly appreciated by GenZ who are attracted by experiences and authentic values. Instagram stories are a wonderful tool for involving donors in sharing their experiences, showing themselves at the front of the pack in supporting a campaign and spreading a message among their network of contacts. A clever use of the hashtags on Instagram can also help organizations to shape and address their communications so their campaign is more likely to go viral.

Owing to its direct, short, and informative communication protocols, Twitter is very suitable for keeping supporters aware of campaign developments; it can also be used to boost donations as a campaign deadline approaches. Endorsements are particularly effective on Twitter, as it is possible to tag relevant profiles in support of crowdfunding activities, which might result in retweeting, or to use hashtags to insert the campaign in trending topics that relate to the crowdfunding.

Companies based in the United Kingdom, Canada and the United States also have the chance to exploit YouTube to raise funds. By posting free videos on their YouTube channels, arts organizations can launch crowdfunding campaigns related to a particular streaming and raise funds from viewers. Live streaming of community activities is an especially effective way to solicit donations on YouTube.

### 10.5.3 *Matched crowdfunding*

Matched crowdfunding is a mixed funding technique that can have interesting implications for digital fundraising. Pilot research has been conducted by Mitchell et al. (2017), and we focus here on the relevance of matched crowdfunding in raising funds for arts projects in the United Kingdom.

The rationale for matched crowdfunding is achieving a funding goal by matching the efforts of the online crowd and a private or a public grant-maker, such as a corporation or a foundation. In respect to this, matched crowdfunding is similar to other kinds of matched grants. The main difference is that matched crowdfunding exploits the internet's connection powers to build a bridge between large and small donors. When opting for matched crowdfunding, arts organizations can apply to specific crowdfunding platforms designed for the purpose, relying on the support of an institutional funder who has a direct agreement with or is even the owner of the platform where the fundraising will be hosted. For a better fit, platforms and funders can create a significant variety of structures and opportunities that manage the connections and relations between the crowd and larger donors.

The crowdfunding platform is the fundraising marketplace for the different projects to be supported. Usually, a page on the website is dedicated to each project, in order to present it and to describe the features of the related fundraising opportunities. The funder usually sets the criteria for the funding match in agreement with the crowdfunding platform. These parameters refer to the object of the possible matched funding (e.g., the fundable project's size and scope, the territory of service) in order to clarify with applicant organizations whether their project is appropriate. Among these disseminated funding criteria, the institutional funder and the platform list in detail what matches are possible, including their type and size, and how, when the fundraising is concluded, the funder will transfer money to the arts institution. Typically, the relationship between the funder and the crowdfunding platform is exclusive (i.e., one platform for one funder, who can also, as noted, own it), but partnerships among one funder and several crowdfunding platforms are not rare. Moreover, when joining matched crowdfunding initiatives on different platforms, grant-makers have the opportunity to benefit from greater flexibility in their choices and to find projects that fit best with their institutional purposes. Marketing and institutional endorsement provided to the crowdfunding project by the institutional funder incentivize small donors to support the initiative.

When supporting matched crowdfunding initiatives, institutional funders may act as "one of the crowd" (Mitchell et al., 2017). In this case, they play an active role in assessing the initiative, focusing on a specific project, and they contribute exactly as an individual donor does, with the only difference that funders match via substantial gifts. Typically, the institutional funder provides its "one of the crowd" donations under specific conditions, such as, for instance, the raising of a defined percentage of the fundraising goal by the remainder of the backers. The ratio of matches (e.g., 25, 50 or 75 per cent of the total funding target) can influence small donors' behavior. For example, a smaller matching ratio may be a sign that the funder's attention is spread among differed crowdfunding projects. Alternatively, larger ratios may work as a powerful incentive for small backers.

Mitchell et al. (2017, 19) outline four primary models that funders can follow to apply a matched crowdfunding initiative:

- *In first model*: in this case, the grant-maker gives a substantial contribution with a sizable up-front investment. The fundraising project developed by the cultural institution on the crowdfunding platform will cover the remaining amount to be funded. This model is preferred when funders want to have a closer, institutional connection to the project or the funded institution.
- *Top up model*: this model works from the opposite standpoint, as top-up funders promise to cover the remainder of financial needs of the arts crowdfunding initiative only when the crowd has raised a specific percentage of the total funding target. Top-up funders prefer to engage with the crowd, following their endorsement choices and interests.
- *Bridging*: this approach to matched crowdfunding sees the involvement of big funders' contributions not only when a fixed percentage of the funding goal has been achieved, but also to balance the different levels of contributions recorded at the beginning, in the middle and at the end of the crowdfunding campaign. As previously noted, crowdfunding campaign efforts are U-shaped: typically, backers tend to be less active in the middle of a crowdfunding campaign.
- *Real time*: when matched crowdfunding occurs in real time, the institutional funder reacts immediately to every single donation (e.g., for every $/€/£1 donated/invested by the crowd, the institutional funder matches with the same, smaller or larger sum). An ongoing alignment of the funding actions of the institutional funder with those of the crowd will help the backer to feel that the project is progressing more quickly. However, managing this type of match requires higher development costs because prompt responses to the crowdfunders' behavior are required.

*Figure 10.1* Different institutional funder's approaches to matched crowdfunding

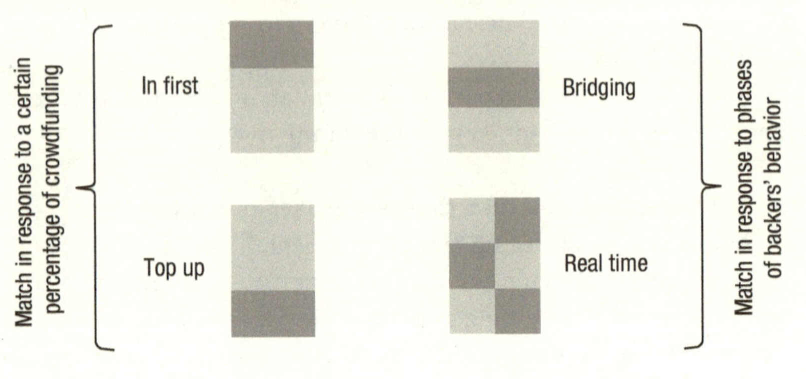


*Source*: Author's elaboration from Mitchell et al. (2017)

Figure 10.1 outlines the institutional funder's different approaches to matched crowdfunding.

In their research, Mitchell et al. (2017) also give evidence of the results of matched crowdfunding in the arts in the United Kingdom, showing that Arts Council England and the Heritage Lottery Fund have matched £251,500, helping to raise an additional £405,941 from 4970 backers. Moreover, researchers highlight how crowd engagement that is incentivized by matched crowdfunding initiatives can provide arts institutions with a dynamic network of volunteers and small donors, and can help institutions improve their digital and community management skills. This means that adopting matched crowdfunding initiatives can have ancillary benefits for arts institutions. Box 10.4 provides a further example of matched crowdfunding in the European context: Crowd4Culture.

**Box 10.4 Crowd4Culture: an Italian example of matched crowdfunding**

In June 2018, Fondazione Cariplo and Intesa Sanpaolo began a partnership to promote ForFunding (the Intesa Sanpaolo crowdfunding platform) in its funding of projects proposed by community foundations.

The ForFunding crowdfunding platform is hybrid. Although it works as a "keep-it-all" crowdfunding platform, Fondazione Cariplo's matches are not transferred to community foundations if the targeted crowdfunding goal is not achieved.
To achieve the agreed promotional goal, in 2020 Fondazione Cariplo involved more engaged community foundations to launch Crowd4Culture, an initiative that supports local crowdfunding projects for the arts via the ForFunding platform. In this project, Fondazione Cariplo plays the role of grant-maker, matching the funds raised by the crowd on the platform. Through the involvement of community foundations, Fondazione Cariplo aims to engage local stakeholders and communities more effectively and to encourage the use of new fundraising methods for the arts, based on digital and community management.
Crowd4Culture has multiple steps, as outlined on the Fondazione Cariplo website:

1. Publication of the Crowd4Culture open-deadline call for proposals of community foundations (in partnership with local organizations in their respective communities).
2. Review and selection of submitted proposals by the evaluation panel and subsequent approval by Fondazione Cariplo's board of directors.
3. Training of community foundations and their partners in the selected projects to maximize the effectiveness of crowdfunding campaigns.
4. Admission of projects into the ForFunding platform and launch of the fundraising campaigns.
5. Attainment of the fundraising goal, end of the campaign, transfer of the funds raised via ForFunding and of Fondazione Cariplo's matching grant.
6. Start and execution of the projects.

*Source*: Author's adaptation from https://www.fondazionecariplo.it/it/progetti/arte/crowd-4culture.html

### 10.5.4 *Online fundraising events*

Another interesting opportunity that digital media offers to arts organizations when raising funds is the organization of online fundraising events. They can be streams of performances, exhibitions or even auctions during which organizations can ask for individual donations, with the specific feature that all happens online. Usually, online events are live and organizations try to involve the highest number of donors during the event. Organizations frequently use Facebook and/or YouTube to organize such fundraising activities, as they provide easy and free tools to let organizations stream contents live and, simultaneously, ask for money. Live chat tools also enhance the possibility of being in touch with supporters during the event and to increase people's involvement in the initiative.

As the success of such fundraising campaigns often depends on communication activities and the viral word of mouth related to the project, fundraisers should pay great attention to the non-financial impact of their virtual events. In fact, as previously noted, digital fundraising has the potential to help organizations not only raise money, but also gain new volunteers and build organizational skills and knowledge. Web funders are ideal promoters, as they can share their supporting experiences in their web networks, helping organizations to meet new potential supporters. Furthermore, online backers can provide feedback and advice on the supported virtual event. This implies that "the crowd" can be more than a pool of small funders, as it can influence and shape virtual experiences in order to achieve funding targets.

### 10.5.5 *Website donation pages*

Most arts organizations' websites now have a page that allows supporters to make donations online using mobile or other devices. This makes giving a very simple process. People get in touch via organizations' internet sites, look at content, posts and projects, and make their choices. The easier the donation process, the more likely people are to engage.

Website sections dedicated to fundraising or donation newsletters typically include a donation button (with a clear call to action), conceived as the perfect equivalent of an online purchasing button (e.g., for tickets or merchandising). Money raised goes direct to the organization's general account. Donation web pages can be used for specific projects or for general operating support. Although creating a donor button is relatively easy, widgets from different providers can also be used. Among its tools for developers, for instance, PayPal offers free donation button codes to embed in a website or in any other web interface; the only requirement is to have a business PayPal account through which donations are collected.

When raising donations online, organizations ask web donors to complete a basic form with their personal details (name, surname and email address). In this way, they can identify and analyze new leads, try to understand their behavior and involve them in future initiatives. This is a functional connection point between digital marketing and fundraising techniques: thanks to management of the database of their web donors, arts organizations can segment and target givers and develop the best follow-up actions, for instance by using customized newsletters. As online giving is immediate, it is very important to ask donors only for required information, in order not to lose their attention and thereby causing them to abandon the donation form.

Compared with crowdfunding platforms or social media, donation pages on an arts institution's own website give the message a different appeal as they address people that are already interested in the organization. They could be spectators, regular donors or partners, but they have all made a conscious decision to visit the donation section of the web site.

Finally, arts institutions should be aware of the role cryptocurrencies are now playing in philanthropy. Indeed, market evidence shows that cryptocurrency donations to charity are booming (Dore, 2021). Tony Oommen, vice president of Fidelity Charitable, has stated that "as investors – particularly millennials – combine their interest in digital currency with their charitable values, digital assets have the potential to become a significant source of funding for philanthropy."[6] Consequently, arts organizations should invest in the resources necessary to seize the opportunities provided by cryptocurrencies: these can represent not only a new channel for digital fundraising, but also a perfect strategy to orient efforts toward new and younger donors.

## 10.6 Guidelines for implementing digital fundraising in arts institutions

Digital fundraising has helped arts organizations find new ways to raise money by exploiting the relationship-based opportunities offered by technological progress. However, even if digital technologies can expand fundraising firepower on a massive scale, using digital means as a tool to

[6] Roh, Association of Fundraising Professionals (AFP) website, 1 January 2022. https://www.afpgoldengate.org/index.php?option=com_content&view=article&id=195:the-future-of-fundraising--the-rise-of-cryptocurrency-giving&catid=31:bay-area-voices-of-philanthropy&Itemid=170

raise money should not be an excuse for organizations to lose their focus on people and their involvement in a cause or a purpose.

Digital is just a language, not a meaning, a way and a space to reach people differently, but it does not alter or corrupt the original philanthropic message. Successful conventional and digital fundraising both require organizations to share their values, and not just consider charitable gifts as transactions to be processed. This is the real value of digital fundraising relations. Currently, digital fundraising provides incremental revenue from numerous small and modest givers and cannot replace the major gifts and/or public subsidy that have been the backbone of support for European and American cultural institutions. That being said, the digital revolution has, at some level, democratized fundraising, bringing many new donors to the cultural sector. When considering digital fundraising in the arts, we can make some concluding comments. As just noted, digital fundraising provides arts organizations of all sizes with the opportunity to broaden significantly their fundraising reach. If compared with the offline philanthropy market, the internet and digital routes offer a wider set of contacts and potential relationships that can improve the effectiveness of organizations' fundraising activities, with relatively modest investments. For example, by using their Facebook page and its communication and donation tools, even a small arts organization can share a fundraising project with followers and ask them to support it, without having the expense of developing a specific platform. Furthermore, the more viral the "ask" becomes, the greater the possibility of reaching fundraising goals. Additionally, the low-cost barriers allow organizations to experiment with minimal risk to develop a potentially boundless and heterogeneous web community. Lastly, digital fundraising is an effective way of establishing a first touch with new small donors (as contrasted with attempting to influence the behavior of stable multi-year donors). The biggest challenge for arts fundraisers then becomes how to engage their small web donors in regular membership programs, thereby ensuring regular donations that hopefully will increase over time.

Digital fundraising allows arts organizations to measure the effectiveness of their fundraising actions in real time, measuring and evaluating the results of their actions. This is possible not only in terms of total money raised, but also in terms of donor retention, value per contact (e.g., interactions or money raised per contact) and so on. This feature of digital systems helps organizations to set and redesign (if necessary) their strategies and tactics efficiently, which is always important when expense budgets are tight.

By working on emotional involvement combined with user-friendly call to action tools, digital fundraising can shorten reaction times when people are deciding whether or not to support a cause or a project. By focusing on storytelling and on the sharing of personal experiences, many digital fundraising campaigns work on emotional involvement and on "word of mouth" (even viral) to raise money. The ease with which individuals can make donations in real time via the web (e.g., donation buttons related to a video posted on Facebook or YouTube) boosts the effectiveness of bottom-up strategies. A good project description, effective images or pictures, and in particular good stories to share, can make people react almost immediately and prompt them to give in just a few clicks. As arts organizations work regularly on emotional involvement of their audience, they can usually rely on a great amount of self-produced content that will engage their web community. However, it is critical that the content shared is compelling, consistent and of the right amount: too much might overload a web audience, while if it is scarce people can lose interest and decide not to follow an organization's initiatives. In addition to looking for consistency, it is therefore wise for organizations to ask users to share their own content, related to the project or the case for support, in order to increase their personal involvement and create something valuable for the online community to which they belong. Digital fundraising enhances feeling of belonging among supporters, multiplying the effectiveness of engagement strategies. Matters such as storytelling, content, vision and value sharing or the feeling of being part of a big community – crucial for the development of any fundraising strategy – are essential for arts organizations. Moreover, so-called web democracy can boost the interest in supporting and donating more than ever because people meeting online can feel part of a large group of equals, who can choose to act together to let an idea develop or help a project become reality. As already noted, that is particularly effective in the arts sector. Arts have to do with personal genius, but also with collective creativity. To make a cultural project possible, many people must work hard and together, each with a specific task. As donors, people can feel part of this process, which involves artists, artisans, staff and donors. Online content sharing can help them to show others what they have done and enhance their feeling of worth as a part of the team. If the organization endorses this (e.g., by tagging or replying), the mutual positive effect is understandable and palpable. Furthermore, as cultural bodies, arts institutions play a generally accepted public role in enhancing the personal and social growth of a community of people. Those who support their activities can feel actively involved in improving societal progress, thereby improving their self-perception. By sharing donation experiences online, donors can increase that positive feeling by connecting with other supporters who share interests and values. When these organizations are consistent in their online storytelling, people trust what has moved them to donate in the first place, and this makes them consider future giving.

Digital fundraising strategies should mainly focus on relations, not just on transactions. As we have already underlined, digital and social media have enhanced the power of concepts such as sharing and sense of community. To that end, arts organizations have worked to enrich their digital tools and contents, to deliver tangible elements of value for their web community in the mutual content sharing process required online. However, in addition to free sharing, some of them are experimenting with methods such as digital ticketing to monetize their web content. Other cultural institutions that have begun digital fundraising have adopted a model that is somewhat similar to selling tickets, providing enhanced content in exchange for contributions. Even if benefit exchange can be effective, the most successful examples of digital fundraising strategies have been those where organizations have made emotional and value-related connections with their online community. What makes the difference is their ability to make their story relevant for potential donors. Donors should feel involved in all that happens on stage or in the exhibition rooms. They should feel the emotion of being essential players and be convinced that their contributions make a difference. If the relationship with the opera house, the museum or the concert hall becomes merely a financial exchange for a digital product, the organization will perform very poorly, because a digital experience will never be able to replace a live event. Moreover, occasional online individual donations never reach impressive amounts, so organizations should focus on enhancing the strength and breadth of their communities to achieve their goals. However, the perception of being always in touch that digital tools offer has revealed itself to be very useful in strengthening relationships with donors. In other words, the most challenging aspect in creating a digital fundraising strategy is properly exploiting online potential by developing a sizable network of people actively committed to a purpose, basing this on membership development, not just on giving to receive benefits. Successful arts institutions focus on sharing values with the community that they serve. Donations should be the way in which the community declares its endorsement and involvement in espousing the values shared with arts organizations, not just a price to pay to receive something in return. By involving web donors in defining the value of what they are supporting together, arts institutions can make the digital monetization process more effective in this increasingly digital world.

### Keywords for arts fundraisers

Digitalization, digital technology, CRM software, web platforms, web transparency, earned media-approach, response time, immersive storytelling, web community, brand activism, online buzz, digital fundraising, digital reputation, content accessibility-based approach, community interaction-based approach crowds, PWYW + Donation scheme, digital ambassadors, donation-based or reward-based crowdfunding, "All or nothing" or "Keep it all" crowdfunding, social media crowdfunding, GenZ, matched crowdfunding, online fundraising events, live chats, donation pages, donation button, cryptocurrencies, web democracy

### Suggested questions for meetings and discussion

- How would you evaluate the impact of digitalization in arts management?
- What digital fundraising tools are used in your organization and in arts organizations you know?
- What kind of digital fundraising technique would you adopt to raise money for the arts disciplines (e.g., opera, theatre, music, visual arts)? Do you see any "best fit" match for specific fundraising projects?
- Which steps would you follow to design and implement a digital fundraising strategy for the arts?
- How does digital community management influence fundraising for the arts?

- How can digital marketing and digital fundraising be bridged in arts organization management?
- From your standpoint, are digital arts marketers also good digital arts fundraisers? What skills are required for these roles?
- What are the most frequently adopted digital fundraising tools for the arts? Which would you recommend?
- What are the opportunities for arts organizations when raising money online? In your experience, what are the primary challenges and threats when raising money online?
- Can you give some examples of best practices in digital fundraising? What are the mistakes or pitfalls to avoid?
- What role does communication play in digital fundraising?

## References

ABA (Advisory Board of the Arts) (2019). *Arts organization digital monetization survey*, November.

Burnett, K. (1992). *Relationship fundraising: A donor-based approach to the business of raising money* London: The White Lion Press, International Fund Raising Group.

Burnett, K. and Fowler, J. (1997). "How to make sure your donors read your publications," *International Journal of Nonprofit and Voluntary Sector Marketing*, 2 (4): 299–309.

Dore, K. (2021). "Crypto donations to charity are booming. What to know before making a year-end gift," *CNBC*, 24 December. Available at: https://www.cnbc.com/2021/12/24/what-to-know-about-making-cryptocurrency-donations-to-charity.html.

Liu, Y., Chen, Y, and Fan, Z. P. (2021). "Do social network crowds help fundraising campaigns? Effects of social influence on crowdfunding performance," *Journal of Business Research*, 122: 97–108.

Lovett, M. J. and Staelin, R. (2016). "The role of paid, earned, and owned media in building entertainment brands: Reminding, informing, and enhancing enjoyment," *Marketing Science*, 35 (1): 142–157.

Mitchell, S., Beack, P. and Bone, J. (2017). *Matching the crowd: Combining crowdfunding and institutional funding to get great ideas off the ground*, Nesta Report.

Sarkar, C. and Kotler, P. (2018). *Brand activism: From purpose to action*. Idea Bite Press.

# Essential Glossary for Arts Fundraisers

**Accountability** Responsibility that arts organizations have to convey information about their activities, finances, accomplishments and decision-making processes.

**"All or nothing" crowdfunding** Crowdfunding model according to which crowdfunding platforms do not release funds unless a project meets its financial goals.

**Altruism** Disinterested and selfless attitude of donors willing to give to the arts.

**Anchor-organizations** Not-for-profit organizations that are unlikely to move location, usually because their mission is tied to a particular city or local area. Examples of this type of organizations are schools, hospitals, museums and theatres.

**Annual giving program** Broad range of activities that take place to collect small gifts and keep smaller givers consistently active. In arts organizations they take the form of membership programs.

**Arm's length principle** According to this principle, there must be a clear administrative separation between political institutions and the agency that finances or manages cultural programs. In other words, the government decides the overall amount of the investment in culture, but a separate and independent agency establishes which organizations or programs will receive it.

**Arts voucher** Piece of paper exchanged for goods or services that entitles the holder to a discount or free tickets to participate in an arts event. Vouchers can also be supplied digitally.

**Baumol's cost disease** According to this theory, arts organizations always experience an income gap, as they are labor-intensive organizations and are a so-called stagnant industry.

**Bequest** Giving of assets to individuals or organizations through the provision of a will.

**Board of directors** Governing body of a not-for-profit organization. It is responsible for aiding organizations in setting goals and ensuring support and resources.

**Board standing committees** These committees are formed within the board in order to engage committed volunteers in decisions that are fundamental for the organization.

**Built-in dataset** Dataset containing contact information that is captured during fundraising events or actions.

**Campaign kick-off** Event that starts the public phase of a capital campaign.

**Campaign pledge** Promised gift from a donor, which may result in a future donation.

**Campaign steering committee** Committee made up of advocates, supporters and community leaders who help to make a capital campaign successful.

**Capital campaign** Effort that is focused on a capital project and may require a period of three to five years to be completed.

**Case for giving/Case for support** Organization's core message to its donors about the whys they should give.

**Cause-related marketing** Association of a brand or business with a cause or an institution.

**Charitable gift annuity** Planned giving vehicle according to which donors can confer cash or securities irrevocably on an arts organization and have in return an annual fixed payment for life (i.e., annuity).

**Charitable lead trust** Planned giving vehicle according to which a donor decides to elect an arts organization as beneficiary of the income from a trust composed of the donor's assets.

**Charitable remainder trust** Planned giving vehicle according to which a donor might confer assets on a not-for-profit organization (the trustee), receiving an annual income. At the termination of the trust, the remaining capital passes to the arts organization.

**Charitable vehicle** Fundraising tool provided by a charity to its prospective donors to raise funds.

**Chief advancement officer** Senior executive in charge of the engagement of all stakeholders in an arts organization. Typically supervises both the marketing and the development department.

**Civil economy** Way of thinking about the economic system based on certain principles – such as reciprocity, gratuity and fraternity – that go beyond the supremacy of profit or the mere instrumental market exchanges in economic and financial activity. It is therefore proposed as a possible alternative to the capitalist conception of the market.

**Community donors** Donors sharing the desire to contribute to the development of their community.

**Community foundation** Grant-making foundation facilitating and pooling donations used to support local not-for-profit organizations.

**Contributed income** Revenue coming from private and corporate contributions, private grant-makers or statutory fundraising.

**Contribution level** In a membership program, this is the tier that allows members to choose the benefits that appeal to them and consequently what they are willing to pay for such benefits.

**Corporate foundations** Philanthropic organizations financially supported by corporations, created as separate legal entities with close ties to them.

**Corporate philanthropy/Corporate giving** Unconditional transfer of cash or other assets to a not-for-profit organization from a business.

**Cost per dollar raised (CPDR)** Amount of money it takes an organization to raise one dollar.

**CRM systems** Combination of customer-related tools and activities that not-for-profit organizations use to manage and analyze customer behaviors.

**Crowdfunding platform** Website that enables interaction between fundraisers and potential donors.

**Crowdfunding** Raising money from the crowd; in other words, reaching fundraising objectives by relying on a huge volume of small contributors.

**Crowding in/out effect** Concerns the effects of direct public funding on the level of private philanthropy. If public funding displaces private gifts, there is a crowding out effect. If public funding enhances the reputation of the arts organization, a crowding in effect might occur.

**Cultural philanthropy** The word "philanthropy" comes from the Ancient Greek meaning "love to mankind." Cultural philanthropy includes any act of giving and altruism that is addressed to sustain arts and culture. Arts collecting – seen as an effort to preserve, protect and promote some form of art or artist – might be included in this definition.

**Cultural policy** Government actions, laws and programs that regulate, protect, encourage and financially (or otherwise) support activities related to the arts and creative sectors.

**Culture of philanthropy** Part of the organizational culture. It implies that everybody in the organization is involved in the development process and that everybody shares the fundraising efforts of the organization.

**Dashboard** Visual summary of key performance indicators.

**Development committee** A working with the staff to develop and fund the organization's development plan.

**Development** Continuous activity of relationship-building. Compared with fundraising, development activities are more aligned with a long-term commitment to support the empowerment of the arts institution as a whole.

**Digital ambassadors** Those donors asking (less or more directly) their online network to join and give as well.

**Digital fundraising** Fundraising using digital technology, also online. It can take place on smartphone apps, social media and online platforms.

**Direct costs** Costs that are directly linked to the production of arts events/services.

**Direct margin** Income percentage generated when all direct costs are subtracted from revenue.

**Discovery visit** Meeting at a prospect's home/office aimed at gathering more information about the prospect and his family.

**Donation button** Button on a non-profit's website leading donors to a landing webpage, allowing an easy online donation to the organization.

**Donation page** Web page located on a non-profit's website that gives individuals the opportunity to donate online.

**Donation-based crowdfunding** Crowdfunding technique based on the involvement of donors who give small amounts to a larger target while receiving no benefits themselves.

**Donation-reward systems** All prizes or benefits that an organization provides for its donors in exchange for the contribution they provide.

**Donor awareness** Donors' concern about a particular situation or need.

**Donor motivations** Reasons why donors give. A fundamental distinction is between extrinsic motivations (having tangible benefits after the gift) and intrinsic motivations (having intangible benefits such as the joy of giving) after the gift.

**Donor pyramid** This traditional model outlines how not-for-profit arts organizations rely on a multitude of small or first-time donors that contribute with reduced-size donations and – as we move towards the top of the pyramid – on a pool of few major donors, granting the largest gifts.

**Donor qualification** Process to understand donors' capacity to give (i.e., in terms of estimated income or endowment).

**Donor retention** The ability of keeping donors engaged in order to make them give through the years.

**Donor upgrading** All the actions taken to increase a donor's giving throughout a year.

**Donor's advised fund** Giving account established at a public charity (a mutual fund company or a community foundation) that collects a donor's gifts. The gifts give a donor an immediate tax deduction as they are irrevocable, but he or she can then recommend grants to charitable organizations over time.

**Donor's stewardship** All the activities after a donor's gift is received in order to create connections and increase loyalty.

**Donors' recognition** Thanking donors for their support and recognizing the value of their contribution. This is a crucial follow-up action after a gift has been secured.

**Dual internal system** System characterizing arts organizations' way of operating. Income from the sale of core or ancillary services (i.e., ticketing, merchandising, rents) only covers only a portion of the production costs so they require another system to develop resources, collect funds and fill the gap.

**Dynamic pricing** Pricing strategy according to which the price for a product or service changes according to changing market conditions (i.e., higher demand).

**EDI** Acronym standing for equity, diversity and inclusion/. Equity is about providing fair access and opportunity for everyone. Diversity is defined as the practice of including individuals from a range of ethnic, racial and social backgrounds. Inclusion addresses the extent to which individuals within all groups have a sense of belonging. Within an inclusive culture, differences in backgrounds are embraced and celebrated.

**Earned income** Revenues coming from the sale of some services such as earned tickets, royalties and space rental.

**Endowment fund** Donation of money or assets to a not-for-profit organization, which uses the resulting investment income for a specific purpose. An endowment can also refer to the total of a non-profit institution's investable assets, also known as its principal.

**Face-to-face solicitations** Strategy used when a fundraiser and/or volunteer meets with a prospect to personally request a gift.

**Feasibility study** Commonly carried forward by external consultants, its aim is to give arts organizations an overview about what they should know before starting a capital campaign.

**First-time donors** Donors who are giving to a non-profit for the first time.

**Friends membership scheme** Broadly speaking, circles of friends work with annual unrestricted contributions from a larger group of smaller donors who typically get functional benefits in return (e.g., free entry to exhibitions, discounted tickets for performances, retail discounts).

**Fundraising** Is the technique, the plan, the programs and the tactics that are implemented to persuade individuals and organizations to make gifts to an arts institution or other type of not-for-profits.

**GenZ (Generation Z)** Individuals born in the early 21st century who are digital natives.

**Gift range chart** A chart that lays out the number of gifts within various value ranges that you'll need to secure from donors in order to reach your capital campaign's goal.

**Giving ladder** A series of gift levels that go from small to big donations.

**Impacts** Significant or lasting changes in people's lives, brought about by a given action or series of actions.

**In-kind contribution** Non-cash gifts such as donated goods, services, labor or use of facilities.

**"Keep it all" crowdfunding** Is the crowdfunding technique allowing not-for-profit organizations keep any funds raised regardless whether or not the goal is achieved.

**Licensing agreement** Arts organizations let the licensee corporations to use their brand or image in return for royalties.

**Life time value** An estimate of the average revenue that a donor will generate throughout her lifespan as a giver.

**Major donors** Individuals who make significant, private gifts in favor of a not-for-profit organization.

**Major donors' profile folder** A folder collecting all the information about major donors together with major-gift prospects' contacts.

**Matching grants** Grants designed to complement other grants coming from different public/private sources.

**Membership program** The main annual giving program in arts organizations. Through a membership program, an organization might transform ticket-holders or subscribers into donors.

**Mission statement** Brief statement about an organization's ultimate purpose, its goals and how it intends to meet them.

**Move record** Document that highlights the status of the cultivation process by recording the target major gift size and the different actions undertaken together with related outcomes.

**Naming opportunity** One of the highest benefits for major donors. In return for a gift, benefactors receive public acclaim. (e.g., the donor's name posted where everyone can see it).

**Nucleus fund** Aggregate of all of the early gifts in a quiet phase of a capital campaign.

**Online buzz (online buzzing)** Viral technique focused on maximizing the word-of-mouth potential of a fundraising campaign or event.

**Online fundraising events** Streams of performances, exhibitions or even auctions during which organizations can ask for individual donations, with the specific feature that all happens online.

**Opinion elite** Individuals who shape and ultimately influence perceptions of institutions, other noteworthy individuals, political movements and so on; they exist at every level of government and society. Occasionally, elites are grouped into governing elites and non-governing elites.

**Patron membership scheme** Donors underwrite a non-transferable membership with the cultural institution.

**Patronage** Support and money given by someone to a person or a group such as a charity.

**PEST(EL) analysis** Strategic assessment about political, economic, socio-cultural and technological (environmental and legal) factors that can influence, as external drivers, the activities of an arts organization.

**Philanthropy** Cultural attitude that shapes and gives consistency to fundraising its purpose is to build enduring relationships and a stable social infrastructure so the arts organization can survive.

**Planned gift** Any significant contribution made during one's lifetime or after death as part of the donor's overall financial and/or estate planning.

**Pooled income fund** Irrevocable gifts (i.e., cash or marketable securities) from many donors that the arts organization manages as a mutual fund, distributing the income proportionately to the beneficiaries. Upon the death of the beneficiary, the remaining principal passes to the organization.

**Pro-forma budget** Predicted budget based on possible changes to contributed or earned revenues.

**Project scope and scale** The scope of a project identifies the activities for addressing the issue, while the project's scale refers to the size of the target.

**Prospect cultivation** Process aimed at building a relationship, gathering information about prospects' interests and giving capacity, and sharing information about the arts institution's programs.

**Prospective donor** Potential donor who has been identified and who the fundraiser officer decides to cultivate.

**Prospect identification** Preliminary check about who is a likely donor and if he or she might be willing to donate consistent gifts.

**Quiet phase** A limited period during a capital campaign when planning and the preparation of a campaign are usually known only to the organization's internal consistencies, as the campaign has not *yet* been presented to the public.

**Relational goods** Produced by not-for-profit organizations. They are non-material goods/services that are not consumed individually but together with other individuals or in groups. They are tied to interpersonal relations.

**Restricted funds** Can be spent only for a given project or cause.

**Retained life estate** When donors donate their property but keep the right to live or use it for life.

**Return on investment (ROI)** Metric used to understand how much the investment earned compared with its cost.

**RFP (request for proposal)** Tool commonly used by public and private grant-makers that establishes the ground rules for submitting a grant proposal.

**Sin companies** Companies involved in fields that are considered controversial or harmful, such as tobacco, drugs or weapons manufacture.

**Social balance sheet** Report that outlines and quantifies the social impact of an arts organization.

**Social capital** Networks of social ties among individuals who live in a community.

**Solicitation** Any attempt to raise funds from donors.

**Special project campaign** Fundraising effort to raise additional money beyond annual fund-raising that is focused on a specific situation or immediate need.

**Sponsorship** Act of a company that provides money to another organization (e.g., arts, communication, sport) for a specific activity or project in exchange for advertising/visibility.

**Stretched gifts** Gifts seemingly out of proportion to a donor's giving capacity.

**SWOT analysis** Strategic tool examining the key factors influencing an organization's activity and strategies in respect to the environment in which it operates.

**Tax benefit** Tax laws/provisions allowing the reduction of the individual tax burden. Benefits range from tax deductions and tax credits to exclusions and exemptions.

**Tax expenditures** Fiscal losses attributable to provisions of tax laws that allow a special exemption or deduction from gross income.

**Third sector** Comprises non-governmental and not-for-profit organizations such as associations and foundations, including charities, social enterprise and social cooperatives.

**Top-down-inside-out approach** According to this approach, engagement with the organization mission should start from within the cultural institution (starting with the strategic apex) before extending to the external environment and donor base.

**Unrestricted funds** These can offset expense centers that might be more difficult to raise funds for, such as staff salaries, utilities and maintenance.

**Victory celebration** Final event in a capital campaign when the achievement of the capital campaign's financial goal is celebrated.

**Virtual volunteering** Any form of volunteering online or through digital media on behalf of an arts organization.

**Vision statement** Clear declaration of what the cultural institution hopes to be in the future.

www.ingramcontent.com/pod-product-compliance
Lightning Source LLC
LaVergne TN
LVHW050951080826
845145LV00005B/1475